THE NEW VIEW FROM CANE RIVER

THE NEW VIEW FROM CANE RIVER

CRITICAL ESSAYS ON
Kate Chopin's
At Fault

Edited by Heather Ostman

Louisiana State University Press
Baton Rouge

Published by Louisiana State University Press
lsupress.org

Designer: Barbara Neely Bourgoyne
Typefaces: Adobe Text Pro and Didot

Cover illustration: Detail of *Standing Woman with Man in Outline,* ca. 1880,
by Thomas Hovenden. Courtesy The Metropolitan Museum of Art, New York,
metmuseum.org.

Cataloging-in-Publication Data are available from the Library of Congress.

ISBN 978-0-8071-7733-4 (cloth: alk. paper)
ISBN 978-0-8071-7777-8 (pdf)
ISBN 978-0-8071-7778-5 (epub)

CONTENTS

Contents

ACKNOWLEDGMENTS

I would like to thank two prominent Chopin scholars for their incomparable contributions to this work. Barbara Ewell's meticulous and thoughtful guidance was essential to the preparation of this volume. Her knowledge and insights were invaluable—a tremendous gift from someone who has given so much already to Chopin studies. For many years, she has been committed to broadening Chopin's audience and deepening their appreciation of her fiction. And I am not sure there are words to accurately express my appreciation for Bernie Koloski's continual support of this work and of every Chopin project I have taken on in the last fifteen years. His knowledge and guidance have been essential to my understanding of Kate Chopin's works over the years—and I know I am one of many. Like Barbara, Bernie has been untiringly supportive of thousands of students, teachers, and readers of Chopin's fiction: this volume is a testament to what his kind words of encouragement and insight can do.

Thank you both.

THE
NEW VIEW
FROM
CANE RIVER

Introduction

HEATHER OSTMAN

Using a range of meaningful critical approaches, *The New View from Cane River: Critical Essays on Kate Chopin's "At Fault"* offers a rich collection of essays that introduces new lenses for a fresh look at Kate Chopin's 1890 novel. Within the context of Chopin's body of work, *At Fault* poses unique challenges to its readers, as it presents a complicated moral universe composed in the aftermath of the American Civil War. Drawing from contemporary theories and synthesizing well-established perspectives in new ways, the essays in this collection shine a bright light on Chopin's literary vision by providing in-depth readings of this complex, lesser-known novel. Such a refreshed reading is timely, given the relevance and the urgency of many of the issues the novel raises—particularly racial and class injustice, as well as women's autonomy—precursors to the themes and concerns that present in Chopin's later works, as well as today, in our own historical moment.

American author Kate O'Flaherty Chopin (1850–1904) is best known for her landmark novel *The Awakening* (1899), which energized a generation of readers and scholars almost sixty years after *The Awakening* had been all but forgotten, following the author's death. Chopin's protagonist, Edna Pontellier, has inspired contemporary reading audiences since the 1960s, to explore, examine, and critique nineteenth-century social roles—the forebears to today's social and cultural landscape. She offered a literary model for speaking to and ultimately transcending the limits of gender roles for the generations since the novel's late twentieth-century revival. In the years that followed, Chopin's groundbreaking work has been become synonymous with feminist theory and women's studies in the context of literature, as it has become one of the most widely read and widely taught novels in the English-speaking world.

The prelude to *The Awakening* was *At Fault,* Kate Chopin's first novel, which she self-published in 1890, several years after becoming widowed in 1882. Living in Louisiana, where she had spent her entire married life, Chopin continued to raise her six children and settled the accounts of her husband, Oscar. About eighteen months after Oscar Chopin's death, she moved her family to her native St. Louis and then wrote *At Fault* during 1889 and 1890, at the start of her writing career (Chopin vii). Initially, Chopin had sought to publish the novel in *Belford's Monthly,* but the periodical, which published novels within its issues, rejected *At Fault.* Records show that Chopin sent the manuscript to Charles Deyo, who was a journalist, but according to her biographer Emily Toth, she made no account of his impressions. However, following *Belford's Monthly*'s rejection, Chopin paid for the printing herself through the Nixon-Jones Printing Company, which was located in St. Louis. Nixon-Jones produced one thousand copies on September 27, 1890, and Chopin promptly had them sent to a distributor and to reviewers (Toth 189). Suzanne Disheroon Green and David J. Caudle point out in the introduction to their 2001 scholarly edition of *At Fault* that likely due to Chopin's private printing of the novel, it contains numerous spelling, punctuation, and other errors (xvii). Recognizing the literary significance of *At Fault,* the editors—and others—sought to reconcile the errors in their early twenty-first-century editions.

Like *The Awakening, At Fault* speaks directly to deep societal and cultural issues, many of which, like post-Reconstruction relationships between Black people and white people, between North and South, between men and women, were fraught with complexity and opaqueness. Similar to many of Chopin's short stories, *At Fault* draws on the local-color genre, depicting a southern plantation setting where Black and white people *seem* to live in relative harmony—at least for most of this novel—and certainly appear unconscious of the South's recent past; there is never a direct mention of the Civil War or of its subsequent devastating loss. However, the external world of relative harmony is only a façade: Chopin's story of a southern white woman and a northern white man who fall in love on her post–Civil War plantation would seem to be a metaphor for national unity, where racial and social hierarchies are neatly inscribed. And yet, fraught with divorce, murder, alcoholism, and betrayal, the novel wrestles with the intricacies of doctrine, morality, legal rights, and social issues—all within the context of the tectonic shifts in the political, cultural, and aesthetic landscape of the United States. Despite its relative brevity, *At Fault* is not a read for the faint of heart.

Because *At Fault* is certainly ambitious: it presents complex human relationships and subsequently raises broader issues about the political and social contexts of the post–Civil War period and the dawn of modernism. But the novel's challenges also show Chopin as the protomodernist visionary she was: she draws no hard-and-fast conclusions about how the world ought to be in 1890; instead, she synthesizes the complexities of the post–Civil War era with the emergent modern world, engaging characters on their own terms, as they, like their real, human counterparts might, struggle to reconcile the doctrines of the recent past with the new world. *At Fault* presents competing narratives among characters who seek order and justice as much as they desire love; they rely on preconceived notions of morality that do not always serve their very human desires for love and connection once these notions are enacted in absolute terms. As a result, the novel invites a multitude of readings that align with contemporary concerns.

Set on the banks of Louisiana's Cane River, *At Fault* tells the story of Thérèse Lafirme, a thirty-five-year-old widow who has chosen to uphold religious-based ideals at the expense of happiness with the man she loves. Until David Hosmer, a northerner, enters her life, Thérèse has been ably managing her deceased husband's Louisiana plantation, Place-du-Bois, although once Thérèse learns her workers are stealing from her, she enacts a firmer hand at managing the plantation in this post–Civil War era. The plot is engaged when Hosmer approaches Thérèse about using timber on her property and he becomes the manager of the Place-du-Bois mill. This work-setting context is fertile for a conventional romance, and Hosmer soon declares his love for Thérèse in the early pages of the novel. However, when Thérèse, who is a Catholic, learns that Hosmer is divorced from his first wife, she insists that he return to his native St. Louis and remarry his ex-wife, Fanny, even though the loss of their young son and her subsequent alcoholism have destroyed any possibility of their united happiness. Although she is aware of the couple's profound misery, Thérèse remains adamant, so Hosmer relents, remarries Fanny, and brings her to Place-du-Bois. Parallel to the narrative of Thérèse and Hosmer are several competing narratives in which other characters also confront idealism and morality, leading each of them in an array of directions, some to newfound independence and others to death. For instance, Hosmer's younger sister, Melicent, also comes to live at Place-du-Bois; she and Grégoire, Thérèse's nephew, become romantically linked. But by the end of the novel, Melicent is independent and mobile, and she rejects Grégoire because of the deadly crime he commits. Unlike Thérèse, who has partly raised Grégoire, Melicent cannot accept him and eventually leaves, bewildered by Thérèse's request of her to forgive him. This narrative thread and others layer the novel with complexity and raise issues that speak to our current cultural and historical moment, particularly in terms of a divided nation, one struggling to reconcile deep-seated sociopolitical opposition and steep racial, class, and gendered inequities, even as milestone advances in each of these areas have occurred.

These complex issues arise within another contextual layer of *At Fault,* which features the changing economic and technological landscape of the American South. We see evidence of this transition most clearly through the prominence of the railroad that brings the Hosmers back and forth from St. Louis and the presence of the northern man's mill on Thérèse's land—a change she reluctantly accepts. Additional evidence is found in the subsequent shifts in relationships between Black workers and white employers. Many of the long-term Black servants demonstrate no resistance or resentment toward their white employees, with a few very notable exceptions, like Joçint, a young man of mixed ethnicity who works for Hosmer at the sawmill. Apparently angry about working at the mill, Joçint eventually sets fire to it, and Grégoire then murders him in response.

The murder sets off a moral dilemma for nearly every speaking character in the novel; they respond in myriad ways, ranging from compassion toward Grégoire, who is eventually killed himself, to contempt, as shown by Melicent. Other characters who respond to this event as well as the encroachment of technology suffer a variety of consequences, not least of all Marie Louise, Thérèse's former nurse. Marie Louise, resistant to change and contemptuous of religious doctrine, loses her life in a flood of the Cane River. Despite Hosmer's attempt to save his wife, the same flood also takes the life of Fanny, who likewise appears unable to change and resumes her alcoholic habits. The sequence of these events leads Thérèse to question her own moral rigidity. However, a year of separation enables Hosmer and Thérèse to reunite and marry on new terms of equality and vision. How much she has changed is questionable—which appears to be a challenging outcome of the novel—but Hosmer and Melicent have definitely changed, as one has married into a "new" southern way of life and the other seeks her independence, embodying the lifestyle of the period's emergent New Woman.

As mentioned, Chopin wrote the novel by drawing from the local-color genre. Her characters represent the post–Civil War South: Black characters speak in dialect, and white characters appear largely unaware of and unrepentant about the poverty of their Black servants—and certainly about prewar horrors of enslavement. The local-color elements depict a rich natural southern landscape and incorporate the details of rural Louisiana culture, including the quiet presence of the Catholic Church. But the local-color elements also veil the deeper, more complex moral issues that underlie the characters' multiple dilemmas, and the church serves as a lens for viewing the limits of doctrine and the relentless human grasp upon immutable "laws" that govern social behavior. Yet very few characters enjoy clear absolutism, even as they may speak to absolutes. Thus, Chopin demonstrates the fallibility of all of her characters: no one is steadfast all the time; humanity, love, and grief tread upon the best ideals, and nearly all slide into moral relativism at some point or another during the story.

Typical of Chopin's work, the characters in this novel must make choices that leave readers uneasy. Thérèse and Hosmer's marriage at the end of the novel, while appearing to conform to romantic literary conventions, does not deliver the closure a marriage between a protagonist and her love interest might have produced in a sentimental novel or a romantic novel. Instead, the readers are left to piece meaning together on their own, to compose meaning in the depiction of a community where fire, flood, and murder have destroyed the landscape and human life.

Written at the beginning of Chopin's career, *At Fault* did not receive the same critical attention as Chopin's *The Awakening* did, as its reception was somewhat delayed and certainly uneven. The novel received its first review in October 1890, published in the *St. Louis Spectator,* which offered it moderate praise for its prose and characterizations. Another St. Louis reviewer, in the *Post-Dispatch,* approved of Chopin's work similarly but also registered some disappointment: "One shudders at hearing Hosmer tell his wife to 'shut up,' and we protest against Melicent's five engagements. If she really was engaged five times it ought not to be mentioned" (quoted in Toth 190). Still, *At Fault* received generally supportive praise, until a year later a reviewer for the *Nation* delivered some varied, at times harsh, criticism of the novel. But as Emily Toth has pointed out, the major win for Chopin was that her work had finally garnered some attention through book reviews; prior to the novel's publication, she had been an unknown author.

Overshadowed by *The Awakening, At Fault* was slower to attract recognition during the revival of Chopin's works in the late twentieth century too. The early 2000s saw the publication of two edited editions of *At Fault,* both of which have been instrumental in the development of this collection: a 2001 scholarly edition with some additional readings, edited by Suzanne Disheroon Green and David J. Caudle, and a 2002 edition, edited by Bernard Koloski, whose essay on what the male characters in *At Fault* want is included in this volume. In the time since, the novel's recognition has accelerated, and it has received some notable critical attention. Because of its complex narrative as well as its publishing history, *At Fault* has attracted comparisons to *The Awakening,* a critical approach that frequently has left this early novel coming up short in estimation. In more recent years, critics have been more appreciative in their comparisons of *At Fault* to other well-known works by authors such as Charlotte Brontë, Edith Wharton, Willa Cather, W. D. Howells, and Mary Wilkins Freeman, among others. Additionally, critical work has largely been devoted to situating *At Fault* within literary traditions of local color and regionalism or within critical discussions focused on race, gender, or French influence. But as Green and Caudle point out, there are several important departures from these more conventional approaches that have yielded rich discussions of this novel. For instance, several scholars have explored the symbolism in the novel, such as William Warkin, who explores the symbols and imagery in *At Fault* with particular attention to African American characters, and Robert D. Arner, who recognizes the symbolism in the landscape as a precursor to William Faulkner's fiction, even more than it is to *The Awakening*. In a 2010 collection of conference proceedings, Jeremy Wells compares *At Fault* and Faulkner's *Light in August* within the context of American plantation fiction, and Jules Kares compares the appearance of widows in "How Merry Were the Widows in Chopin's *At Fault* and Faulkner's 'There Was a Queen'?" Other critics like Barbara C. Ewell have noted the novel's misleading appearance as a sentimental novel; she and others, like Pamela Glenn Menke, have argued that beneath the apparent sentimentalism and domesticity in the novel lies its subversive vision (Green and Caudle xxx–xxxi).

The scholars mentioned above and others have provided a firm critical foundation for Chopin's lesser-known novel. With thousands of university syllabuses listing the author's other work nationally (*Open Syllabus*), *At Fault,* although not as widely taught, is an essential novel for understanding the critical underpinnings of Chopin's larger body of fiction and to understanding her as an author with unique vision. *The New View from Cane River: Critical Essays on Kate Chopin's "At Fault"* offers a critical, panoramic view of the novel, providing rich contextual, theoretical, and interdisciplinary approaches to Chopin's compelling 1890 novel. The only one of its kind, this essay collection synthesizes the novel's complex and often interdependent issues, reframing them for a reading audience within the context of today's fraught and divisive political, social, and cultural landscape. Read as a volume, they present an interconnected highway of themes that locate this particular novel at the threshold of modernity and draw from current theoretical frameworks, with emphases on race, class, and gender, as well as focused readings on religion, narrative, "things," and emotions. The essays collectively engage the density of the novel's social issues—its overlaying of widowhood, divorce, remarriage, second marriage, and murder—and enable readers to plumb the uncomfortable depths of ambiguity, as the text resists a singular reading. In its evasion of a solitary message, *At Fault* clears a swathe through the literary woods for Chopin's short fiction and her later literary masterpiece. The emergent themes that elevated *The Awakening* to its status as an American classic derive from Chopin's earlier experimentation with narrative in *At Fault*. For readers who are committed to understanding Chopin's later novel, *At Fault* is required reading, and the essays here help readers navigate it.

The New View from Cane River: Critical Essays on Kate Chopin's "At Fault" presents ten critical essays written by a range of seasoned and well-regarded Chopin and American literature scholars, including emergent and international scholars. The contributors draw from their rich expertise as well as from previous critical scholarship on this novel to produce a spectrum of diverse approaches to Chopin's complex early novel. The effect is a continual repositioning of the novel, shifting the view from the novel's nineteenth-century context to its status as a precursor to the next century's modernity, as if each contributor were turning the novel over and over like a precious stone to see the different colors it casts. All of the essays approach the novel as an artifact from a time of massive transition in the American South. With a sensitivity that surely derives from our complex modern moment, the contributors each read the novel with an eye for interconnections and interdependency; they eschew general, categorical approaches for a reverence for the novel's narrative ambiguity and multilayered complexities, knowing that for today's readers, the challenges of Chopin's first novel in many ways mirror the transitions, divisiveness, and anxieties of our own historical moment.

Therefore, the first three essays in this collection situate *At Fault* within current, nuanced discussions of gender, class, and race that focus on the intersections among these elements as well as the objects and characters that function as signifiers of those relationships. Read together, these essays demonstrate the myriad ways current American culture and politics are inextricably linked to the nation's pre– and post–Civil War past. The first essay opens the conversation by addressing *who* is at fault and explores the interdependent relationships between cosmopolitanism, regionalism, and women characters in *At Fault*. In this essay, "Absent Babies and Cosmopolitan Bananas: Fault Lines, Networks, and Modernity in Kate Chopin's *At Fault*," Deborah Lindsay Williams examines these interdependent factors as elements of networks that privilege white women in the novel, particularly as they are expressed through their mobility as well as their financial and social independence. Williams sets the stage for *The New View from Cane River* as she reveals the political, social, and cultural contexts that surround the romantic challenges Chopin's characters face. Her discussion serves as a point of departure for the volume, as several other contributors explore "things," objects, and other familiar features in the essays that follow as evidence of historical and cultural transitions.

The second essay, "Reconciling the (Post)Plantation in *At Fault*: Reunion Romance, Western Expansionism, and the (Neo)Liberal Turn," by Natalie Aikens, examines the novel within the context of American reconciliation. Here, Aikens extends Williams's discussion by exploring the intersections among three critical points in the novel: the reunion-romance genre, western expansionism, and the politico-economic (neo) liberal turn. Through the confluence of these critical elements, she argues that while Chopin *may* reject white-supremacist presumptions and rhetoric, the novel reveals the failure of the post-Reconstruction era to ultimately deconstruct pre–Civil War hierarchies. Aikens's exploration of *At Fault* resonates with sociopolitical issues still present in American politics to this day. Similarly, the third essay takes a deep dive into racial politics in "'Miss T'rèse's System': *At Fault* and Antebellum Nostaglia." In this essay, Nadine M. Knight deepens the conversation about race with a frank look at the ways the failures of post-Reconstruction are expressed in the novel through several narrative threads that link race and masculinity to a sociopolitical hierarchy: through the perception of a northern siege upon the southern plantation, through northern characters who are constructed as inept and lacking in moral and physical strength, through the emasculation of southern chivalry, and through the corruption of peaceful Black laborers. Read together, these narrative strands echo through the twentieth century and into our current century, which has witnessed the American sociopolitical system grapple with imposed power structures based on regionalism, race, gender, and class.

The collection then shifts gears and introduces several new approaches to the novel, beginning with the fourth essay, Emily Toth's "So Melicent Is a Unitarian: Who's *At Fault?*" In this essay, Toth examines the Unitarian subtext to the seemingly Catholic pretense of the novel. An early predecessor to *The Awakening, At Fault* drives fault lines through Catholic conventionality, as it restores the pursuit of truth over fear and even tradition. But Toth sees Unitarianism providing a foundation for the novel's approach to its moral questions, as well as expressing the author's inherent critique of Catholic dogma. The fifth essay, written by Bernard Koloski, "What Hosmer Wants: Male Aspirations in *At Fault,*" focuses on the character of David Hosmer as the predecessor to Edna Pontellier herself in Chopin's *The Awakening.* Koloski identifies the parallels between the two characters' deep-seated desires, as well as comparing Hosmer's aspirations to characters in other, selected shorter works. This essay reminds readers of Chopin's wholistic vision, one in which women's autonomy could only be achieved through the liberation from gendered social roles for women and men.

In the sixth essay, Michael P. Bibler takes the conversation in another direction by introducing the sexological subtexts in *At Fault* in "Kate Chopin's Queer Etiologies: What's *At Fault* in the History of Sexuality." Here, Bibler redirects the well-tread conversations that have surrounded *The Awakening,* which have discussed gender, women's autonomy, and sexuality, to the author's nuanced representation of sexual etiologies in her earlier novel and the ways they manifest in the characters' behaviors and idiosyncrasies, as well as reshape the ways readers may read sexuality. Importantly, Bibler's essay contributes to more recent scholarly efforts to bring the conversation of sexuality in Chopin's work up-to-date and away from traditional binary notions of gender and sexuality.

The next two essays turn the reader's gaze toward the act of aesthetics and narrative. In the seventh essay, John A. Staunton focuses on the "unwholesome" narratives Fanny Hosmer reads in her adopted Louisiana, stories that seem to parallel the drama of her new married life. In

"Quick, Dead, and Widowed: Failed Reading of 'Unwholesome Intellectual Sweets' and the Importance of Knowing Whose Story You're In," Staunton traces Fanny's reading as a prelude to discussing the literary influences on Chopin herself and the author's ideas about women and fiction. In the eighth essay, "Divorce and the New Woman: Precedents to Modernism in *At Fault*," I argue that Chopin's 1890 novel demonstrates protomodernist elements, pointing to the author's understanding of the shifts in American literature and the dawn of the modernist period, as seen through the phenomenon of divorce and the construction of the New Woman in the text.

The final two essays introduce innovative theoretical frameworks for reading how "things," particularly objects and emotions, take on agency and causality in *At Fault*. In the ninth essay, "Personified Matter: Empowered Things in Kate Chopin's *At Fault*," Susan Moldow departs from conventional analysis of symbolism and metaphor and draws from "thing theory" in her analysis of the ways certain mundane material objects in the novel trigger change and inspire characters with renewed ideas about who they are. And in the final essay, "'Thérèse Was Love's Prophet': The Emotional Discourse and the Depiction of Feelings in Kate Chopin's *At Fault*," Eulalia Piñero Gil argues that the emotional discourse and epistemology of emotions in the text provide new ways of considering the dimensions of Chopin's novel, particularly in terms of the affective world. In this essay, Gil shows how emotions and feelings take on causal dimensions, as well as register profound changes and transitions occurring during the novel's historic period.

The New View from Cane River: Critical Essays on Kate Chopin's "At Fault" offers fresh, new essays that individually bring depth and collectively bring breadth to the exploration of Chopin's challenging and lesser-known novel. Read independently or together, the work in this collection provides a rich critical discussion of one of Chopin's most complex narratives for today's readers. All of the contributors are experienced, highly competent instructors—in addition to their scholarly credentials—which has made them experts in distilling complex ideas into accessible, compelling prose, providing an essential supplement to the reading of Chopin's challenging novel.

WORKS CITED

Chopin, Kate. *At Fault.* 1890. Edited with an introduction and notes by Bernard Koloski. London: Penguin, 2002.

Green, Suzanne Disheroon, and David J. Caudle, eds. *"At Fault": A Scholarly Edition with Background Readings.* Knoxville: University of Tennesee Press, 2001.

Open Syllabus Explorer. English Literature. Columbia University. 2020.

Toth, Emily. *Kate Chopin.* Austin: University of Texas Press, 1990.

Absent Babies and Cosmopolitan Bananas
Fault Lines, Networks, and Modernity in At Fault

DEBORAH LINDSAY WILLIAMS

At the conclusion of *At Fault* (1890), Kate Chopin's first novel, the heroine, Thérèse Lafirme, takes the train from New Orleans back to Place-du-Bois, her plantation along the Cane River near Natchitoches. After six months in Paris and a visit to New Orleans that was "filled with pleasant disturbances," she is eager to get home. We first see her in this chapter through the eyes of another female passenger, a "little grey-garbed conventional figure," who admires Thérèse's Parisian fashions. Thérèse doesn't notice the other woman because she's too engrossed in trying to open the train window to let in the fresh air; nor does she notice, a few seats away, "an interesting family group." The family consists of a "husband, but doubly a father, surrounded and sat upon by a small band of offspring. A wife—presumably a mother—absorbed with the view of the outside world and the elaborate gold chain that hung around her neck" (161). A few paragraphs later, "the husband and father had peeled and distributed his second outlay of bananas amongst his family. It was at this moment that Thérèse, looking towards the door, saw Hosmer enter the car" (163). Given that the novel's primary plot has centered on the love triangle of David Hosmer, Thérèse, and Hosmer's ex-wife, Fanny, readers might notice only this moment of reunion, six months or so after Fanny drowned in a flash flood. But there is more than just a lovers' reunion happening in this train car: the vignettes of the car's other occupants serve as concentrated reminders of the novel's key concerns and show us that nothing in *At Fault* is as simple as it seems.

Questions about gender roles, about mobility, and about the relationship between the urban and the rural, run like fault lines through this novel, which has long been overshadowed by the critical acclaim given to *The Awakening,* published nine years later. Donna Campbell suggests that *At Fault* should be seen as being "about change and resistance to change" (33), but ultimately, I think, change is not so much resisted as it is embraced. Even the simple fact that Thérèse and the "grey-garbed figure" are traveling alone and unchaperoned suggests a change: a new attitude about women in public space. The woman in gray understands the international provenance of Thérèse's clothing: everything, even Thérèse's umbrella, "had Paris written plain upon them . . . points likely to have escaped a man" (161). After she inventories Thérèse's clothes, the woman "betake[s] herself to the absorbing pages of a novel which she read through smoked glasses" (161, 163), which are themselves quite *au courant.* The car has another occupant, whose seat is marked with a "large valise, an overcoat, a cane and an umbrella," while the owner of these items is "likely to be at present in the smoking car" (161). It seems quite possible that this absent traveler, mingling with the other men in the homosocial space of the smoking car, is a traveling salesman, like Jack Dawson, one of Hosmer's St. Louis acquaintances. The gray-garbed female traveler underscores the independence of the modern nineteenth-century woman, and the traveling salesman in the smoking car reminds us of the circulatory power of commerce, which brings us novels, smoked glasses, Parisian fashions—and enables the transport of lumber from the mill that Hosmer established on Thérèse's plantation.

It is the "interesting family group" at the far end of the train car, however, that pulls together the novel's fascination with networks, exchange, and the shifting roles available to women. We notice that the wife is only "presumably" a mother and seems utterly disinterested in her family. We don't know what has "absorbed" her attention outside the train window, but whatever it is seems as interesting as the other woman's novel and far more engrossing than the domestic scene arrayed alongside her on the train seat. We are told twice that it is the "husband and father" who deals with the children, as if to underscore the reversal of conventional nineteenth-century gender roles. Even more interesting than these blurred gender roles, however, are the bananas that the father hands around as a snack—the "second outlay," no less. How did those bananas get in the hands of that husband and father? And why bananas, rather than a fruit more local to New Orleans, like satsumas (akin to mandarin oranges), apples, or strawberries? Were his children aware of their great good fortune, to receive *two* outlays of what was, in the late nineteenth century, still a luxury product? Eating their bananas on the train, the family literalizes a Veblenesque demonstration of conspicuous consumption, nine years prior to the publication of *Theory of the Leisure Class* (1899). By providing these luxurious treats to his children, the man upholds his position as economic provider, even as his caretaking role feminizes him. This family scene illustrates a crack in the façade of conventional nineteenth-century gendered domesticity that runs through the entire novel and results in the unusual marriage between Hosmer and Thérèse that takes place in the final pages of the book. Taken in its entirety, then, the scene in the train car, coming as it does so close to the end of the novel, affirms the novel's ultimate commitment to change and to finding modes of cosmopolitan engagement with the new.

The train car is full of new things—bananas, smoked glasses, French fashions—and new behaviors (single women traveling unchaperoned)[1] that are in transit between the rural and the urban. The train is stillness and motion, a specific site and a liminal space, an "instrument of progress," as Campbell calls it (37), and an emblem of the status quo in that it is an all-white car, a fact that Chopin takes so much for granted it doesn't even warrant mention. In the enclosed space of the train car, the unchaperoned white women can travel in safety, although they "undergo the ordeal of having [their] tickets scrutinized [and] commented upon" by the "suave conductor," who is also white (163). All these passengers enjoy the luxury of individual seats, windows that can open and shut, and the mobility that comes with privilege. Neither transformation nor transportation is readily available for anyone other than whites: the networks that crisscross the landscapes of the novel seem able to bring change to almost everything, except to the constricted tangle of post-Reconstruction racial politics.

Caroline Levine points out that "networks and enclosures are constantly meeting, sometimes sustaining and reinforcing one another, at other times creating threats and obstacles . . . neither form has the final organizing word—neither always regulates the other" (119). *At Fault* offers myriad examples of the constant interactions between enclosures and networks, and when we track these relationships, we see that far from being suffused in nostalgia, the novel fully engages with the new.[2] It attempts to establish a nonhierarchical relationship between the local and the global, the rural and the urban, that might be seen as enabling a regional cosmopolitanism. Susan Mizruchi argues that at the turn into the twentieth century, "American social life demanded a disposition of cosmopolitanism, which might be characterized as openness to other cultures and to cultural others, as well as to the global interconnectedness that such others implied" (76). The networks and fault lines that run through Chopin's novel show us that the seemingly hyperlocal world of the plantation is acutely aware of the world of innovation, technological advancement, and the circulation of ideas. *At Fault* is deeply engaged with, and supportive of, modernity, mobility, and transformation; cosmopolitan engagement becomes a cardinal virtue that, if avoided or disregarded, results in dire consequences.

Cosmopolitanism emerges from, and demands, what Mizruchi calls "global interconnectedness," but those connections are not without complications and difficulties, all of which are neatly emblematized by the bananas being eaten so happily and inconsequentially by the family on the train. Bananas were introduced to the United States at the 1876 Philadelphia World's Fair, in the Horticultural Hall, where it was possible to buy a single banana for ten cents (a cost that for some, represented an hour's wages); they remained a luxury item until the early twentieth century. When large-scale production and refrigerated transport became the standard, bananas became ordinary, but in the 1880s,[3] when the novel is set, they were fancy fruit.[4] The fortunes of the banana are themselves a lesson in change and exchange: they were seen initially in the Americas "as a food for slaves [and] became in the nineteenth century an exotic luxury for wealthy and well-traveled North Americans" (Jenkins 57). This history resonates with the history of the slave-owning American South, both in terms of the human cost of capitalist success and in the complex relationship between the rural/agrarian landscapes and the urban spaces of national and international exchange.

The exotic snack that the father offers to his family probably came from a small banana plantation in Central America, perhaps even a family-owned farm similar to Place-du-Bois. By the turn into the twentieth century, bananas were grown on agricultural factory farms, but in 1880, banana plantations were still relatively small operations that were trying to figure out how to capitalize on the innovations of refrigerated shipping and transport. The bananas on Thérèse's train found their way from the Honduras to a steamship to New Orleans to the hands of a man about to get on a northbound train. The simple action of a father offering a banana to his children ripples outward to signify the novel's awareness of international commerce and the concomitant need for information networks that support those transactions—information about crops, ports, markets, and consumers.

The networks that result in bananas being available for train rides suggest that there is not a clear-cut relationship between rural and urban, familial and foreign: the fruit is proffered in a moment of domesticity that takes place within a symbol of modern mobility that is itself moving along a track somewhere between rural and urban. The boundaries, in other words, between enclosures (the train car, the plantation) and networks (the train, the shipping industry) are neither fixed nor absolute. People and things are constantly on the move, and while Thérèse's plantation and Hosmer's lumber mill seem geographically isolated, they are in fact very much enmeshed in a series of networks—the postal service, the railroad, telecommunications—that mitigate, even eradicate, that isolation.

Syntactically, the bananas and Hosmer are linked: the narrator tells us that the father "distributed his second outlay of bananas amongst his family. It was at this moment that Thérèse . . . saw Hosmer enter the car" (163).[5] We don't know why Hosmer is on this train—he'd left Place-du-Bois months earlier, to take Fanny's body to St. Louis for burial, and then he'd fallen ill and gone to the seashore with his sister to recuperate. His sudden presence is as surprising as his unheralded arrival at the Place-du-Bois train station at the beginning of the novel, when he appears on Thérèse's veranda with a "moneyed offer for the privilege of cutting timber from [Thérèse's] land" (8). How had he known the timber was there? Some unspoken but efficient information network must have been at work, bringing details about Louisiana timber to St. Louis and setting Hosmer's plans in motion. Technology—the conveyance of information, ideas, and people—collapses the distance between his office in St. Louis and Natchitoches Parish.

Trains are the most visible network in the novel, and it is easy to imagine an oppositional relationship between the train and the fixed pastoral space of the plantation—the dialectic that gave rise to Leo Marx's famous configuration of the "machine in the garden." But as Levine reminds us, networks and enclosures—such as the bounded space of an estate—function together; neither has the final word. This linked relationship is what we see in *At Fault,* in which enclosure and network come together in such a way that we need to rethink oppositional relationships and instead see how rural and urban, local and global, come together and blur any clear distinctions. The relationship between enclosures and networks enables cosmopolitan encounters that reaffirm the novel's commitment to modernity and change. Thérèse herself is "not disposed to rebel against the changes which Time brings" (30): she is a "clever enough businesswoman" to recognize the benefit of Hosmer's offer, for example, and after a brief bout of tears in her "beloved woods," she settles the deal. In her shrewdness and independence, Thérèse challenges conventions not only because she is a woman who refuses to stay a disconsolate widow but also because she is not afraid to remake the world as she thinks it should be. As her last name implies, Thérèse is formidable and firm in all things: if grieving about her husband is going to become such a distraction that people can steal from her, she will put aside her sorrow and "awaken unsuspected powers of doing" (6); if someone wants to buy lumber rights on her property, she will sigh and sign the contract; if she no longer likes the view from her house, she will build a new house with a different view.

Thérèse's huge plantation—four thousand acres—stretches farther than the eye can see, and while the bayou on its far side is "sluggish," life on and around the plantation moves briskly. Even Thérèse is always on the move: Marie Louise, her former nanny, says, "Why do you run about so much, *Tite maîtresse*? You are always going this way and that way; on horseback, on foot" (90). Everything circulates: people, books, fashion, fruit, information, and even voices, through the use of telegrams and telephones. Hosmer "speaks a few words through the telephone which connected with the agent's desk at the station" (13), almost as if the telephone is an extension of the train line, and at another point, "certain late telegrams" arrive at the plantation (32). In a curious coincidence, the telephone was introduced at the same world's fair as the banana, two very different objects that signify the development of networks bringing the remote into contact with the local. Telephone service in the South lagged behind the rest of the country (Fischer 89), which suggests that the presence of a phone at Hosmer's mill is all the more remarkable, but it is presented without comment. Place-du-Bois is connected to the world beyond its immediate borders; it is in the vanguard rather than trapped in some nostalgic haze of yesteryear.

The only other person who uses a phone is Jack Dawson, a traveling salesman whose wife, Lou, is a friend of Fanny's, and whose phone calls ensure that people and goods stay in constant movement. When he's at home in St. Louis, Dawson's activities turn the household "inside out and upside down" (56). He uses the telephone to call a "large circle of acquaintances who happened not to be on the road," so that he can plan card parties, picnics, and other social activities (56). With his cronies, Dawson talks business and refers to being "in Houston, Texas, the other day" or "over in Albuquerque," itself glancing reference to movement beyond national borders—New Mexico did not become a state until 1912. Dawson's counterpart in the novel is the bookish Mr. Worthington, another St. Louis friend of Fanny's. Worthington has a job at the customs office, a post he's maintained through "various changes of administration," although it's not clear if his longevity is due to being "unobtrusive" or to his "many-sided usefulness" (54). He works in the office that regulates the flow of goods coming into St. Louis—he may even be the person who notes the tariffs on the shipments of bananas headed for St. Louis grocery stores. The customhouse is an enclosure, a fixed entity through which goods circulate. Dawson and Worthington embody the links between enclosures and networks that enable the flow of goods and ideas, offering the possibility of cosmopolitan engagement.

Through these innovations in telecommunication, the rural spaces of lumber mill and the plantation are engaged in two conversations—literally, with those at the other end of telecom systems, and symbolically, with the very concept of modernity itself. In *Cosmopolitanism,* Kwame Anthony Appiah stresses the importance of conversation, a word that he says connotes "not only . . . literal talk but also a metaphor for engagement with the experience and the ideas of others. . . . [These] encounters, properly conducted, are valuable in themselves. Conversation doesn't have to lead to consensus about anything, especially not values; it's enough that it helps people get used to one another" (85). Encounters with difference happen throughout the novel, in face-to-face conversations, through telecoms, and through what Appiah calls "imaginative engagement" with books. The material objects that circulate through the novel—or are themselves the means of circulation—reveal the networks of commerce and exchange that make Place-du-Bois a full and vital participant in global conversations.

But these networked conversations also occur through the vehicle of "imaginative engagement" that Appiah mentions: books. Chopin's books themselves were marketed as conduits for encounters with "cultural others," to use Mizruchi's term, as the introduction to the *Cambridge Companion to Kate Chopin* notes: "The publisher's advertisement for [Chopin's] first collection of short stories, *Bayou Folk,* in 1894, drew attention to the fact that Chopin's characters were 'semi-aliens' and featured in narratives 'quite unlike most American tales'" (Beer 1). The world of New Orleans was seen as a bit of Europe in the United States, and Creoles, according to Helen Taylor, "talk[ed] as if they were Parisians; they read French newspapers, visited French relatives, and discussed French politics" (149). Books can be seen as commodities to be bought and sold—Mr. Worthington has "small hoard [of books] which he had collected at some cost," for example—but as the contents of Thérèse's bookcases demonstrate, books also further challenge the distinction between the rural and the urban. When the Worthingtons visit Place-du-Bois from St. Louis on their way to "Muddy Graw" in New Orleans, Mr. Worthington is entranced by the sight of Thérèse's bookshelves. At home in St. Louis, he has to hide his books in a closet, lest his wife use them to prop up wobbly tables or smooth out wrinkled linens. As he looks at Thérèse's books, he notices some titles in French, "to him an unfamiliar language," as well as Balzac, the Waverly novels, Racine, Moliere, Bulwer, Shakespeare, and "five imposing volumes in dignified black and gold, bearing the simple inscription, 'Lives of the Saints—Rev. A. Butler'" (133). Hundreds of miles from both cosmopolitan New Orleans and modern St. Louis, this bilingual bookshelf speaks to the transatlantic perspective of the Lafirme household; French language and culture do not stop at the New Orleans border.

Taylor claims that in the late nineteenth century, New Orleans was "cosmopolitan but still in thrall to its rural hinterland" (149), but this characterization seems to rely on the urban assumption that the rural is always somehow laggard. Chopin's novel demonstrates the need to see both urban and rural as valuable; the one needn't dominate the other, and cosmopolitanism was not exclusively urban. Even in a small town like St. Martinville (or Saint-Martinville), which is more than one hundred miles from New Orleans, for instance, French language and culture were so pervasive that it was known as Petit Paris. Networks, as Levine points out, are "neither consistently emancipatory—freeing us from a fixed or dominant order—nor always threatening—trouncing sovereignty or dissolving protective boundaries" (115). The cosmopolitan city and the rural hinterland are linked in this novel but not necessarily in tension or in conflict. Instead, the novel presents us with the idea that encounters with difference can be mutually transformative; "conversations" between rural and nonrural might present problems, but they can also offer new possibilities for those who are willing to engage.

Books provide the opportunity for Hosmer and Worthington to engage in the sort of conversation about religion and philosophy of which Appiah would approve, in that the two men explore their differences of opinion without trying to convert or demean one another. Their conversation is quite different from the way Worthington's daughter Lucilla talks to Aunt Belindy, one of Thérèse's servants. Aunt Belindy asks about the paper that Lucilla carries with her, which is "stuck with myriad tiny pin holes" (128). Lucilla tells the older woman that each pinprick represents an act of virtue and with enough acts—"thousands and thousands"—she will gain "twenty-five years of indulgence" and thus not spend as much time in Purgatory. The novel appears to mock Aunt Belindy's seeming inability to accept pinpricks as representations of acts and her apparent lack of knowledge about Purgatory; Campbell reads this scene as another instance of the novel's "stereotyped humor" around the African American characters (40). But the scene also mocks Lucilla's facile religious sentiment: she cannot explain what an "act" is, for example: "an act is something you do that you don't want to do—or something you don't want to do, that you do—I mean that you don't do. Or if you want to eat something and don't. Or an aspiration; that's an act, too" (128). It's no wonder that Aunt Belindy is confused, although she asks a question that strikes right to the heart of the matter: how does Lucilla know that these pinpricks will result in avoiding Purgatory? Lucilla's only response is "because I know."

Lucilla's simplistic certainty sounds similar to Thérèse's assertions about Catholicism and morality, claims that seem at first to be implacably conservative. When Hosmer seeks her out in the seldom-used parlor of her house and confesses that he loves her, Thérèse rebuffs him because he is divorced, a status that her "moral principles" cannot accept. Although he tries to engage her in an intellectual discussion about her morals, suggesting that her principles might be mere "prejudices [that] may be set aside by an effort of the will" (36), she refuses to entertain his perspective and remains adamant that hers is the only correct view. She loves Hosmer but insists that he return to St. Louis and remarry Fanny, to "face the consequences of his actions" (39); she ignores his evident misery at this request, and after one passionate kiss, Hosmer leaves the parlor—and Place-du-Bois—in "blind submission" to her command. It is easy to see this scene as Thérèse falling back into the narrowest and most local of ideological perspectives here, relying on a moral absolutism that we see nowhere else in the novel.[6]

If we think about the space in which this scene happens, however, we might see Thérèse's refusal in a slightly different light. The parlor, which the servants view as a "holy sanctuary," is the most conventional room in Thérèse's house and is decorated with "tasteful pictures" that alternate on the walls with "family portraits [that are] stiff and unhandsome" (35). In this sanctuary, where Thérèse imagines herself "secure from intrusion," it is difficult to imagine how a relationship with such an unconventional suitor—northern, Unitarian, industrial—might flourish. The "miserable story" that Hosmer tells about his first marriage does nothing to suggest that a more positive marital narrative is possible, especially when we consider that his description of young Fanny as "pink and white and merry blue eyes and stylish clothes"—makes her sound quite similar to Thérèse herself, who is fair-skinned, blue-eyed, and fashionably dressed. Hosmer's marriage story ends with the death of his young child, his wife's descent into alcoholism, and her subsequent request for divorce. In refusing Hosmer's affections, Thérèse seems appalled by the sordid misery of his tale; she chooses the solitary life of her two namesakes—sixteenth-century Teresa of Ávila and nineteenth-century Thérèse of Lisieux, "Little Flower of Jesus"—who renounced domesticity and marriage in order to live contemplative and scholarly lives. Her decision seems to favor tradition and conservatism over the risk of a new love affair.

If we consider Thérèse's legal status as a widow, however, which allows her full control over her plantation and her finances, the conservatism of her decision seems less absolute. Louisiana property laws in the late nineteenth century did not give a married woman full right to property; if she were to remarry, she could stand to lose her financial independence.[7] So while on the one hand, we could see her rejection of Hosmer as uncharacteristically retrograde, her decision also reaffirms her status as an unconventional woman who is "not steeped in the agony of remorse which many might consider becoming in a widow of five years" (31) and who is steadfastly, unapologetically, childless, a detail that is mentioned in the second sentence of the novel and never again. Refusing to marry Hosmer and then sending him away (perhaps to avoid the temptation of further passionate embraces) can be seen an "effort of the will" to challenge conventional behavior, even as it is also an illustration of Thérèse's inability to imagine any possibility outside that convention. It seems no accident that when the two are finally reunited—and then married—the only scene we have of them is outside on the veranda, a less confined space and one that is not watched over by stiff portraits of ancestors.

Thérèse's decision might look like a refusal to change and, in a sense, it is: she wants to remain fully in control of her property. She loved to "walk the length of the wide verandas, armed with her field-glass, and to view her surrounding possessions with comfortable satisfaction" (6). Her insistence on independence, couched in the language of religion, however, suggests that while she appreciates the need for complexity and change in her professional life, she cannot imagine similarly complex or unusual possibilities in her emotional life. Her single-mindedness about Hosmer makes her, according to a letter that Chopin wrote to the *Natchitoches Enterprise,* the character most at fault because she has given into "blind acceptance of an undistinguishing, therefore unintelligent code of righteousness" (quoted in Campbell 30). Thérèse cannot imagine any narrative for herself other than what she already knows—a conventional marriage and a sense of right and wrong she'd always assumed was "easy of interpretation" (127). Thérèse's apparent failure of imagination could be seen in terms of Appiah's ideas about "contamination": "Cultural purity is an oxymoron. The odds are that, culturally speaking, you already live a cosmopolitan life, enriched by literature, art, and film that come from many places, and that contains influences from many more" (135). Through networks of commerce and innovation, Place-du-Bois is situated in this cosmopolitan context, contaminated, as it were, by ideas that come from many places, not just the local. And in a similar fashion, Thérèse's refusal of Hosmer also resists easy definition: it is both an instance of moral absolutism and a modern insistence on female autonomy. The lovers are reunited only after Fanny's death and after both Thérèse and Hosmer experience "staggering doubt" (127) about their choices.[8]

The inability to change, as Donald Ringe points out, is dire: those who resist—Grégoire, Joçint, even Fanny—perish. Joçint, the son of African American Morico and a Native American mother, resents having to work at Hosmer's mill because his "heart is in the pine hills" (13). In his rage and powerlessness, Joçint sets fire to the mill (after first killing his dog so it doesn't betray his whereabouts by barking) but is caught in the act by Grégoire, Thérèse's handsome but feckless Creole nephew. Grégoire kills Joçint, and when Morico sees his son's body in the fire, he tries to pull Joçint to safety and is killed in the process. Hosmer's sister Melicent hears Grégoire say that Joçint "ain't goin' to set no mo' mill afire," and thinks that perhaps Grégoire "arrested" Joçint, but Thérèse suspects the truth (105). There are no legal consequences for killing a "half-breed" in the middle of committing a crime; in this novel, there seem only to be laws governing business, marriage, and property. Grégoire is sure that he's done the right thing in killing Joçint and does not understand why Thérèse and Melicent are so appalled. He is sure that Melicent, with whom he fancies himself in love, will get over her disgust at his actions and "melt, perhaps, to the extent of a smile or one of her old glances" (111). But instead, she leaves Place-du-Bois with an icy good-bye, and Grégoire leaves soon after. He ends up dead in a barroom brawl in Cornstalk, Texas, information that is conveyed to Thérèse by Rufe Jimson, a man who stopped by Place-du-Bois while he was "in transit" to tell her the news. Thérèse realizes that Grégoire was "killed by the hand of a stranger with whom perhaps the taking of a man's life counted as little as it had once counted with his victim" (140). Neither Grégoire nor Joçint are willing (or able) to adapt to the changing world; they both pay the ultimate price as a result.

Ringe includes Marie Louise in his list of those who resist change, but this easy interpretation of her death does not necessarily render the full picture, which we can see if we think about the network of history that brought Marie Louise to live on the bank of the Cane River in the first place. She drowns when the river floods and washes away the bank where her house stands. She had refused to have the house moved, despite Thérèse's entreaties. Prior to the flood, Thérèse had said that she was going to "insist on having [the] cabin moved back; it is silly to be so stubborn about such a small matter. Some day you will find yourself out in the middle of the river—and what am I going to do then?—no one to nurse me when I am sick—no one to scold me—nobody to love me" (90). Marie Louise, unlike Hosmer, refuses Thérèse's attempts to manage her life, telling her "*Non—non, Tite maîtresse, Marie Louise 'prè créver icite avé tous son butin, si faut* (no, no, *Tite maîtresse*, Marie Louise will die here with all her belongings if it must be)" (91, translation in original). Her refusal, in the language that she and Thérèse share, becomes Marie Louise's assertion that she will do what she likes with her body.[9] In the aftermath of slavery and Reconstruction, this claim of physical autonomy seems particularly significant. Were she to move, it would be the second time: the first time is at the behest of Thérèse's husband, Jérôme. Marie Louise reminds Thérèse of that fact, telling her, "I said [to Jérôme], Marie Louise will move no more; she's too old. If the good God does not want to take care of me, then it's time for me to go" (91). Perhaps her religious faith is an illusion, a certainty that leads to her undoing. But it is also possible, if we think about the history that brought her to this cabin, that this former slave is claiming the right to live (or die) as she sees fit rather than according to the needs of her former owner. When we situate Marie Louise's death in this fashion, her decision becomes a demonstration *of* change rather than the refusal *to* change and an indication that the fault line of race is so deeply entrenched that it will not be easily bridged or repaired.

Marie Louise's decision to control her own fate thus seems similar to Thérèse's refusal of Hosmer and her rejection of conventional domesticity. Thérèse defies local expectations about femininity because she successfully manages her vast estate and because she is childless. As a seemingly devout Catholic, Thérèse might be expected to express concern about her childless state, but she never mentions it. There are, in fact, very few children in this novel: Hosmer and Fanny had a son who died at the age of three; the Worthingtons have Lucilla; Thérèse's friends the Duplans have a daughter named Ninette; Joçint is Morico's adult son. Thérèse's plantation may be "rich in its exhaustless powers of reproduction," but the people themselves are not (6).

The train that Thérèse takes back to Place-du-Bois at the end of the novel not only reunites her with Hosmer but also provides one of the few images of a seemingly happy family, if, that is, we disregard the presumable mother's disinterest in the "small band of offspring" on the train seat next to her. This mother, staring out the window, adds to the novel's subtle and ongoing interrogation of femininity, marriage, and motherhood. In her disaffection, the presumable mother seems similar to Fanny, who is seen earlier in the novel enroute from St. Louis to Place-du-Bois (the only other scene in the novel actually set inside a train).

After Fanny remarries Hosmer, she greets his announcement that they will return to Place-du-Bois with "martyred resignation" (65). And although she initially thinks of the journey as holding "the promise of novelty," the novelty fades, and she sees out the windows only "an unfamiliar country whose features were strange and held up no promise of welcome." She takes no pleasure in the modernity of the journey, and she is mystified by the fact that Hosmer recognizes "the faces of those who loitered about the stations at which they stopped" (73). He shakes hands, exchanges greetings (using the few words of French he's learned), and makes it clear that what to Fanny is "unfamiliar country" is no longer strange to him. Hosmer comes to Place-du-Bois in search of commerce but made the decision to engage, not merely observe. He has been changed by his time in Louisiana, which Fanny cannot imagine, and their differing experiences on the train suggest that there will be no happy ending waiting for them at the conclusion of their journey. Theirs is yet another in a series of unconventional marriages that the novel portrays.

The white women in *At Fault* enjoy the luxury of mobility, which speaks to their relative affluence, and to the networks that enable their movements. Thérèse goes to New Orleans and Paris; the Worthingtons go to New Orleans from St. Louis; Melicent comes to Place-du-Bois after going "North, West, or East as alternating caprice prompted" (14), and the last we hear of her, she is planning an expedition to the American Southwest with a female friend; Bert Rodney, with whom Lou Dawson has an affair in St. Louis, does so while his wife and child are vacationing in Narragansett. These peripatetic women are enabled in their travels by the additional fact that most of them are childless (the "training and education" of the Worthingtons' daughter have been taken over by an aunt [55]). It is as if in this novel, Chopin can imagine a world in which "woman" does not necessitate "mother," an option that she does not extend to Edna Pontellier in *The Awakening*. We might even imagine that the presumable mother on Thérèse's train, "absorbed with the view of the outside world and the elaborate gold chain that hung around her neck," foreshadows Edna, chafing at the elaborate leash of her marriage and daydreaming about what's happening outside the enclosure of domesticity.

When we consider the ambivalent portrayals of marriage and motherhood in *At Fault,* the portrayal of Thérèse and Hosmer's happy domesticity in the novel's final pages becomes a slightly more complex affair, particularly because they have no children, a fact that has gone unremarked in most critical commentary. Some critics, such as David Russell, read the novel's conclusion—Thérèse and Hosmer reunited at Place-du-Bois—as negative: "a hierarchical geography in which the plantation is restored as the primary unit of social organization" (9). For the most part, however, the novel's conclusion is seen as a happy union of opposites—the northern industrialist reunited with the southern agrarian; the Unitarian and the Catholic; the urban and the rural. Ringe says that with the marriage of Thérèse and Hosmer, the "Cane River past flows into a future that is filled with promise" (165). But Place-du-Bois is a place of the future long before Thérèse and Hosmer marry. They do not usher in this new future; they are in fact recipients of it. The final scene of the novel takes place on the veranda: the now-married lovers have escaped the gaze of the staid family portraits in the parlor. Just as the veranda is both a public and private space, so too does their marriage make space for both public and private selves. When Hosmer tells Thérèse he has investors in the lumber mill, which will give him more time to spend with her, she thinks he wants to be more involved in running the plantation, but he assures her that's not the case: he will "not rob [her] of [her] occupation . . . put no bungling hand into your concerns" (167). His comment makes clear that in their marriage there is room for professional success, even as the novel's final image also suggests sexual intimacy. Hosmer whispers something in Thérèse's ear that makes her blush, and the narrator asks, "can that be Hosmer? Is this Thérèse? Fie, fie. It is time we were leaving them" (170). Our last vision of the married pair, then, is of the two of them canoodling on the veranda at twilight. At the moment of transition between day and night, in the liminal space of the veranda, this unusual couple seems to have achieved their unconventional version of a "happy ending."

Given the novel's emphasis on networks, mobility, and change, however, it is difficult to see this happy relationship as "the future." It is only a node on a network—one marital possibility among many. Thérèse and

Hosmer have no children, and it seems unlikely that they will, given that when they marry, Thérèse is thirty-six and Hosmer is in his early forties. Nor is there any sense that anyone other than Thérèse will be able to run the plantation: the "impecunious old kinsman" she'd left in charge of Place-du-Bois while she traveled spent his time hunting and fishing, with the result that "things had not gone well" in her absence (163). What, then, will be the legacy of this modern marriage, which is under-girded by cosmopolitan engagement and offers the space for a woman to be professionally powerful and *not* be a mother? The narrative of marriage that Chopin creates for Thérèse and Hosmer is all the more unusual when we compare it to other marriages in the novel and to Edna Pontellier's marriage in *The Awakening*. Edna cannot reconcile the competing tensions of wife/mother/woman; the power of conventional narratives defeats her. The power of that narrative—that a woman un-satisfied by marriage or motherhood has no options—perhaps explains why *At Fault* has languished at the margins of Chopin's career: Thérèse's radical reinvention reverberates along a fault line that still exists.

NOTES

1. For a discussion of the single woman traveler in the United States during this period, see, for example, Catherine Cocks, *Doing the Town: The Rise of Urban Tourism in the United States, 1850–1915* (2001), or Karin M. Morin, *Frontiers of Femininity: A New Historical Geography of the Nineteenth-Century American West* (2008).

2. Place-du-Bois is often seen as a pastoral space that is "ruptured" by progress, as Alice Petry Hall says in her introduction to *Critical Essays about Kate Chopin*, a view that is echoed by Donald Ringe characterizing modern industry as an "intrusion" into the Cane River Valley. Nostalgia takes on a slightly different cast in Sandra Gunning's view of the novel, in which Place-du-Bois is a "white domestic haven" (120) and Thérèse is a symbol of respect for "traditional racial codes and racial balances of power [as well as] the Southern white need for black labor" (122).

3. Donald Ringe, for example, estimates that the novel is set in 1881 because that's when the Texas and Pacific Railroad reached Natchitoches.

4. United Fruit, which would come to dominate the tropical fruit industry, was not formed until 1899. At the moment of the novel's composition—and even more so at the time the novel is set—bananas were still a luxury item.

5. We wonder if Chopin chuckled as she created this syntactically racy image, linking Thérèse's would-be lover with bananas.

6. It is interesting to note that after her nephew Gregoire dies, Thérèse pays for masses to be said on his behalf, "not that Thérèse held very strongly to this saying of masses" (143), yet another indication that her Catholicism seems to be strategic rather than foundational.

7. Suzanne Lebsock notes that "major statutory changes in the law of married-women's property in . . . Louisiana awaited the 1880s and beyond" (215).

8. When Thérèse tells him that he's a coward for leaving Fanny, Hosmer suddenly sees himself differently, even though he was not eager "to accept a view of the situation that would place him in his own eyes in a contemptible light" (39). Her words "carried an element of truth" that forces him to reconsider his actions and his attitudes.

9. Marie Louise's self-assertion results in her death, in a way similar to Edna Pontellier's decision at the end of *The Awakening,* in which her decision to swim out to sea is an act of self-destructive autonomy.

WORKS CITED

Appiah, Kwame Anthony. *Cosmopolitanism: Ethics in a World of Strangers.* New York: Norton, 2006.

Baron, Mathew. "A History of Bananas." August 21, 2017. https://gourmetnuts anddriedfruit.com/a-history-of-bananas.

Beer, Janet, ed. *The Cambridge Companion to Kate Chopin.* Cambridge: Cambridge University Press, 2008.

Campbell, Donna. "*At Fault:* A Reappraisal of Kate Chopin's Other Novel." In *The Cambridge Companion to Kate Chopin,* edited by Janet Beer, 27–43. Cambridge: Cambridge University Press, 2008.

Chopin, Kate. *At Fault.* 1890. Edited with an introduction and notes by Bernard Koloski. London: Penguin, 2002.

Cocks, Catherine. *Doing the Town: The Rise of Urban Tourism in the United States, 1850–1915.* Berkeley: University of California Press, 2001.

Fischer, Claude S. *America Calling: A Social History of the Telephone to 1940.* Berkeley: University of California Press, 1992.

Gunning, Sandra. *Race, Rape, and Lynching: The Red Record of American Literature, 1890–1912.* Oxford: Oxford University Press, 1996.

Hall, Alice Petry. *Critical Essays on Kate Chopin.* Boston: G. K. Hall, 1996.

Jenkins, Virginia Scott. *Bananas: An American History.* Washington, DC: Smithsonian Books, 2000.

Lebsock, Suzanne D. "Radical Reconstruction and the Property Rights of Southern Women." *Journal of Southern History* 43, no. 2 (1977): 195–216.

Levine, Caroline. *Forms: Whole, Rhythm, Hierarchy, Network.* Princeton, NJ: Princeton University Press, 2015.

Mizruchi, Susan L. *The Rise of Multicultural America: Economy and Print Culture, 1865–1915.* Chapel Hill: University of North Carolina Press, 2008.

Morin, Karin M. *Frontiers of Femininity: A New Historical Geography of the Nineteenth-Century American West.* Syracuse, NY: Syracuse University Press, 2008.

Ringe, Donald A. "Cane River World: Kate Chopin's *At Fault* and Related Stories." *Studies in American Fiction* 3, no. 2 (1975): 157–66.

Russell, David. "A Vision of Reunion: Kate Chopin's *At Fault.*" *Southern Quarterly: A Journal of the Arts in the South* 46, no. 1 (2008): 8–25.

Taylor, Helen. "'The Perfume of The Past': Kate Chopin and Post-Colonial New Orleans." In *The Cambridge Companion to Kate Chopin,* edited by Janet Beer, 147–60. Cambridge: Cambridge University Press, 2008.

Reconciling the (Post)Plantation in *At Fault*

Reunion Romance, Western Expansionism,
and the (Neo)Liberal Turn

NATALIE AIKENS

Lisa Hinrichsen writes in *Possessing the Past: Trauma, Imagination, and Memory in Post-Plantation Southern Literature* (2015) that "the post-plantation white southern imagination is marked by ambivalence about lingering modes of mimicry and mastery" (2). In *At Fault*, mimicry and mastery exist simultaneously; the novel highlights both the repetition of old systems and mastery in the sense of hegemonic authorities over near-powerless subordinates as well as mastery, in the sense of moving forward and changing. Kate Chopin's *At Fault*, in fact, wavers between two tonal registers—one obscuring and the other recording the violent, racist plantation legacy shaping the novel's present.

Considering *At Fault* in the context of reconciliation in the US South and the larger nation in the late nineteenth century, these two tonal registers—obscuring and recording—correlate respectively to (1) projecting a national fantasy of white supremacy that erases or disposes of Black, multi-ethnic, precariat, and otherwise marginalized workers and persons as well as their liberties, rights, and economic potentialities; and (2) critiquing the historical fait accompli of the Compromise of 1877 in order to suggest its failure, its fault.[1]

While both tonal registers exist, suggesting conceivably Chopin's own ambivalence to white supremacy, the ambivalence of the nation at large to this project, Chopin's early development as a writer, or some combination thereof, Chopin amplifies the national critique over the national fantasy she juxtaposes with it in her first novel.

Fantasies emerging from and/or incorporating the US South, according to Hinrichsen, often envision it as homogeneous and harmonious.

Invoking W. J. Cash's canonical text *The Mind of the South,* Hinrichsen suggests that "Cash's 'one South' is predicated on the obscuring of real diversity within the region, including the imaginative eradication of feminine agency and African American presence: the South, inherently diverse and heterogeneous, can only be seamlessly integrated and made ideologically coherent and whole through fantasy" (8). Hinrichsen emphasizes the way in which fantasies edit out groups and agents active in the southern region, especially Blacks and women. What remains, then, is the fantasy propagated by the US South of whiteness and maleness, "a (mythic) stable, patriarchal, white power structure in which pain can be kept at bay" (6). Hinrichsen notes that another one of the common myths of the US South found in its literature is "the nostalgic, pastoral visions of plantation harmony still anachronistically found in modern southern literature" (12).

Although Chopin's text does traffic in some "nostalgic, pastoral visions," it generally refrains from what George Handley calls "collective amnesia"—the partially deliberate forgetting of traumatic and violent events in the Americas (26). Instead, the novel's critique exists through its exposure of the oppressive social and economic mechanisms of the plantation system and by locating the plantation system within a northern/western /US network of violent, oppressive systems. In short, Chopin exposes the abuses of authority and power, its functions, and its tensions, maintaining that it is not the South, but the North and the larger nation that needs "reconstruction." Speaking of the inner workings of power, Foucault writes in *Discipline and Punish: The Birth of the Prison:* "Effects of domination are attributed not to 'appropriation,' but to dispositions, manoeuvres, tactics, techniques, functionings; that one should decipher in [this power] a network of relations, constantly in tension, in activity, rather than a privilege that one might possess; that one should take as its model a perpetual battle rather than a contract regulating a transaction or the conquest of a territory" (26). In other words, power functions not because of inherent might, right, or possession of power, but through the methodologies and practices of power that are recognizable through the conflicts that arise because of and through the exercise of power. Chopin makes plain the workings of the postplantation's power through three nodes of critique in *At Fault:* the reunion-romance genre, western expansionism and imperialism, and the politico-economic (neo)liberal turn.

In the first node of critique, Chopin largely subverts the stereotypical imperial implications of the reunion-romance genre by changing or expanding the genre's plotting, its setting, and its cast. Chopin also wields the popular late nineteenth-century genre to point out the North's own flaws needing "reconstruction," to criticize northern militarism and imperialism, and to decry the Compromise of 1877 for sacrificing individual interests to large corporations. In a second node of critique Chopin employs tropes of frontier novels to connect the North's imperialism in the US South during Reconstruction to western expansionism and imperialism throughout US history. In doing so she excuses and stresses the exploitation and violence of the United States' imperial project. Finally, Chopin uses mimicry to underscore the staying power of exploitative systems based on plantation capitalism, showing the institution of the plantation to be, in some ways, impervious to change and yet, marking the ways in which Black characters utilize plantation capitalism to stimulate their own economic gain and produce their own precarious upward mobility. Chopin critiques the (post)plantation system itself as well as the classical liberalism fueling the system's fin de siècle success.

At Fault *as a Reunion Romance*

> In every generous bosom . . . rose the thought—"These are not of another nation, but our citizens." Their mistakes, their evil cause, belonged to the system under which they were reared, but their military skill and heroic bravery belong to the nation.
>
> —HENRY WARD BEECHER, *Norwood,* a reunion romance

At Fault considers the heroine Thérèse Lafirme, recently widowed, who has inherited a four-thousand-acre Louisiana plantation from her husband just after the end of Reconstruction. Thérèse contracts with a westerner with northern capital named David Hosmer to allow part of her plantation to become a sawmill. A romance ensues until Thérèse becomes aware that David is divorced, which she cannot countenance as a Catholic. She encourages David to remarry his young alcoholic bride from St. Louis and return with her to Place-du-Bois, Thérèse's plantation. A romantic relationship has also been budding between Thérèse's nephew Grégoire and David's much younger sister Melicent, but after David's return with his wife social relations between the two families are somewhat strained until Fanny Hosmer relapses into alcoholism and dies, along with Thérèse's "mammie," Marie Louise, in a great flood that washes away the northern woman and the would-be Black female plantation competitor, allowing Thérèse and David to reignite their romance, which ends in marriage.

In addition to the main arc of the romantic relationship between Thérèse and David there are several subplots worth noting that help to subvert the usual conventions of the genre. Throughout the novel whether the Black servants are meant to be picking cotton, working in the mill, or doing housework, these characters rebel in significant ways, the most common being not performing the duties their white employers request them to carry out. However, several characters engage in more active rebellion too. Before the action of the novel begins, Marie Louise, Thérèse's childhood nanny has become so grotesquely overweight that not only can she "not" work, she can no longer visit her former charge. Marie Louise lives what seems, based on the description of the food she consumes, a relatively lavish lifestyle across the river from Thérèse, where Thérèse visits her frequently. Marie Louise exudes a power of influence over Thérèse that no one else in the novel does. Joçint is an even more clearly rebellious character. The half-Black, half-Indian character does not listen to his father, Thérèse's faithful Black servant Morico. In fact, Joçint has been dismissed from his work on the plantation several times, but he has always been given another chance because of his father's faithfulness (22). Joçint's greatest and final act of rebellion is burning down David's mill, at which point Grégoire, Thérèse's nephew, shoots and kills him. Grégoire's act of aggression without command demonstrates that it is not only the Black servants who take liberties. Grégoire seldom follows his aunt's instructions. Eventually, Grégoire is killed in a bar fight long after the romance between Melicent and him has dissolved. On several occasions, Melicent, David's younger sister, is obviously in awe of the power that Thérèse wields, and Melicent mimics Thérèse's exertion of authority later in the novel. Melicent hires an English maid and ends the novel pursuing her amateur interest in botany, an activity that Mary Louise Pratt terms a "hegemonic reflex" (15). All of the characters assert, mimic, or resist imperial authority.

In terms of her use of genre in *At Fault,* Chopin both supports and subverts the stereotypical imperial implications of the reunion-romance genre. Considering only the plot trajectory of the main protagonists— David Hosmer and Thérèse Lafirme—Chopin depicts a late nineteenth-century world in which whites appear as victors. Chopin's novel is a reunion romance with elements, I argue, of a frontier "Western." Both the reunion romance and the Western are imperial genres that promote the domination of "abject" peoples by "winners"/conquerors tradition-ally labeled US "heroes."[2] In fact, these genres, especially in the late nineteenth century, might be considered propaganda, advertising and bolstering US governmental policies. The traditional northern-authored version of reunion romances portrays the domination of southerners; the "Lost Cause" intersectional romance portrays the domination of African Americans; and the Western generally features a victorious cowboy who wins because of his domination or extermination of the Indian.[3] As Nina Silber suggests in *The Romance of Reunion: Northerners and the South, 1865–1900,* a regional power differential was inherent in the reunion romance: "This image of marriage between northern men and southern women stood at the foundation of the late-nineteenth-century culture of conciliation and became a symbol which defined and justified the northern view of the power relations in the reunified nation" (7), and "The specific pairing of a Yankee husband with a south-ern wife offered the northern man a symbolic vehicle for reasserting authority. . . . Northerners enshrined the image of their victory in this metaphor, using it to reflect the political and economic leverage they hoped to exercise over Dixie" (10). Indeed, as Silber insinuates, the metaphor of reconciliation was part of northern imperialist propaganda (ironically) in which southerners participated. As Edward Said iterates in *Culture and Imperialism,* "the main battle in imperialism is over land, of course; but when it came to who owned the land, who had the right to settle and work on it, who kept it going, who won it back, and who now plans its future—these issues were reflected, contested, and even for a time decided in narrative" (xii–xiii). In other words, Said suggests that the conflicting ideologies inherent in stories about imperialism are doing important cultural work to uphold or resist imperialism. Again, focusing on only the outcome of the romantic plotting suggests Chopin wholly approves of the results of the North's domination of the South during Reconstruction; however, focusing on Chopin's efforts at publication and the literary marketplace itself lends some uncertainty to this conclusion.

To Chopin critics like Sandra Gunning and David Russell, the marriage at the close of *At Fault* between Louisianian Thérèse Lafirme and David Hosmer of St. Louis enacts the quintessential merger of "white development in the context of North-South social and economic alliances" (Gunning 72) and functions as the overarching symbol for the work. Examining the reunion-romance genre and the literary market's political climate at the historical moment in which Chopin self-published her novel, as well as Chopin's own motives for publishing (as far as they can be known), suggests Chopin may have utilized a stereotypical ending to pander to editors and readers to sell her novel. Motivations for a stereotypical finale may have included publication, money, and success on Chopin's part. Tellingly, the late nineteenth-century literary marketplace strongly favored writers whose fiction advocated North/South reconciliation, which Chopin likely would have known as "she studied the literary marketplace" (Koloski, introduction x). According to Edward Ayers, "The editors of the major magazines of the North were ... convinced that sectional reconciliation best served the interests of the nation, that the course of Reconstruction had been a mistake" (*Promise* 340). Furthermore, and more importantly, conservative white-supremacist ideology about sectional reconciliation sold. A prime example is Thomas Nelson Page's *Red Rock* (1898), which Ayers considers "the embodiment of the Southern white conservative view of Reconstruction, full of stock emotions and cardboard characters" and which "reached number five on the bestseller list, even though some Northern critics recognized it for the mixture of propaganda and fairy tale that it was" (*Promise* 348). Chopin, writing in this climate and genre eight years earlier than Page's *Red Rock,* but after Page had made his presence in the reunion-romance genre felt with his short story "Meh Lady" (1886),[4] and, acquainted through correspondence with major editors such as William Dean Howells, must have felt the pressures to conform, especially because she wanted her work to be successful.[5] Heather Kirk Thomas even conjectures about Chopin's short-story writing in the 1880s that "as some stories were repeatedly rejected, Chopin . . . needed to temper or sanitize . . . components to sell her work" ("White League" 102). In light of Thomas's speculation, we cannot clearly confirm or reject Chopin's beliefs about post-Reconstruction sectional reunion in the United States.

Likewise involved in the ambiguity of the reunion-romance ending is the political "policy of non-interference" that Chopin alludes to twice in her novel (89). This is the policy that Thérèse invokes when she realizes that encouraging David to remarry Fanny likely impedes not only her own happiness but potentially also the happiness of the two people in whose relationship she meddled. This approach of noninterference reverberates in the final chapter after David and Thérèse's marriage when David announces that he will "put no bungling hand into [Thérèse's] concerns" when it comes to the plantation on Place-du-Bois (167). Russell notes that "*At Fault* emerges from a political period in which 'a policy of non-interference' had become the order of the day" and then goes on to cite the Supreme Court's 1883 decision to overturn the Civil Rights Act of 1875 in an 8–1 decision that eroded the rights Blacks had only recently gained (20). The political period that Russell references, however, begins with the Compromise of 1877, which "compelled President Grant to give up his own policy of intervening with force in the South" and "laid the political foundation for reunion" (Woodward 10, 3). In addition to pertaining to reunion itself that the genre in which Chopin is writing is concerned with, the unwritten Compromise of 1877 more specifically affected southern Blacks such as those Chopin portrays in *At Fault* who had been sheltered under the cloak of Reconstruction until 1877 but would be hereafter without legal and military protection. Thérèse and David both supporting this policy gives the novel a clear conservative bent that might support the eventual rights of African Americans but essentially takes a "go slow" approach so as not to upset the primary reunion.

Beyond the plotting, moreover, *At Fault*'s setting in the multi-ethnic post-Reconstruction Creole South is noteworthy. Chopin's reunion romance subverts the stereotypical reunion-romance genre's focus on whites as it highlights the complexities of the geographies, cultures, and races/ethnicities that have shaped Louisiana. With the textured realm of Louisiana—not simply a fertile territory with the potential for profit to be produced—Chopin widens the scope significantly to depict a palimpsest of current and former inhabitants exhibiting what Handley terms "creoleness." "Creoleness," Handley explains, is "an attractive conception of cultural heterogeneity that stresses two important ingredients missing in most Americanist attempts to redefine 'American' culture": "the comparative *interaction* of cultures. That is . . . not los[ing] sight of the mutual agency of contestatory cultures, and secondly [a] focus on the brutal and at times violent nature of this interaction" (45).[6] Instead of a reductive binary focus (North/South, Black/white), Chopin showcases the multicultural origins and *agencies* of the peoples of the United States that include Black, American, Creole, French, and Native American and their geographical diversity. Her characters, emanating from the North, the West, the South, St. Louis, the Cane River region, and Texas, commingle and (violently) clash as they negotiate the Place-du-Bois plantation and the places connected to it.[7]

Indeed, the multi-ethnic cast of *At Fault* further disrupts the too-easy acceptance of a totally "happy" ending in the novel's central plot outcome with the marriage of Thérèse Lafirme and David Hosmer. In her history of the reunion-romance genre Silber notes that the "1890s racial politics and reunion . . . paved the way for northern acceptance of some of the most virulent forms of racism which American society had ever produced" (124). The racist politics of the era was recorded in reunion romances by southern female authors. Chopin's ending in *At Fault* may not be as heavy-handed as Sherwood Bonner's reunion

romance *Like unto Like* (1878) that features an unhappy romantic conclusion with the northern Roger Ellis parting from the southern Blythe
Herndon as well as the death of a young Black boy named Civil Rights
Bill; still, it similarly critiques the fait accompli of the Compromise of
1877. A problematic resolution at best, the compromise allowed Ruther-
ford B. Hayes to become the nineteenth president of the United States,
and it ended the US military's occupation of the US South and formal
Reconstruction, thereby abandoning the southern Black populace to
white southerners' rule. The denouement of *At Fault* emphasizes the
way in which Blacks and other minorities were cut out of the immediate national project. Rather than celebrating this historic compromise,
however, Chopin seems, instead, to point to the significant losses it
necessitated, embodied in the deaths of Marie Louise, Fanny, Grégoire,
Joçint, and Morico, and the departure of Melicent.

When David and Thérèse reunite near the end of the novel on a
train going to Place-du-Bois, the reunion, although a happy one, seems
blighted by loss, and for Thérèse, the pain of almost losing David to
the storm, given that she cannot bear to look at him, though David
twice asks Thérèse to do so (164). Chopin furthermore potentially
points out that "small" business owners like David and Thérèse were
not the supreme winners in the Compromise of 1877; men and women
like them were now, more than ever, subject to Republican conservative concerns: "an elaborate system of tariffs, subsidies, currency laws,
privileged banks, railroads, and corporations" (Woodward 35). Chopin
represents big business with the train that David and Thérèse meet on
in the penultimate chapter. No more are trains and corporations in the
periphery; no longer can such entities be represented as a single "brown
and ugly intruder" that can be kept at bay, visible only through field
glasses (6).[8] Now, David and Thérèse and their business ventures are
riding on and subject to the desires and the direction of the train and
other corporate, capitalist interests.[9] As Richard Slotkin notes in *The Fatal Environment: The Myth of the Frontier in the Age of Industrialization:
1800–1890:* "The settlement of North-South differences by the 'Compromise of 1877' (through which Hayes was elected and Reconstruction
ended) had been shaped by the pressure of railroad men and railroad

interests. A common economic crisis had brought those competitors . . . together for a common political end: the redirection of federal concern from southern politics to railroad finances" (478). Slotkin thus implies the way that the Compromise ignores individuals while it safeguards corporate—specifically railroad—advantages.

My reading of Fanny Hosmer augments the role of these capitalist interests. Fanny, a character generally ignored or excused in Chopin criticism, is also among the major subversions to the genre of the reunion romance and Chopin's vision of national "reconciliation" (83). Jane Censer, in "Reimagining the North-South Reunion: Southern Women Novelists and the Intersectional Romance, 1876–1900," notes at least one other southern female author, in M. G. McClelland, also writing in the reunion romance genre whose southern female protagonist (named Pocahontas Mason) chooses a partner "who is an 'outsider,' a northerner, and a divorcé" similar to David Hosmer (70). Thus, it isn't the fact of David as a divorcé that is unique in the genre—it is Chopin's inclusion of his first love in the plotting. Fanny is the weak-willed, frivolous, and even at times crass, first wife of David Hosmer. Fanny is Chopin's tongue-in-cheek revision of Reconstruction. In Chopin's view it is not the US South that needs the North's help to rehabilitate it into the national union; it is the North/West, represented by Fanny from St. Louis (in 1890 considered the West), that needs reconstructing and reform for the tenuous reunion to work. Thérèse's gesture and advice to the rewed Mrs. Hosmer just after Fanny arrives to Place-du-Bois are telling: "laying her hand gently on Fanny's arm, 'I know you'll be strong, and do your share in this reconciliation—do what you can to please him'" (83). Here in this scene, as usual, it is Thérèse (representing the South) who is in control as she is for the majority of the novel. The loss of the Civil War and Reconstruction were for white southerners embarrassing conditions of "domination" and "conquest" portrayed in the reunion-romance genre by the metaphor of marriage (Censer 66, 67). The condition of remarriage and Thérèse's "gentle" (southern) intervention/attempt to reconstruct/rehabilitate Fanny is similarly unbearable for Fanny once she realizes in the chapters before the storm that David is in love with Thérèse.

In terms of the national metaphor, Fanny, hailing from the ambiguously located North/West of St. Louis, symbolizes vice, especially the effect of unrestrained capitalism on the uncivilized (upper) middle class. The eminently dressed but supremely uncouth Belle Worthington, and the "handsome," adulterous Lou Dawson (Fanny's best friends) help to emphasize this characterization (52). Chopin scathingly describes Mrs. Worthington and Mrs. Dawson as "two ladies of elegant leisure, the conditions of whose lives, and the amiability of whose husbands, had enabled them to develop into finished and professional time-killers" (54). Importantly, Fanny's "reconstruction" suggests the substantive power of the South represented by Thérèse. Maureen Anderson, for example, views Thérèse's persuasion of David to remarry Fanny as "the most explicit display of Thérèse's control" (9). Alternately, Fanny's failed reconstruction emphasizes the depravity of northern/western capital, imperial interests in the West, South, and beyond—she cannot be reconstructed; while alive Fanny will find a way to engage in her vice of alcoholism at any cost just as Fanny's St. Louis friends and acquaintances while in possession of capital will continue to squander money throughout their frivolous, commodity- and acquisition-driven lives.

Even as Chopin reenvisions Reconstruction as benevolent but mildly "at fault" southern interventionism, Chopin unequivocally rejects northern militarism by leaving out the stereotypical northern soldier in the reunion romance and eschews northern imperialism as she abstains from casting the South as a potentially willing partner in the northern imperialist project (165). As Silber suggests, "the specific pairing of a Yankee husband with a southern wife offered the northern man a symbolic vehicle for reasserting authority" (10). Chopin, with David's St. Louis origins and Thérèse's French origins (and her trip late in the novel to France) and clear authority, softens the idea of Yankee superiority and alludes to a broader collaboration among worldwide whites of various ethnic backgrounds to dominate the darker people of the world. As Censer implies, the stereotypical ending of the reunion romance used by popular authors in the genre, including Thomas Page and John W. De Forest, whose "depictions of northern military supremacy" (67) supported (knowingly or not) an imperialist (northern) project.

This imperialist project, as Harilaos Stecopoulos in *Reconstructing the World* and others have noted, quickly moved beyond the borders of the United States, so that "as the twentieth century began, northerners revealed a new respect for the South as an equal and willing partner in imperialist expansion" (Silber 11). With Melicent's letter coming from the outside world in the last scene, David and Thérèse seem in a position to consider how to use their influence beyond their own sphere when the mill has consumed all of the cypress trees. Overall, Chopin's genre modifications expand the genre and critique the North's methods and its motivations.

Western Expansionism and Imperialism

> "Cultural imperialism" . . . still lives, still trivializes the West and the South, still reduces the people of both regions to character parts in a national drama. (We divide up the violent roles between us.) Unfortunately, progressive history encourages the belief that the West and the South can be easily characterized and contained, and done so in relation to the North and East.
>
> —EDWARD AYERS, "The South, the West, and the Rest"

Chopin expands her depiction of the nation's regions beyond the sectional North/South to both critique the detrimental effects of US imperialism and to decry a lost past—a nostalgic assertion. In the novel, David represents both the North and the West. David, as he himself says, is "from the West," specifically from St. Louis (8), and Thérèse Lafirme is Creole (5), what Bernard Koloski defines in the explanatory notes to *At Fault* as "a comparatively wealthy, sophisticated descendant of settlers from France or Spain" (171).[10] Mixing tropes of frontier novels with the reunion-romance genre emphasizes the ways in which the North's imperialism in the US South during Reconstruction mirrors western expansionism and imperialism throughout US history. In doing so, Chopin both excuses and stresses the exploitation and violence of the United States' imperial project.

Like her protagonists, Kate Chopin herself had multiregional ties. Although today's readers typically associate Chopin with the South in which she set much of her fiction, Chopin's first novel reminds readers of her ties to the West by differing in one major respect from all of her other work: a significant portion of it is set in St. Louis, a city considered in the late nineteenth century as part of "the West." The author, who was not only born and raised in St. Louis but lived there from 1884 until her 1904 death, also used a St. Louis printing company to self-publish her novel. Critics or individuals first introduced to Chopin's literary acumen through *At Fault* praised and/or criticized the writer and her fiction that hailed, according to nineteenth-century reviews, from either the West or both the South and West. None of Chopin's contemporary reviewers addressing *At Fault* labeled its author a southern writer alone.[11]

Furthermore, considering the western expansionist elements of *At Fault* makes sense given the fact that Chopin seems to have, in Heather Kirk Thomas's words, "considered herself a vital working member of the Western literary movement" ("Development" 70). Thomas's evidence for this statement is a review-essay Thomas refers to as "newly discovered" in 1990 ("Development" 69). The *St. Louis Republic* published Chopin's piece in its December 9, 1900, Sunday edition under the heading, "Development of the Literary West. A Review. Written for the Sunday Republic by Mrs. Kate Chopin" ("Development" 70). In this essay written ten years after *At Fault* was published, Chopin praises and critiques a list of western writers from Bret Harte to Hamlin Garland and Ambrose Bierce writing "away off in California" (quoted in Thomas, "Development" 71).[12] While Harte, Garland, and Bierce continue to be thought of as western writers in twenty-first-century literary studies, the line Chopin traces around western writers includes a far broader range of authors and geographies than our current century envisions. She claims as western the works of Mark Twain, those of the Northwest and Indiana as well as the recent writings of Chicagoans—which Chopin pans—(potentially alluding to, among others, Theodore Dreiser and his *Sister Carrie,* published in 1900), and hometown St. Louis writers Chopin touts—such as the curiously named Winston Churchill (quoted in Thomas, "Development" 72). Given that in Chopin's own categorization a decade after she published *At Fault* she and her first novel would have fit squarely into her own definition of western writers/western writing, it seems apt to query how *At Fault* signals its hallmarks as an "intensely interesting story developing in the West," which, Chopin notes, "hundreds of men and women, keen with artistic perception, are telling . . . and telling . . . well" (quoted in Thomas, "Development" 71).

Chopin's geo-literary taxonomy is not without precedent; classifications of "southern" and "western" have fluctuated throughout the United States' political and literary history, problematizing the idea of static regional affiliations. Areas we now think of as the "South" or the "Midwest" such as Louisiana and St. Louis, respectively, were thought of as the West through the mid- to late nineteenth century. Early in the United States' nationhood its western border was the Mississippi River as of the 1783 Treaty of Peace with Great Britain (Lawson and Seidman 17). And Louisiana wasn't acquired from France until the Louisiana Purchase in May 1803. In literary lore, Thomas Mayne Reid's novel of 1856, set primarily in Louisiana and St. Louis (and the inspiration for Boucicault's *The Octoroon*), was titled *The Quadroon or, Adventures in the Far West.* Dion Boucicault's play *The Octoroon,* similarly set in Louisiana, first premiered in 1859 with a scene in which vigilante justice is about to be enacted wrongly on the Indian when the good northern overseer Scudder suggests, "you call yourselves judges—you ain't—you're a jury of executioners. It is such scenes as these that bring disgrace upon our *Western* life" (163, my emphasis). Additionally, the region we know today as the South was linked to the movement alternately called "'frontier humor,' 'pioneer humor,' 'Western humor' and 'Southwestern humor'" with authors such as Mark Twain most famously in his 1884 novel *Huckleberry Finn* (Chamberlain 201). Finally, in the 1930s, according to Bob Brinkmeyer, the South and West were culturally aligned by the Agrarians, who "for a while dreamed of teaming up with like-minded regionalists from the American West, with whom they shared a fundamental conviction that the South and West were colonies of the North and the forces of finance capitalism" (8–9). And, in a far more problematic association, the Agrarians also "embraced the resistance to American expansionism, lionizing instead Native Americans and their efforts to stop American's westward progression. Native Americans, by the Agrarians' regionalist model, were obvious victims of the same pioneering spirit from which they saw Dixie suffering" (Brinkmeyer 9). Chopin traffics in proto-Agrarian sentiment, as *At Fault* incorporates some ambiguous nostalgia for an "Old South" myth and a myth of the lost frontier, the West, which Frederick Turner would famously note was "gone" in his address of 1893, *The Significance of the Frontier in American History*, three years after Chopin's *At Fault* was published. Significantly, however, the US Census of 1890 declared the frontier eliminated the same year that Chopin published her novel (Lawlor 1).

David Hosmer, in his journey south, in fact, fits many of the classic hallmarks of a frontier hero, associating him with western expansionism and marking him as an agent of US imperialism that Chopin seems to both revere and censure. On the one hand, David, the male protagonist whom readers are meant to cheer in *At Fault*, springs from a celebrated heroic tradition. As Brinkmeyer writes, "Fiction in the classic American tradition, or at least what was once deemed classic—Melville, Cooper, Thoreau, Hemingway, and a few others—tends to celebrate a solitary hero breaking out *from* a restrictive society and *into* a world of uncharted freedom" (4). David leaves the contrived social world of St. Louis with its matinées, dinner parties, and general frivolity for the more restful, "natural" world of Louisiana, replete with natural resources available to be mined.[13] To say this another way, at its base, David's is a tale of man who leaves home for the wild frontier, where he establishes and becomes king of a new order like a Prospero or a Huck Finn, only by first confronting his adversary the (native) Indian(s). David Hosmer, in other words, is a Daniel Boone figure leaving his home and setting out into the deep (southern) woods, a fact emphasized by the name of the Lafirme plantation, "Place-du-Bois," "a wooded area" (Chopin 171).

On the other hand, overcoming the Indian and laying claim to and "conquering" territory (or at least trees) associates David with settler colonialism rampant in the late nineteenth-century West and denounced, for example, in María Ruiz de Burton's *The Squatter and the Don,* published five years before Chopin's *At Fault*. Although Thérèse approves David's sawmill and his stay on Place-du-Bois, he irrevocably changes the landscape and insinuates himself (legally, but dominantly) into the realm. Chopin critiques David and "the North as West, a manifestation of the forces of rapacious expansion" (Brinkmeyer 5). As other scholars have noted, David's arrival comes on the heels of the arrival of the railroad, which Thérèse judges "a brown and ugly intruder"; and the forces that brought the railroad and David both have their roots in industrial production and modernization (4). In a telling discussion between David and Mr. Worthington, David's friend maintains that David's philosophical alter ego, Homeyer (closely aligned with David himself) "would tear down and leave devastation behind him; building up nothing. He would deprive a clinging humanity of the supports about which she twines herself, and leave her helpless and sprawling upon the earth" (68). David demurs, replying, "No, no, he believes in a natural adjustment" but "is a little impatient to always wait for the inevitable natural adjustment" (68). Although Hosmer denies the correctness of Mr. Worthington's charge, the reader cannot help but wonder if there is more than a grain of truth in what he alleges, given the mill's efficiency and the time that passes in the novel (more than two years from beginning to end).

Nevertheless, David clearly welcomes the progress of modernity. David and his sister Melicent, though most recently from St. Louis and the West, because they had not been long in St. Louis (their parents were from elsewhere), lack distinct origins and geographical ties (8, 32). Chopin thus associates both Hosmers with newness and leaving the past behind. This further associates them with characteristics of western heroes such as "romantic westernism" and "originality." Mary Lawlor, for example, in *Recalling the Wild: Naturalism and the Closing of the American West,* emphasizes in her explanation of "romantic westernism," using Daniel Boone as a prime example, Boone's "originality" or "the will to be new, to start things over again" (22). As Lawlor indicates, Boone is "ever a new man, he is not placed by any of his surroundings, but rather places them in his wake" (22–23). David brings a fresh start to Place-du-Bois, while Melicent, leads a whirlwind, peripatetic lifestyle, linking her to a western classification as well.

However, this mythological view of the West as "the space unburdened by history, space where a person can begin anew, leaving the past behind" is undercut by both theorists and Chopin in *At Fault* (Brinkmeyer 16). Scholars like Annette Kolodny and Anne McClintock urge us to see beyond such an easy conception of the West.[14] As McClintock clarifies: "The myth of the virgin land is also the myth of the empty land, involving both a gender and a racial dispossession. With patriarchal narratives, to be virgin is to be empty of desire and void of sexual agency, passively awaiting the thrusting male insemination of history, language and reason" (30). Additionally, if Chopin likens David to Daniel Boone, or, closer to the character's name, Davy Crockett, it is important to remember Richard Slotkin's caution in *Regeneration through Violence,* that "men like Davy Crockett became national heroes by defining national aspiration in terms of so many bears destroyed, so much land preempted, *so many trees hacked down,* so many Indians and Mexicans dead in the dust" (5, emphasis added). Chopin, obviously critical through Thérèse of the "Cypresse Funerall" Place-du-Bois undergoes throughout the novel in service to David's mill, similarly critiques the violence at the mill that David indirectly brings to the plantation (10).[15]

Through their dual backgrounds of southern/French-descended and northern/western, Chopin links her main protagonists to regional imperialism and racial dispossession and denies an optimistic reading of white rule or imperialism by any entity. Thérèse's French descent links her to French imperialism and colonialism in Louisiana; her plantation mistress status links her to the imperialism of slavery; and her affiliation with the US South links her to the North's imperialism and military, juridical, and economic occupation of the South during Reconstruction and the lingering effects of this occupation after Reconstruction. David, too, is connected to imperialism in more than one way. Through his northern capital he is linked to a commercial imperialism of the South, and through his commercial enterprise in the South he is linked to postslavery's virtual reenslavement of Blacks. Through his western roots, he is linked to the destruction of land and Native Americans in the pursuit of manifest destiny.

One of the two "western-style" gunfights in *At Fault* shows Chopin's pains to limn Thérèse's and David's ancestral and individual roles in the displacement and deaths of Indians, Blacks, and the working class in the West and in the South, underscoring her critique of the nation's imperialism. When Grégoire comes upon Joçint in the process of burning down the sawmill, he promptly shoots the unarmed half-Indian, half-Black character, showing disregard for both populations' lives—violence that epitomizes the history of the West and the South. In *The Fatal Environment* Richard Slotkin asserts that terminology associated with "Indian warfare" was often employed with respect to class warfare, far more common after 1877 (477–80). This further connects Joçint to industrialism and union strikers (and thus, white agitators in addition to those of color). Gunning implies that Grégoire serves as an "enforcer" for Thérèse's and David's racial politics in this violent moment, helping them to propagate and conceal a "system based on a subjugation of black labor," "masked behind the figure of Grégoire" (70). Grégoire's killing of the Native American, Black, and working-class Joçint, however, serves to underscore more than regional, sectional, or temporal policies; Grégoire and his off-site, narrated death, represent the open secrets that are emblematic of longtime imperialism integral to the founding of the United States and nineteenth-century expansionism.[16]

While Grégoire may have pulled the trigger and is thus the sole party directly responsible for the death of half-Black, half-Indian Joçint, national US policies of abandoning Reconstruction in the South and promoting settlement of the West, aided by disease and the Indian Wars that decimated the numbers of Indians in the West, are "at fault" as well and should be blamed for killing Black and Indian children either literally (through lynching or warfare) or figuratively (by condemning future children and generations of Blacks to sharecropping and Jim Crow laws and by ensuring that Indian children because of the Indian Removal Act of 1830 and infamous boarding schools would grow up not knowing their ancestral homelands or their cultural ways). While Chopin may or may not have been alluding to contemporary events, knowledgeable contemporary readers might have made such connections. Nevertheless, it is clear in *At Fault* that white power structures are to blame for Black and Indian deaths. Chopin herself signaled her awareness a decade after the publication of *At Fault* in her review-essay on Western literature that "the [Indian] is vanishing" (quoted in Thomas, "Development" 71).[17]

NATALIE AIKENS

The (Post)Plantation Economy and the (Neo)Liberal Turn

> Colonial women made none of the direct economic or military decisions
> of empire and very few reaped its vast profits . . . nonetheless, the rationed
> privileges of race all too often put white women in positions of decided—if
> borrowed—power, not only over colonized women but also over colonized
> men. As such, white women were not the hapless onlookers of empire but
> were ambiguously complicit both as colonizers and colonized, privileged
> and restricted, acted upon and acting.
>
> —ANNE McCLINTOCK, *Imperial Leather*

If investigating elements of the frontier novels associated with western
literature in *At Fault* highlights a macrocosmic view of the imperialist
nature of US history, investigating the elements sustaining the postplantation economy of the late nineteenth century limns the effects of
imperialism on a microcosmic level: its exploitative conditions causing
precarity for workers seeking upward mobility, the enduring power of
capitalism, and little real social or economic change. While the stereotypical plot points and character tropes of the genre of (post)plantation
fiction bolster plantation-era ideals, the divergences from the stereotypical form in Chopin's (post)plantation novel serve to question such ideals. The postplantation operates by utilizing the same well-established
racial and class hierarchies utilized during formal slavery and by valuing
profit and production above all else, undercutting the idea that the pre-
fix "post" can appear alongside "plantation" without thoughtful qualifi-
cation. The postplantation is both a social and an economic institution
with the two components functioning to reinforce one another. Handley
implies, however, that the social aspect is the more important quality in
postplantation literature. Handley maintains that "family history is the
thematic and structural sine qua non of postslavery narrative" (3). But
it is neither family history nor social connections among the characters
that Chopin's *At Fault* chiefly explores. Chopin's *At Fault* concentrates
less on social relations than on economic relations; this focus is evident in Thérèse and David's relationship founded on and predominately
steeped in their business association upon Thérèse's property.

Chopin's depiction of (post)plantation economies makes clear that both Black characters' resistance to the plantation structures and white characters' reinvention of these structures in the post-Reconstruction era demonstrate little real change because of the mimicry of old systems in the resistance to and reinvention of plantation structures. New groups have come to power, but systemic change has not occurred. Those newly in power, no matter their status, too often act exactly like the white male imperialists in power before them, continuing policies privileging profit and employing violence and exploitation. For example, as scholars have argued, Thérèse's gentler authority upon the plantation nevertheless means many of the same "traditional racial codes and racial balances of power" (Gunning 70). Yet Chopin's text tends to mark rather than mask this fact.

Even more telling, potentially, are Chopin's investigations of Black economies. Two Black characters, Marie Louise and Nathan, underrepresented in *At Fault* criticism, epitomize the changes and upheavals of the capitalist-focused (post)plantation economy as well as underscore Chopin's critique of classical liberalism and its contradictions. It is through two Black characters' mimicry in *At Fault* that the slippage/parody allows Chopin to further emphasize the ties to the old system (and the difficulty of eradicating them), the precarity of individuals engaged in profit-based systems, and the presence of plantation capitalism in postslavery economics not directly tied to the plantation. Additionally, Chopin notes the ways in which the marginalized utilize plantation capitalism to stimulate their own economic gain and produce their own precarious upward mobility.

An ironic courting scene between Thérèse's nephew Grégoire and David's sister Melicent, whose flirtations initially forecast "a conventional double love plot" (Campbell 28), help to illustrate Chopin's critique of postplantation frameworks mirroring plantation-era frameworks. The stark contrast of the white lovers relaxing and the Black laborers picking cotton in the field blurs the line between terms such as "antebellum" and "postbellum," "slavery" and "postslavery," and "plantation" and "postplantation." During the scene, Melicent, resting in a pirogue, imagines herself "an Indian maiden of the far past, fleeing and seeking with her dusky lover some wild and solitary retreat on the borders of this lake" (16). Chopin, perhaps, subtly alludes to the fact that it is the displacement of Indians that allows this scene to take place at all. Moments later the couple passes the grave of old McFarlane, who, according to Grégoire, is "the meanest w'ite man that ever lived, seems like. Used to own this place long befo' the Lafirmes got it. They say he's the person that Mrs. W'at's her name wrote about in Uncle Tom's Cabin" (17).[18] On another trip, specifically to visit old McFarlane's grave, the narrator observes the scene around Melicent and Grégoire: "There were patches of the field before them, white with bursting cotton which scores of negroes, men, women and children were dexterously picking and thrusting into great bags that hung from their shoulders and dragged beside them on the ground; no machine having yet been found to surpass the sufficiency of five human fingers for wrenching the cotton from its tenacious hold" (42). The narrator later outlines Grégoire's part in the cycle of cotton harvesting, contrasting it with that of the black forms picking cotton in the field: "Grégoire's presence would be needed later in the day, when the cotton was hauled to gin to be weighed; when the mules were brought to the stable, to see them properly fed and cared for, and the gearing all put in place. In the meanwhile he was deliciously idle with Melicent" (43). The comparison with old McFarlane's abused slaves and the present picture of Black bodies laboring while white bodies linger idly differs only in the authority exercised to motivate the Black labor force. In McFarlane's case, it would seem to be violence, while in Mrs. Lafirme's case, "gentle influence" (22). But what is most uncomfortable is that the oppressive structure of white leisure and Black labor remains unchanged (not to mention the contrast between the narrator's careful note that the farm animals are "properly fed and cared for" and the narrator's silence as to whether Black workers enjoy similar privileges). These juxtapositions and comparisons are ones that Chopin makes deliberately and instructively.

Marie Louise

Marie Louise, like Thérèse, uses the plantation's structures as a way in which to gain power. She thus replicates the structure that at one time may have enslaved her.[19] Her resistance, therefore, does not go outside the bounds of plantation capitalism and plantation hierarchies. But she does effectively gain power by mimicking these hierarchies and by negating the typical white-Black power structure, at least in her relationship with Thérèse. In spite of critics who have seen her reductively as a forgotten "sign" (Russell 18) or a "stereotypical mammy" (Anderson 6; Castillo 63), and in spite of her death in the novel, Marie Louise, through her role as Thérèse's former nurse/mammy and her consistent resistance to Thérèse's power, contradicts ideas of clear-cut power binaries of master/slave, landowner/tenant, or colonizer/colonized. Chopin employs the grotesque to bring sharp visibility to the subaltern and her subversive behavior, pointing out the subversive in the most respected Black female in white southern mythology: the mammy figure. Where white southern mythology would represent the mammy as obedient and harmless, and thereby "the ideal slave, and the ideal woman" (White 58), Chopin shows that the very characteristics that white planter culture embraced in the stereotypical mammy can also be used subversively. Moreover, her move from slave to owner of a "slave economy" clearly illustrates McClintock's point that "race and ethnicity" is not "synonymous with black or colonized" (*Imperial Leather* 7), even in the last decade of the nineteenth-century South, in which "racial politics and reunion . . . paved the way for . . . some of the most virulent forms of racism which American society had ever produced" (Silber 124). Ultimately, however, Marie Louise, like Thérèse, David, and the rest of Chopin's characters, is trapped in the inherently flawed system of plantation capitalism. Marie Louise, with her slave economy and mimicry of the methods that formerly enslaved African Americans, brings attention to the inherent flaws in that system.

One of the stereotypical traits of the mythological Black mammy figure is her characteristic plumpness, which often points to her asexuality. In Chopin this plumpness is grotesquely amplified in order to brighten the spotlight on Marie Louise's resistance. Yaeger asserts that southern women writers utilize "the grotesque," a process by which "dissonance gets magnified or multiplied; anomaly gets figured as monstrosity, and monstrosity itself becomes a way of casting out or expelling the new"

(7). Thérèse holds no power over Marie Louise, quite the opposite. Marie Louise's size points to this power incongruity. Rather than merely connoting asexuality, Chopin designs a new way of seeing the mammy's bulk. Critics neglect Marie Louise's massive frame itself as being a form of resistance, let alone the main resistance she employs against the woman whom she nursed and cared for, but it is just that. As Chopin's narrator tells us, "[Marie Louise's] ever increasing weight had long since removed her from the possibility of usefulness, otherwise than in supervising her small farm yard" (88). In other words, it is Marie Louise's "cumbersome size" that gains her a cabin of her own and disables her from working for Thérèse and from doing her own farmwork, not the customary cause for retirement of age that allows Joçint's "old father Morico" his freedom (22). Also unlike Morico, whose "brown visage . . . had grown old and weather beaten," and thus portrays his declining health (22), Marie Louise's physique portrays her prosperity. She is able to provide a generous spread when Thérèse visits, including milk, butter, eggs, flour, coffee, and a dish of *croquignoles* (88, "crunchy cookies" [Koloski, "Explanatory Notes" 175]). Finally, the names that Marie Louise and Thérèse call one another also underscore the overt power reversal at work between them: while Thérèse is "*Tite maîtresse*" (88, 90, 91, "little mistress" [Koloski, "Explanatory Notes" 175]), Marie is "*Grosse tante*" (88, 90, 91, "big aunt" [Koloski, "Explanatory Notes" 175]).

Another stereotypical trait of the mammy in white southern mythology is her supreme capabilities. White signals that "Mammy was the woman who could do anything, and do it better than anyone else. Because of her expertise in all domestic matters, she was the premier house servant and all others were her subordinates" (47). While white mythology would see her trustworthiness in this description, Chopin again reinvents the stereotype, imagining the characteristic as descriptive of a ruler, not one who takes rules well. Being linguistically and culturally distinct and distant from other Black servants leaves Marie Louise with a status that is distinct and distant from theirs as well, and suited to rule over those who share her color. As the narrator bluntly informs readers, "[Marie Louise] had little use for '*ces néges Américains*,' as she called the plantation hands—a restless lot forever shifting about and changing quarters" (88–89, "these Negro Americans" [Koloski, "Explanatory Notes" 175]). Marie Louise derives her freedom and status from her employment of underlings, in much the same way that Thérèse derives her own power. Marie Louise "*supervise[s]* her small farm yard," implying her own workers. Marie Louise is no servant then; she is, instead, her own minor plantation mistress.

After Thérèse allows Marie Louise a tenuous freedom, Marie Louise, it seems, begins her own mini-colony/plantation across the river from her former charge. The novel opens with the narrator telling of the tragic loss of Thérèse's husband. But it is what brings Thérèse out of mourning that propels her toward her role as plantation "master" and hints to readers (and perhaps Thérèse herself) of a competitor, later insinuated to be Marie Louise. It is a house servant by the name of Hiram who sets into motion Thérèse's reign upon the plantation. He does this by telling her a simple fact meant to startle her out of her bereaved state: "Things is a goin' wrong; dat dey is. I don't wants to name no names 'doubt I'se 'bleeged to; but dey done start a kiarrin' de cotton seed off the place, and dats how" (5). Hiram's words immediately have their desired effect as Thérèse is "rouse[d] from her lethargy of grief" because "wrong doing presented as a tangible abuse and defiance of authority, served to move her to action" (5).

The stolen cotton seed points to a larger operation in place, what Ira Berlin and Philip D. Morgan call a "slave economy," or in this case, a postslavery economy at a time when post-Reconstruction conditions all too closely resembled slavery for large numbers of Black men, women, and children in the US South. Berlin and Morgan define a slave economy by dividing the work a slave did for his master and the work he did himself: "The work slaves did for their masters accounted for most of their labouring time, but the independent economic activities of slaves . . . had far-reaching consequences. By producing food for themselves and for others, tending cash crops, raising livestock, manufacturing finished goods, marketing their own products, consuming and saving the proceeds, and bequeathing property to their descendants, slaves took control of a large part of their lives" (1). In other words, a slave economy can be a form of economic subversion against the imperial institution of slavery, that "form of labour organization in which masters forcibly expropriated the slaves' person, plus the lion's share of the surplus that slaves produced" (Berlin and Morgan 2). The Black workers in Chopin's novel perhaps tacitly acknowledge with their theft an awareness of their own exploitation at the hands of white planters with this criminal act that in part balances the system's power inequity.

With their act of theft, the unnamed plantation hands have reversed power dynamics in a number of ways. In "kiarrin' de cotton seed off de place" (5), not stealing gold or silver, or money (if much of either existed after the fall of the Confederacy), and not even the product, the saleable cotton itself or something akin to it, which might be sold and immediately turned into profit, the workers are in fact appropriating the product of their own labor. Eighteenth-century philosophers such as Locke would regard the theft as the plantation hands taking what rightfully belongs to them by virtue of just that—their having produced it with their own labor. Instead of "stealing" a product, cotton, in and of itself, the unnamed "thieves" procure the means to produce again through their own labor a product of their own. Thus it can be inferred the plantation hands have developed their own production system separate from the one that only decades before had enslaved them. We don't know what happens to the cotton for sure; it is never mentioned again. But it would seem that the former slaves have become (momentarily) the masters of land, the possessors of capital, and have, thereby and therewith, the means to oppress others.

Mimicry lays bare the workings of exploitation. For McClintock, discussing Homi Bhabha's and Luce Irigaray's theories of mimicry, "mimicry is . . . a strategy of the disempowered" (*Imperial Leather* 64). Copying their former plantation master(s) allows Marie Louise and her Black workers to elevate themselves and their status—to get ahead, marginally. But ultimately, in the "slippage" between the plantation and Marie Louise's version of the postplantation it is apparent that conditions have not changed and that considerable precarity/danger is necessary to continue these operations. Marie Louise's location of herself on the other side of the river, "high up and perilously near the edge" illustrates this precarity necessary for upward mobility (88). The undesirable location potentially makes it permissible for her to inhabit this site without competition for it, but it fatally exposes her to a natural disaster. Marie Louise, thus, exemplifies the limited gains possible for marginalized persons, especially Blacks, in the US South in the post-Reconstruction era without systemic change.

Nathan

Perhaps the clearest image of the postplantation economy is the image of the raft upon the river during the storm; it demonstrates the chaos of change, the precarity of workers and goods, and the workings of old and new capitalism. This scene also contains explicit reference to a Black worker receiving remuneration for his labor—marking one systemic change in the postplantation world. Nathan is the ferryman who controls the ferry's departure and guides its path back and forth across the "red turbid stream" (154). Nathan's deft performance of his labor under the difficult circumstances of the storm impresses David, who, as he watches, remarks, "I guess you earn your money, Nathan" (158). Minutes later, however, as the imperiled Fanny struggles to stay afloat, Nathan freezes and David takes command, shouting at him: "Take hold that oar or I'll throw you overboard" (159). With an aim to lighten the load and rescue Fanny, David also threatens the white teamster with whom David quickly negotiates a deal to pay for the loss of his horses, which David forces him to drive into the river (160). In the course of a few minutes, David emerges as the captain of the raft due likely to both his status and his wielding of his capital, his ability to "pay [the teamster] twice [the horses'] value" (160). A rigid hierarchy is still firmly in place—even in the postplantation economy; David as the highest-ranking white male is the master; the white working-class male is subject to the wishes and whims of his superior; the Black working-class male is still treated as expendable; and the older Black woman, Aunt Agnes, with her "very battered umbrella" signifying that she is without sufficient protection against the natural and human elements, bears witness to the spectacle of death, violence, and loss (158).

In this scene Nathan and the teamster exhibit their capitalist motivations. Nathan does not wish to launch the raft to the other side until the raft's load is full (158). The raft is then subject to greater danger but also greater reward—more capital. Although Fanny is in danger and time is of the essence, the teamster still elects to discuss compensation for the goods the horses were carrying rather than immediately jumping into action to help save Fanny. Seemingly calm, the teamster wonders to David, "You 'low to pay fur the cotton, too?" (160). The capitalist structures and plantation hierarchies ultimately weigh down the raft and prevent the men from saving Fanny. This failure marks the way that free and unrestrained capitalism fail economically, socially, and humanistically. Instead, in (neo)classical liberalism unfettered capitalism means perpetually fettered laborers—human beings fettered to and at the mercy of a system.

Scholars have mapped the ways that the era of classical liberalism in the late nineteenth century and our own era of neoliberalism echo one another. John F. Henry suggests that "the roots of the neoliberal program are found in the late 19th century" (543), and Thomas O. McGarity has noted that "'laissez faire minimalist' ideology" dominates the thinking and influences the workplace conditions in both the late nineteenth century and the late twentieth and early twenty-first centuries (5). Ultimately, Chopin neither wholly espouses nor rejects classical liberalism, but she criticizes the politico-economic (neo)liberal turn by making plain its insidious workings in numerous scenes of her novel.

While Chopin in *At Fault* perhaps forecasts an unheralded era of white supremacy in the fin de siècle United States subject only to corporate railroad interests and capitalism itself, by expanding and subverting the genre of the reunion romance her first novel also forecasts the incredible toll of this reign, connects the toll of loss to the imperialism at the roots of the founding of the United States, and elucidates the economic peril and thwarted agency for marginalized peoples in the United States under this course of action.

NOTES

1. Here I use the neoliberal term "precariat" anachronistically because it is more fitting than "proletariat" and in order to show the link between the era Chopin was writing about and our own. According to Alexandra Perisic in *Precarious Crossings: Immigration,*

Neoliberalism, and the Atlantic (2019), precariat workers experience more instability and "contingency" than do proletariat workers (10).

2. I follow a number of New Southern Studies scholars including Riché Richardson, Leigh Anne Duck, Jennifer Greeson, Harilaos Stecopoulos, and Melanie Benson (among others) who utilize Julia Kristeva's term "abject" in referring to the US South. I would also like to extend the usage of the term "abject" beyond the US South to include the US West (following Brinkmeyer and Slotkin), and beyond the geographical to include the female, Black, and Indian (following Stecopoulos and Norton). As Stecopoulos observes, Anne Norton argues that from the antebellum period the South was "represented as an 'alternative America' variously coded as female, Black, and Indian" (3).

3. As Leslie Fiedler suggests, the frontier hero of the Western contends "with the confrontation in the wilderness of a transplanted WASP and a radically alien other, an Indian—leading either to a metamorphosis of the WASP into something neither White nor Red (sometimes by adoption, sometimes by sheer emulation, but never by actual miscegenation), or else to the annihilation of the Indian (sometimes by castration-conversion or penning off into a ghetto, sometimes by sheer murder)" (24).

4. Censer suggests that Page was "the most famous southern author of romantic reunion" (66).

5. Chopin's biographer Emily Toth writes: "Now at midlife [after sending *At Fault* out for publication], Kate was impatient for literary recognition. After *Belford's* rejected *At Fault* she decided to have it printed at her own expense. . . . One thousand copies, with pale green covers, were ready on September 27, 1890, and within a week, Kate had sent them out" to various distributors, libraries, editors (including William Dean Howells), magazines, and periodicals (189). Earlier in her biography, Toth also makes clear that the success Chopin was seeking was financial as well as critical (175).

6. George Handley is actually explaining the benefits of Jean Bernabé, Patrick Chamoiseau, and Raphael Confiant's definition of "creoleness" (*"créolité"*) from the Martinican *Créolité* manifesto "In Praise of Creoleness," which Handley applauds yet has reservations about (see Handley 44–45).

7. See also Susan Castillo's "'Race' and Ethnicity in Kate Chopin's Fiction" for more on *At Fault*'s multi-ethnic cast.

8. Maureen Anderson sees the train in the novel as "a symbol of industry, movement, and progression" seemingly more positively in this penultimate scene (11).

9. As Katherine Donahue explains and points out in *Freedom from Want: American Liberalism and the Idea of the Consumer* (2003), there were inherent contradictions in classical liberalism. Donahue suggests that "at the center of classical liberal theory was the idea of laissez-faire. To the vast majority of American classical liberals, however, laissez-faire did not mean no government intervention at all. On the contrary, they were more than willing to see government provide tariffs, railroad subsidies, and internal improvements, all of which benefited producers. What they condemned was intervention on behalf of consumers.

10. Only Pamela Menke specifically terms David a westerner (92).

11. Chopin's and *At Fault*'s regional designation in reviews appears highly subjective. In general, southern reviewers note Chopin's and *At Fault*'s southern connections, and St. Louis reviewers note western connections in the same manner, but one enterprising St. Louis review notes both "South and West" connections. The only national review of Chopin's first novel, in the *Nation* (Toth 193), does not note a regional affiliation (see Toth 192; and Petry 38).

12. Thomas's essay contains a reprint of the entire contents of Chopin's December 9, 1900, review-essay.

13. Chopin, here, is hinting with David as resource seeker to denounce the mythology of "virgin land." As Slotkin reminds us, "Behind the mystique of the 'virgin' land lay the principle of the 'resource Frontier': the economic doctrine which holds that the Frontier is the discovery and conquest of new lodes of valuable resources—precious metals, industrial ores, supplies of cheap labor, 'virgin' markets" (*Fatal Environment* 531).

14. See Kolodny's *The Lay of the Land: Metaphor as Experience and History in American Life and Letters* (1975) and *The Land before Her: Fantasy and Experience of the American Frontiers, 1630–1860* (1984).

15. It's worth noting again that Place-du-Bois's name means "a wooded area," a description that would be less and less fitting as the novel and the work at the mill continue (Koloski, "Explanatory Notes" 171).

16. Slotkin further explains: "Behind the mystique of the Indian war lay a concept of social relations that insisted on the racial basis of class difference, and insisted that in a society so divided, strife was unavoidable until the more savage race was wholly exterminated or subjugated. This was a doctrine applied first of all to social relations in industry and the new cities of postwar America; and it could also apply to the governance of nonwhite populations beyond the seas, when an imperial America went in search of those new lands and virgin markets" (*Fatal Environment* 531)

17. Chopin uses a derogatory term to refer to Native Americans.

18. Several critics note that it is supposedly the plantation later owned by Oscar Chopin (Kate Chopin's husband) that Harriet Beecher Stowe represents in her attention-getting novel.

19. If the novel is set in 1881 or 1882 (see Ringe 160; and Leary 61), when Thérèse is thirty years old (5), then "Thérèse's nurse and attendant from infancy" (88), Marie Louise, may have been a slave in the early years of performing this role and/or other roles.

WORKS CITED

Anderson, Maureen. "Unraveling the Southern Pastoral Tradition: A New Look at Kate Chopin's *At Fault*." *Southern Literary Journal* 34, no. 1 (2001): 1–13.
Ayers, Edward L. *The Promise of the New South: Life after Reconstruction*. 15th anniversary ed. Oxford: Oxford University Press, 2007.

————. "The South, The West, and the Rest." *Western Historical Quarterly* 25, no. 4 (1994): 473–76.

Berlin, Ira, and Philip D. Morgan. Introduction to *The Slaves' Economy: Independent Production by Slaves in the Americas,* edited by Berlin and Morgan, 1–27. London: Frank Cass, 1991.

Boucicault, Dion. *The Octoroon.* In *Plays by Dion Boucicault,* edited by Peter Thomson, 133–69. Cambridge: Cambridge University Press, 1984.

Brinkmeyer, Bob. *Remapping Southern Literature: Contemporary Southern Writers and the West.* Athens: University of Georgia Press, 2000.

Campbell, Donna. "*At Fault:* A Reappraisal of Kate Chopin's Other Novel." In *The Cambridge Companion to Kate Chopin,* edited by Janet Beer, 27–43. Cambridge: Cambridge University Press, 2008.

Castillo, Susan. "'Race' and Ethnicity in Kate Chopin's Fiction." In *The Cambridge Companion to Kate Chopin,* edited by Janet Beer, 59–72. Cambridge: Cambridge University Press, 2008.

Censer, Jane. "Reimagining the North-South Reunion: Southern Women Novelists and the Intersectional Romance, 1876–1900." *Southern Culture* 5 (1999): 64–91.

Chamberlain, Bobby. "Frontier Humor in *Huckleberry Finn* and Carvalho's *O Coronel e o Lobisomem.*" *Comparative Literature Studies* 21, no. 2 (1984): 201–16.

Chopin, Kate. *At Fault.* 1890. Edited with an introduction and notes by Bernard Koloski. London: Penguin, 2002.

Donahue, Katherine. *Freedom from Want: American Liberalism and the Idea of the Consumer.* Baltimore: Johns Hopkins University Press, 2003.

Fiedler, Leslie. *The Return of the Vanishing American.* New York: Stein, 1968.

Foucault, Michel. *Discipline and Punish: The Birth of the Prison.* Translated by Alan Sheridan. 2nd ed. New York: Vintage, 1995.

Gunning, Sandra. "Kate Chopin's Local Color Fiction and the Politics of White Supremacy." *Arizona Quarterly* 52, no. 3 (1995): 61–86.

Handley, George. "A New World Poetics of Oblivion." In *Look Away! The US South in New World Studies,* edited by Jon Smith and Deborah Cohn. Durham, NC: Duke University Press, 2004.

Henry, John F. "The Historic Roots of the Neoliberal Program." *Journal of Economic Issues* 44, no. 2 (June 2010): 543–50.

Hinrichsen, Lisa. *Possessing the Past: Trauma, Imagination, and Memory in Post-Plantation Southern Literature.* Baton Rouge: Louisiana State University Press, 2015.

Kolodny, Annette. *The Land before Her: Fantasy and Experience of the American Frontiers, 1630–1860.* Chapel Hill: University of North Carolina Press, 1984.

———. *The Lay of the Land: Metaphor as Experience and History in American Life and Letters*. Chapel Hill: University of North Carolina Press, 1975.

Koloski, Bernard. "Explanatory Notes." In *At Fault*, by Kate Chopin, edited by Koloski, 171–77. London: Penguin, 2002.

———. Introduction to *At Fault*, by Kate Chopin, edited by Koloski, vii–xxii. London: Penguin, 2002.

Lawlor, Mary. *Recalling the Wild: Naturalism and the Closing of the American West*. New Brunswick, NJ: Rutgers University Press, 2000.

Lawson, Gary, and Guy Seidman. *The Constitution of Empire: Territorial Expansion and American Legal History*. New Haven, CT: Yale University Press, 2004.

Leary, Lewis. "Kate Chopin's Other Novel." *Southern Literary Journal* 1, no. 1 (1968): 60–74.

Mayne Reid, Thomas. *The Quadroon or, Adventures in the Far West*. Unabridged facsimile ed. Elibron, 2006.

McClintock, Anne. "Imperial Ghosting and National Tragedy: Revenants from Hiroshima and Indian Country in the War on Terror." *PMLA* 129 (2014): 819–29.

———. *Imperial Leather: Race, Gender and Sexuality in the Colonial Context*. Abingdon, UK: Routledge, 1995.

McGarity, Thomas O. *Freedom to Harm: The Lasting Legacy of the Laissez Faire Revival*. New Haven, CT: Yale University Press, 2013.

McPherson, Tara. *Reconstructing Dixie: Race, Gender, and Nostalgia in the Imagined South*. Durham, NC: Duke University Press, 2003.

Menke, Pamela Glenn. "Chopin's Sensual Sea and Cable's Ravished Land: Sexts, Signs, and Gender Narrative." *CrossRoads: A Journal of Southern Culture* 3, no. 1 (1994): 78–102.

Perisic, Alexandra. *Precarious Crossings: Immigration, Neoliberalism, and the Atlantic*. Columbus: Ohio State University Press, 2019.

Petry, Alice Hall, ed. *Critical Essays on Kate Chopin*. Boston: G. K. Hall, 1996.

Pratt, Mary Louise. *Imperial Eyes: Travel Writing and Transculturation*. 2nd ed. Abingdon, UK: Routledge, 2008.

Richardson, Riché. *Black Masculinity and the U.S. South from Uncle Tom to Gangsta*. Athens: University of Georgia Press, 2007.

Ringe, Donald. "Cane River World: Kate Chopin's *At Fault* and Related Stories. *Studies in American Fiction* 3 (1975): 157–66.

Ruiz de Burton, María Amparo. *The Squatter and the Don*. 1885. Houston, TX: Arte Público, 1992.

Russell, David. "A Vision of Reunion: Kate Chopin's *At Fault*." *Southern Quarterly* 46, no. 1 (2008): 8–25.

Said, Edward. *Culture and Imperialism.* New York: Vintage, 1993.

Silber, Nina. *The Romance of Reunion: Northerners and the South, 1865–1900.* Chapel Hill: University of North Carolina Press, 1993.

Slotkin, Richard. *The Fatal Environment: The Myth of the Frontier in the Age of Industrialization, 1800–1890.* New York: Atheneum, 1985.

———. *Regeneration through Violence: The Mythology of the American Frontier, 1600–1860.* New ed. Norman: University of Oklahoma Press, 2000.

Stecopoulos, Harilaos. *Reconstructing the World: Southern Fictions and US Imperialisms, 1898–1976.* Ithaca, NY: Cornell University Press, 2008.

Thomas, Heather Kirk. "'Development of the Literary West': An Undiscovered Kate Chopin Essay." *American Literary Realism* 22, no. 2 (1990): 69–75.

———. "The White League and Racial Status: Historicizing Kate Chopin's Reconstruction Stories." *Louisiana Literature: A Review of Literature and Humanities* 14, no. 2 (1997): 97–115.

Toth, Emily. *Kate Chopin.* New York: William Morrow, 1990.

White, Deborah Gray. *Ar'n't I a Woman? Female Slaves in the Plantation South.* New York: Norton, 1999.

Woodward, C. Vann. *Reunion and Reaction: The Compromise of 1877 and the End of Reconstruction.* 1951. Oxford: Oxford University Press, 1966.

Yaeger, Patricia. *Dirt and Desire: Reconstructing Southern Women's Writing, 1930–1990.* Chicago: University of Chicago Press, 2000.

"Miss T'rèse's System"

At Fault *and Antebellum Nostalgia*

NADINE M. KNIGHT

The opening chapter of *At Fault,* "The Mistress of Place-Du-Bois," introduces readers to the Louisiana plantation as an operation not much changed in the aftermath of war and Reconstruction. The needs of the plantation outweigh the newly widowed Thérèse Lafirme's "inconsolable" grief and showcase her adept leadership rather than signaling any sense of disarray or decay (5). When one of her now-servants (and likely former enslaved worker), Uncle Hiram, reports that cotton is being stolen, Thérèse "felt at once the weight and sacredness of a trust" (5–6) as she restores oversight among her workers and her land so that "no more seed was hauled under cover of darkness from Place-du-Bois" (6). Thérèse's duty to her workers and her land continues a sense of noblesse oblige that evokes the nostalgic view of benevolent slaveholding that became even more important with the development of the Lost Cause view of the Confederacy in the postbellum era. This view drove the popular reception of the plantation fiction published by many of Chopin's contemporaries, most notably Thomas Dixon, Thomas Nelson Page, and Joel Chandler Harris. *At Fault* reveals a narrative that, for all of its forward-looking gestures, cannot escape nostalgia for the "sacred" way of plantation life that places a white southern plantation mistress as the undiminished moral center of the plantation and the key to its true prosperity.[1] With only one exception in the novel, the Black laborers are eager to continue working for Thérèse and will often only perform work for northerners such as Melicent Hosmer if they understand the work to be part of "Miss T'rèse's system" (21), indicating their ongoing reverence for her authority. This nostalgia for antebellum life is evoked through four narrative strands: the sense of the plantation as still under attack by northern disruption; the unflattering comparison of northern physical and moral fitness in comparison to Thérèse; the ways in which peaceful Black laborers are corrupted through contact with northerners; and the emasculation and reckless failure of the chivalric white southern male. By the end of *At Fault*, characters either bend to Thérèse's system or they are no longer part of the plantation.

Where Chopin stands apart from much postwar plantation mythologizing is in the novel's refusal to allow Place-du-Bois to experience the reduced circumstances that were a common reality and a device for evoking southern sympathy in literature about the Old South. With the exception of the fallen fortunes of Thérèse's Santien relatives, Thérèse's family seems to have weathered the Civil War with no loss of financial viability or social status. This avoids the trajectory of shame, poverty, and pity that was traditionally cured by northern sympathy and love in reconciliation narratives of the postbellum period. As Nina Silber argues, after the Civil War "middle- and upper-class Yankees found the plantation aristocracy especially deserving of sentiment and sympathy because of the tremendous losses that class had endured" (106–7), and romance is often forged "through financial cooperation, an effort usually paid for by northerners" (107). In *At Fault*, Thérèse is gifted with the best of both worlds. Her plantation has escaped hardship, yet still she gains an economic boost—and, eventually, a devoted husband—through northern financial investment in her land. Precisely because Thérèse can allow northern commerce but otherwise resist cultural change at Place-du-Bois, *At Fault* reassures readers that the old ways were best and that northern cooperation could be brought under southern women's control.

Chopin's critics have differed widely in how they position *At Fault* and Chopin's literary sensibilities, with many choosing to set Chopin apart from the plantation tradition and antebellum nostalgia. Chopin's first major biographer, Per Seyersted, argues that Chopin's works were "not retrospective, and she was no antiquarian . . . she concentrated on people living in the present" (82). Similarly, Thomas Bonner declares that Chopin "speaks not for the past but to the present" (142). Maureen Anderson provocatively argues that "*At Fault* is about change" (3) because Chopin "invert[s] . . . old pastoral roles" (2). In *At Fault*, Thérèse's embrace of further monetizing her estate by selling timber rights to David Hosmer affirms that she is "a clever enough business woman" whose pragmatic acceptance of new industry makes Place-du-Bois financially secure (9). Bernard Koloski argues that Thérèse "yearns for a world in which the old traditions and customs help preserve order and harmony," but he also contends that Thérèse "largely through chance, manages to unify her two realms and achieve a sense of peace" (89). But this does not happen by chance; rather, because Thérèse has rigorously maintained her looks, her pleasant demeanor, and the loyalty of almost all of her workers, she avoids desperation and the complete usurpation of her position as the soul of Place-du-Bois.

The novel likely takes place soon after 1881, which would make Thérèse, like Chopin herself, a teen during the Civil War (Ringe 158). Although the war and Reconstruction are not openly referenced in *At Fault,* "the war itself . . . has had its effect on the society she depicts" (Ringe 158). Much of the state avoided large-scale battles during the war, with the most heated conflicts, for control of New Orleans and the Mississippi River, at a remove from the Cane River region of the novel.[2] Although Thérèse must accept some new industry, the overall impression of Place-du-Bois is that it has remained largely unchanged and untroubled by the Civil War. The best parts of her estate are those that have resisted modernization in the intervening years. "In building," the narrator tells us, Thérèse "avoided the temptations offered by modern architectural innovations and clung to . . . a style whose merits had stood the test of easy-going and comfort-loving generations" (6).[3] Much like her architectural preferences, Thérèse's understanding of her Black laborers and her position as their rightful and benevolent supervisor remains similarly unchanged with the times as she surveys the "negro quarters . . . breaking with picturesque irregularity into the systematic division of field from field" (6). Thérèse "loved . . . to view her surrounding possessions with comfortable satisfaction. Then her gaze swept from cabin to cabin" (6). What are certainly ex-slave quarters, now simply "cabins," remain in Thérèse's possession; so, by extension, do the inhabitants. This kind of easy assertion of possession of both land and laborers stands in opposition to any post-Reconstruction changes to the southern way of life to which Thérèse has been accustomed. The novel acknowledges modernity but does not retreat from antebellum values.

Chopin's own Confederate leanings—she was very close with a half brother who fought, and died, for the Confederacy—invite readers to take a keen eye to the persistence of antebellum nostalgia and resistance to northern mores in *At Fault*. Emily Toth, Chopin's definitive biographer, recounts that a teenaged Chopin became locally "famous among southern sympathizers, as one who'd stood up to the Yankees" when she risked arrest by Union soldiers for tearing down a Union flag the soldiers had affixed to her house (64). Chopin's defiance was homegrown and unsurprising for her social milieu. Chopin grew up in a slave-owning household, including one woman named Louise "who may have been Kate's mammy" (Toth 30). According to Toth, "Kate evidently forgot—or chose not to remember—that the slaves had run off" during the war, and, according to a friend, "had seen the 'devotion of which the well-treated slaves were capable'" (69). This selective and nostalgic creation of memories is further underscored when we consider the faithful devotion modeled by the likes of Uncle Hiram and Marie Louise, Thérèse's old mammy, in *At Fault*.

Such examples support the contention that "Chopin also makes use of familiar nineteenth-century stereotypes that serve both sentimental and satiric purposes" (Walker 64). The sentiment outweighs the satire in the novel as a whole, particularly as much of the satire serves to paint northerners in an unflattering, unwelcome light, as will be discussed later. David Russell offers the compelling argument that the novel "reproduces an antebellum social structure that countermands the model of development and race relations set forth during Radical Reconstruction" in order to promote white-supremacist models of order and control of Black bodies (9). Though Thérèse does very little to actively exert control over her Black laborers, her long history with many of them suggests that there has been little turnover of her labor force on Place-du-Bois and, thus, that her authority on the plantation has been benevolent in accordance with popular myths of plantation life.

Chopin echoes Lost Causist concerns about the security of the plantation (and the white mistress at its heart) at the hands of northern invaders in how Thérèse views the industrial changes at the edges of her land. Chopin uses militaristic language to underscore how beleaguered Thérèse initially feels, as the new and nearby railroad depot represents "a visionary troop of evils" and, in "the occasional tramp, she foresaw an army" (7). These hyperbolic turns of phrase, in Thérèse's perspective, collapse the distance between the novel's present and the Civil War past. Similarly, Thérèse's fear that railroad passengers who stop to shop at the depot will become "intruders forcing themselves upon her privacy" summons the popular narratives of Union soldiers invading southern plantations and committing offenses upon the women and their properties (7). Anne Sarah Rubin chronicles the "Confederate letters and diaries . . . filled with stories of women terrorized and property devasted" (89) that heightened the "fears of Confederates regarding Yankee transgressions against women despite the protection of femininity" (92). Thérèse's femininity does protect her, however; within the bounds of her property, Thérèse is unchallenged, secure, and happy. Sandra Gunning sees this as a "revision of the myth of the Southern belle" (*Race* 121) that arose "during the Civil War, when white plantation mistresses had been required to manage the slaves and land" (Gunning, *Race* 122). Thérèse's property is, according to the narrator, "rich" (6) in its fecundity and "perfect" (7) in its landscaping. Thérèse has found the perfect balance in "maintaining the old traditions and values that give dignity and beauty to life . . . because managing her large plantation provides meaningful occupation for her" (Skaggs 78). Notably, Thérèse's successes are not, then, particularly innovative: she simply embraces the plantation mistress tradition that arose during the Civil War and then resists much further progress.

The new "army" that will force itself on Thérèse's bucolic plantation comes in the form of St. Louis inhabitants who are all connected to David Hosmer, the sawmill supervisor. Although St. Louis was fiercely divided, politically, during the Civil War and post-Reconstruction, Chopin paints it as a northern city in contrast to the unquestionably southern setting of Place-du-Bois: as Nancy Walker observes, "In contrast to the Louisiana countryside, St. Louis is depicted as busy, crowded, and impersonal" (67). The characters who make it their home represent what

Walker calls "urban pretentiousness, especially in contrast to Thérèse Lafirme's natural beauty and morality," as they waste time in endless rounds of social calls and gossip (66). In order to heighten the contrast between Thérèse and the northerners who will disrupt the peaceful plantation operations at Place-du-Bois, Thérèse is a paragon of white southern womanhood in looks, moral authority, and ability to elicit happy labor from the Black inhabitants of the plantation.

Thérèse is, of course, naturally blonde, blue-eyed, and "fair, with a warm whiteness" (8). She is pleasingly plump, which Toth notes upholds what was becoming a distinctly southern standard of beauty (in contrast to leaner northern types): "Ever since the Civil War, when millions of southern women had gone hungry, plump flesh had been considered a prime womanly attraction and a sign of health" (Toth 184). Thérèse is a paragon because her weight is "judiciously guarded" (8). In contrast, the narrative repeatedly mocks the statuesque northerner Belle Worthington, whose "one hundred and seventy-five pounds of solid avoirdupois" is revealed by her friend Lou Dawson to actually be 180 pounds on the scale (53, 62). As Lou jeers, "there's no convincing her she's not a sylph" (62). The indiscretion of broadcasting Belle Worthington's exact weight and then further inflating it is meant to shame her for exceeding the ideal plumpness and suggests that, as "professional time-killers," Belle and Lou lack the restraint and sense of duty to self and others evinced by Thérèse (54). Additionally, Belle's blonde hair is cosmetically enhanced, in contrast to Thérèse's natural fairness; as Donna Campbell observes, "Thérèse's blonde 'roundness' signals . . . she is more grounded in reality" (35). Thérèse's ability to carry weight and be admired for it is one of the many ways that she alone represents womanly virtue and restraint. Indeed, the lack of northern restraint is further emphasized when the narrative reveals that Lou Dawson has engaged in an extramarital affair (57, 169)—in stark contrast to Thérèse, who self-righteously denies herself a romance with David Hosmer until Hosmer's status as a widower makes their marriage socially—and, more importantly, religiously—acceptable.

Although Peggy Skaggs finds Thérèse to be "something of a busybody," this does not alienate her Black laborers, all of whom seem grateful for her attention in ways that serve to mythologize antebellum nostalgia (76). The enthusiastic reception offered to her by Old Morico and Marie Louise, in particular, add to what Susan Castillo sees as "rather embarrassing caricatures of the Faithful Retainer stereotype" in Uncle Hiram and Aunt Belindy (Castillo 61). Thérèse's good working relationship with her laborers contrasts starkly to the novel's subplot about Melicent Hosmer's inability to retain any workers for her little cottage on the estate. Melicent, Hosmer's capricious younger sister, has a body and complexion that also lacks in contrast to Thérèse, as she is tall, thin, and has "olive tinted skin" and dark hair (14). But Melicent's true failing is that her northern manners variously offend and terrify the Black laborers at Place-du-Bois, and they either refuse to work for her altogether or are deliberately and aggressively unreliable. Melicent is thus neither as fair of complexion nor fair as an employer as Thérèse.

Melicent is so inept that not even Thérèse's efforts can overcome the way she repels Black workers. Thérèse "had used her powers, persuasive and authoritative, to procure servants for her, but without avail" (20). Melicent, who is clearly unfamiliar with socializing with Black workers, makes an inappropriate joke about cutting a Black child's hair. Donna Campbell identifies this moment as "a colonising gesture that carries with it a remembered legacy of violence" (39). Helen Taylor concludes that Melicent's ineptitude "serves to underline the real understanding that Chopin (following other white southern writers) suggests white Louisianans have for 'their' blacks" (168). Melicent violates unspoken social norms and her inability to recognize this nuanced aspect of Black bodily autonomy on the plantation leads Thérèse to educate her about her missteps: "Thérèse soon enlightened her with the information that the negroes were very averse to working for Northern people whose speech, manners, and attitude towards themselves were unfamiliar" (20–21). In her own way, Melicent evokes another wing of the imagined northern invader, one who mishandles the plantation workers' bodies and disrupts the previously pleasant work ethic. Though Melicent believes that the plantation is "swarming with idle women and children," the narrative had not heretofore noted this as a problem; on the contrary, the manual labor seemed to be done well (19). This mismatch of perception and expectation reveals, as Helen Taylor summarizes, that "Northerners are seen as crass and grasping, while the plantation is on the whole harmonious, fiercely community spirited, and unmaterialistic" (166). Though Melicent is full of enthusiasm for a chance to play house while on the plantation, her ineptitude serves as a reminder that northerners are not a good fit for plantation life, nor do they relate well to Black communities. The old ways of interaction, according to *At Fault,* are far less traumatic for Black laborers.

One key symbol of the old way of life is the reliance on horses in the novel. The emphasis on horseback riding and good horsemanship resists industrialization and venerates a more bucolic past on the plantation. The strongest contrast to Thérèse's benevolent, antebellum-style plantation leadership is with Fanny, Hosmer's alcoholic first wife. Fanny represents the ineptitude and inferiority of northerners in her failure as a horsewoman. Her inability to ride a horse leads to her relapse into alcoholism, thus underscoring the novel's message that traditional life on a southern plantation offered, for white women, the best physical, mental, and emotional preparation for life. Thérèse's fitness as a horsewoman is noted several times in the narrative in order to further emphasize how admired she is among her workers and how easily she has command of all on her property: people, crops, and animals. Thérèse's preferred mount is named Beauregard—a name that recalls, most immediately, Confederate general P. G. T. Beauregard, the Louisiana-born "dapper, voluble hero of Fort Sumter" (McPherson 336).[4] When Thérèse rides, her Black workers narrate with a sense of wonder: "Jis' look Miss T'rèse how she go a lopin' down de lane. Dere she go—dere she go—now she gone," one of the children reports (23). It is not just that Thérèse cuts a fine figure but also that she rides expertly in a way that reinforces her command over the landscape.[5] From horseback, Thérèse can spot "a bridle path where an unpracticed eye would have discovered no sign of travel," and she navigates easily to her destination (23).

Thérèse's northern acquaintances have no hope of matching her riding skills, and this mismatch serves as subtle reminder that they do not truly belong at Place-du-Bois. When Hosmer arranges to encounter Thérèse while riding in the woods, they must slow to a walk. His skills, while competent, are no match for hers, and neither is his horse. When Hosmer compliments her horse, Thérèse responds: "Beauregard is a blooded animal. . . . He quite throws poor Nelson in the shade,' looking pityingly at Hosmer's heavily-built iron-grey" (26). For Hosmer to not understand the importance of good breeding and to be content with serviceable but dull transportation adds to the romantic trope of mismatched lovers. However, it is important to also consider this as another demonstration of how antebellum values are celebrated as necessary and self-protective. Thérèse, in deflecting the romantic trajectory of their conversational exchange, relies on her horse for escape: "At a slight and imperceptible motion of the bridle, well understood by Beauregard, the horse sprang forward into a quick canter, leaving Nelson and his rider" behind until she deigns to be caught (26). That Thérèse can command her horse "imperceptibly" is the mark of highest expertise. Given the encroachment of the railroad, the primacy of horseback travel and the quiet peace of hidden bridle paths are further nostalgic reminders of the past that quite throw railroads and sawmills into the shade.

No other riders in the novel match Thérèse's skill, which is another way in which she and all she stands for seem like cherished relics of the antebellum period. The impatient horsemanship of the Texan who brings her word of her nephew Grégoire's untimely and wasted death symbolizes a lack of respect for women and horses that Chopin critiques as part of the hasty erosion of class and gender barriers endemic to post-Reconstruction modernity. Here, too, the horseflesh is no match for a southern-bred steed like Beauregard. The messenger rides a "scrubby little Texas pony," and his manners are a far cry from Thérèse's subtle skills (138). With alarming roughness, the Texan "jerk[ed] his hitherto patient pony by the bridle" and "loped his horse rapidly forward, leaning well back in the saddle and his elbows sawing the air" (141). The amount of attention given to the Texan's manner could be seen as a comedic part of local-color narrative, but to those familiar with horsemanship it elicits disgust.[6] The Texan's sawing elbows indicate that the rider is being far too active in pulling on the bit in the horse's mouth, which can be unnecessarily painful for the horse and send it mixed messages about its speed, much as leaning backward does. The rider is as uncouth with his horse as he was in addressing Thérèse, when the narrative expressed dismay that he "spoke to Thérèse as he might have spoken to one of her black servants" (139). His familiarity is another reminder of the upheavals to social hierarchies accelerated by the Civil War and Reconstruction. Though Thérèse responds to his lack of manners with equanimity, Chopin invites readers to mourn the imagined decorum of the past in the face of what Gunning identifies as the novel's "strong preoccupation with white adjustment in the wake of black emancipation, with the problem of internal ethnic and class divisions" as well (Gunning, *Race* 112).

Fanny Hosmer also violates the racial and social hierarchies on the plantation, and here, too, her failings are embodied and accelerated by her poor horsemanship. Fanny offers the least flattering depiction of northern physical and moral failings in the novel. Fanny's inability to ride already made her unsuited to her remarried life alongside Hosmer at Place-du-Bois, but perhaps her greater offense is that she turns Black workers into her enablers and overturns the benevolent and largely productive work ethic that Thérèse was lauded for in the plantation's operation. Understanding neither an essential and beloved part of the active southern lifestyle nor her feminine obligation to serve as a benevolent guide to industrious Black workers, Fanny repudiates everything that Thérèse has maintained at Place-du-Bois. It is telling that the northerners are solely responsible for Black dissent. Melicent's poorly received joke prompts the household staff to shirk their duties, and Hosmer's sawmill is the root of dissatisfaction for the "surly Joçint," who resents "this intrusive Industry" (13). Fanny, through her addiction, creates new strife between Joçint and his father, Morico, during her very first meeting with the men, and she corrupts a young laborer, Sampson, into becoming an alcohol smuggler on her behalf.

Though she is largely apathetic about remarrying Hosmer and moving to Place-du-Bois, Fanny initially flourishes under Thérèse's care and the attentiveness of the servants. Even Melicent finds her "less objectionable since removed from her St. Louis surroundings" (79). Northern cities, *At Fault* reminds readers, are unhealthy places that make for unhappy wives. Events become disastrous, however, when a social riding excursion is planned and it is clear that Fanny will never transform into a proper paragon of southern white womanhood. Thérèse and David know that Fanny is no horsewoman and plan accordingly, giving her the ironically named Torpedo to ride. Torpedo, though perfectly safe, is obstinately lazy, and the event is a failure: "Fanny making but a sorry equestrian debut and Hosmer creeping along at her side; Thérèse unable to hold Beauregard within conventional limits" (93). Fanny whines about being unfit and quits on the trail, refusing to try a different mount and exaggerating, "goodness knows if I'll ever get there alive" at the thought of walking back to the house (93). Chopin adds further insult to Fanny's complete inability to approach Thérèse's level with the observation that Fanny cannot even manage to dress like an accomplished southern horsewoman: "her long riding skirt, borrowed for the occasion, twist[ed] awkwardly around her legs" (94). Fanny's physical failings and lack of fortitude hasten her return to active alcoholism.

Fanny waits at Old Morico's cabin for a buggy to carry her back to the plantation, and Morico unwittingly becomes her first enabler when, in an ill-fated offer of hospitality, he gives her a whiskey toddy. Fanny then steals Morico's flask and allows his son, Joçint, to be blamed for its absence. Fanny's immediate dishonesty and provocation of Black anger after a few sips of a stiff drink recall how white southern temperance women correlated "the use of whiskey" with the threat of Black men raping white women (Gunning, *Race* 108). In her study of the violent Joçint, Gunning argues that *At Fault* repudiates the plantation-fiction rape trope in favor of a "clash of racially determined goals over the use of land and labor" (Gunning, *Race* 121). However, it is important to consider that although rape is definitely not a threat in *At Fault,* still Black men become implicated in the threat to Fanny's health and, by extension, her death.

There is a surprisingly passive framing of Fanny's alcoholism from many of the critics that elides the connection between her relapse and the narrative's emphasis of her involvement with Black men. Per Seyersted writes simply that "Fanny falls back into drinking" (91), while Peggy Skaggs notes that Fanny "bribes, begs, and steals to get the alcohol her body demands"—but does not say from whom (73). Maureen

Anderson acknowledges that "Fanny . . . [b]rings with her a lack of con-
science, exhibited by her alcoholism" and is one of the few to note that
Fanny's actions put Morico and Joçint in conflict (8). Additionally, there
is Fanny's corruption of Sampson, the young Black servant who tends
to the fire in the Hosmer home. In contrast to the respect with which
Thérèse is always greeted, Fanny elicits a dangerous transgression of
racial hierarchies. Fanny's failure to properly calibrate her interactions
recollects Melicent's failure to understand plantation norms. Unlike
Melicent, however, Fanny is too friendly, and Sampson "made such
insinuating advances of friendliness towards her, [and] had continued
to attract her notice and good will" (120). This goodwill, however, is
corrupted because Sampson's duties now include smuggling on Fanny's behalf: "He drew something from his rather capacious coat pocket,
and, satisfying himself that Hosmer slept, thrust it in the bottom of the
basket, well covered" (120). As soon as Hosmer departs for the day,
"Fanny hastened to the hanging basket, and fumbling nervously in its
depths, found what the complaisant Sampson had left for her" (121).
Sampson enables Fanny's dishonesty and her addiction; he does not
deliver alcohol to anyone else. Fanny and Sampson become partners
in vice, and together they usher in what Thérèse views as the "spirit of
Disorder" to the Hosmer dwelling and, by extension, all of Place-du-
Bois (121). Thérèse's system has, once again, come under assault by the
postbellum northern invasion, and she regrets forcing David to bring
Fanny down from St. Louis.

The only way that Thérèse's virtuous system can be restored is
through Fanny's drowning on the one day she leaves her cabin unsu-
pervised and in search of alcohol. Fanny again breaks social protocol by
venturing to Sampson's cabin rather than waiting for him to serve her.
Though her trip leaves her feeling "good" and intoxicated, she waits out
stormy weather in Marie Louise's riverfront cabin, and both Fanny and
Thérèse's former mammy are washed away to their death when the river
tops its banks (157).[7] Fanny's death frees Thérèse and Hosmer to marry
and brings the novel to a more traditional reconciliatory romance that
affirms the worthiness of antebellum womanhood and eases anxieties
about divorce that were becoming a cause for concern in Chopin's era.

As Silber argues, "The reunion drama, in reviving the seemingly old-fashioned custom of marriage, urged northerners to look backward, to an early moral standard of domestic harmony and familial integrity" (117). Thérèse is, of course, the novel's fiercest advocate of marriage as she insists first that Hosmer honor his first vows and then is rewarded with the convenient and relatively quick death of the first wife, which clears the path for her to accept his proposal in all propriety.

The end of the novel reaffirms the message that a plantation needs a good wife to run it and that marriage—to a man who agrees to preserve the old traditions—is more satisfying than widowhood. Thérèse's presence is essential to the plantation; matters fall into chaos without her. When she spends time in Paris, we learn that "things had not gone well at Place-du-Bois during her absence," not the least of which that her workers had suddenly become "a troublesome body of blacks" (163). Without the plantation mistress at the helm, it is clear, the plantation will not survive and Black laborers suddenly revolt en masse. Accordingly, when Hosmer and Thérèse agree to marry, their declarations of mutual affection are also declarations of a division of labor in which Hosmer acknowledges that Thérèse should continue to run the plantation and thus continue to keep Place-du-Bois as a monument to antebellum mores: "I'll put no bungling hand into your concerns," Hosmer tells her (167) in a final acknowledgment of all of the ways in which northerners threatened Place-du-Bois. As David Russell argues: "[Thérèse], the 'true' Southerner, gets unhindered control of the area of Southern ideological production. . . . But far from protesting this repressive return, Hosmer also endorses it, if only tacitly" (22). In allowing Thérèse to keep the plantation running in her fashion, Chopin indicates that models of antebellum womanhood remain strong and are essential to post-Reconstruction economies.

While the novel's successful romance plot asserts the importance of antebellum values in causing northerners to compromise more than southerners, the failed North-South romance between Grégoire and Melicent offers a more mournfully nostalgic view of antebellum white southern manhood. Thérèse's dashing nephew turned errand boy and southern tour guide for Melicent, Grégoire represents "a more adventuresome, more passionate past" (Gunning, *Race* 118). Grégoire, by turns now too emasculated and then too violent, cannot adapt to post-bellum expectations, and his inevitable yet senseless death elicits the most poignant responses from Thérèse and Melicent. Grégoire's family, the Santiens, appear in some of Chopin's shorter works as well, and it is important to note that their fallen circumstances are a direct result of the Civil War. As Gunning observes, "The 'damage' inflicted by the Civil War comes visibly in the loss of slaves, and the Santiens find them-selves unable to manage under the economically altered conditions of the South" (*Race* 118). Grégoire is the clearest example of a white family whose circumstances were indisputably better in the antebellum period, and *At Fault* mourns the tragic effects that post-Reconstruction and northern involvement will have on Grégoire's life.

Grégoire's emasculation is signaled by his dependence on Thérèse for a living and for some sense of direction in life. He likes being bossed around, telling Melicent, "I was in Texas, goin' to the devil I reckon, w'en she sent for me, an' yere I am," because "they ain't no betta woman in the worl' then Aunt Thérèse, w'en you do like she wants" (18). In deferring to Thérèse's authority, Grégoire signals the lasting effects of the Civil War, which, in popular perception, left generations of white southern men stripped of authority and power. As Rubin explains, southerners re-sented "the notion, all too prevalent, that the South had somehow been 'unmanned' by its defeat, that Northerners were more masculine and therefore superior to Southerners" (170). Further, "to call something 'manly' in the South was to bestow a compliment of the highest order" and yet, *At Fault* highlights a perceived lack of manliness in Grégoire that anticipates his fall from grace (Rubin 170). Melicent is initially re-pulsed by Grégoire's voice, which she found to be "too softly low and feminine" (15). His physical appearance and bravery are also found lack-ing as Grégoire has become "an androgynous, dandified figure" (Castillo 62). When Grégoire tells Melicent that the Lafirme plantation used to belong to the cruel slave owner who was the inspiration for *Uncle Tom's Cabin*, he appears to be afraid of ghosts whereas Melicent is eager to see the grave. "It'll have to be broad day, an' the sun shinin' mighty bright w'en I take you to old McFarlane's grave," he insists (17). Notably, Melicent fails to find the grave at all scary and evinces more sympathy for McFarlane than Grégoire, in another example of how postbellum social and gender expectations can go astray in the novel.

When Grégoire later overcorrects and exerts hypermasculine extralegal justice by shooting Joçint for setting fire to the sawmill, Melicent repudiates him and abandons Place-du-Bois even though the narrator acknowledges that the broader community found his actions to be "justified . . . and beyond dispute, a benefit" (108). Gunning argues that "Chopin's failure to offer a complete condemnation of Grégoire" indicates that she "respects [the] usefulness" of "white violence" (*Race* 121). Grégoire, hurt by Melicent's condemnation and refusal to even say farewell to him, embarks on a fatally reckless spree of provoking barroom brawls. Melicent's northern morals are thus seen as unnecessarily rigid and cruel, and Grégoire's death an unappreciated waste and further indication of the anxieties about the decline of southern white manhood after the Civil War.

In his self-destructiveness, Grégoire abandons two important signifiers of antebellum white southern male virtue: good horsemanship and the façade of benevolent white supremacy. He can no longer command the respect that would have been due him in the antebellum period, which the novel mourns. As Grégoire begins his fatal trajectory, the narrative takes note of his poor riding, which indicates that he has lost self-control and self-respect; he will even abandon his southern-bred horse. One of the Black members of Place-du-Bois recounts that Grégoire's "hoss look like he ben swimmin' in the Cane Riva, he done ride him so hard" (116). Whereas Grégoire's bold riding received no censure at the start of the novel, now he has clearly overworked his horse and his riding has crossed the line from dashing to abusive. Similarly, when Grégoire departs town, he is again needlessly rough and excessive: "he lean down mos' flat an' stick he spurs in dat hoss an' he go tar'in like de win' down street, out o' de town, a firin' he pistol up in de a'r" (119). With no need to spur his horse other than a violent and flashy impulse, Grégoire departs fully from the kind of imperceptible and gentle riding exemplified by Thérèse and signals his further departure from the plantation respectability she represents.

In addition to abandoning his proper riding skills, Grégoire will also abandon his horse, though at least it is for one final, redemptive cause, as we learn in Chopin's short story "In Sabine." In a last chivalric gasp, Grégoire abandons his "fine sleek horse" in favor of an "unkempt, vicious-looking little Texas pony" at a miserable homestead so that the admirable and beleaguered mistress of the household, 'Tite Reine, can escape her abusive husband, Bud Aiken (Chopin, "In Sabine" 325). Through his actions in this story, Gunning sees Grégoire as "the aristocratic white man made rigid by his adherence to past values" who finds "a certain absolution in the aftermath of Joçint's murder" ("Local Color" 73).[8] However, with the theft of the nasty and unpredictable Texas pony, Grégoire's trajectory becomes vicious and short-lived as well. In *At Fault*, Grégoire dies in a distant "disorderly settlement" over an argument as needlessly pointless and violent as his riding style and mount have become. He takes umbrage at being called "Frenchy," which even the impertinent messenger who delivers the new to Thérèse opines is "a insufficient cause for rilin'" (140). That this news is unsurprising and yet sincerely mourned—far more than Fanny's death—gives an elegiac quality to the figure of the bold and charming antebellum horseman, now dishonored far from home.

Before his departure west, Grégoire escalates matters by upsetting both Black and white patrons of the local store with his insistence on buying drinks for everyone. The white men are outraged, and the Black men are scared: "dey knows Grégor gwine fo'ce 'em drink; dey knows Chartrand gwine make it hot fu' 'em art'ards ef dey does" (117). Grégoire's insistence on forcing everyone to drink is an easy means of provoking anger among his peers by playing upon post–Civil War tensions about Black access to white spaces, and this kind of display "is usually seen as an obnoxious act performed half-seriously by local whites who want to harass their own kind" (Gunning, *Race* 117). It is also important to consider, however, that Grégoire's acts are deeply abusive to the Black men caught up in his game. They are forced, at gunpoint, to drink alcohol to excess in an unwelcoming space, and it is clear that Grégoire will not be around to protect them from any future retaliation for daring to cross the color line of a backroom bar. This, too, violates the antebellum myth of benevolent interracial relationships so aptly demonstrated by Thérèse on the plantation where "there was hardly a soul at Place-du-Bois who had not felt the force of her will and yielded to its gentle influence" (22). Grégoire can no longer fit into the plantation system because he finds his masculinity and his social status under assault by nonsoutherners; the novel mourns him as a man whose charm and talents are wasted in the postbellum diminishment of Creole manhood in Louisiana and farther afield.

In considering Chopin's body of work, Helen Taylor makes the argument that Chopin "did not identify herself as a southern cheerleader" but rather was interested in European models of literature, unlike some of her contemporaneous female authors (Taylor 157). However, the persistence of antebellum values pertaining to the plantation way of life, including its racial hierarchies and anxieties, and the reverence that *At Fault* maintains for the land of Place-du-Bois itself emphasizes a regional jingoism that cannot be overlooked. Antebellum nostalgia may seem peripheral to *At Fault,* but this paradigm is essential to the narrative arcs that drive the novel to its happy ending—one that represents the triumph of white southern womanhood in gaining more than is sacrificed. Donald Ringe argues that the deaths in the novel allow a "symbolic freeing of Thérèse and David from their former selves. . . . The potential for change in the Cane River world can at last be fulfilled" (164). But nothing changes—or at least, nothing changes too drastically. Thérèse ends the novel with most of her property still under her control, still with a full complement of faithful Black workers, and she tacitly approves of lynching any Blacks who fall out of line. Through her skillful deployment of her beauty and good nature, she "rebuilds Place-Du-Bois [*sic*] not to accommodate change but rather to buttress tradition" (Russell 9). The northern invaders that Thérèse feared at the novel's beginning have all been neatly dispatched by the end: the main northern characters die (Fanny), depart (Melicent, last seen chasing adventure on her way to Yosemite and points west), or adapt (Hosmer, who reveres Thérèse and Place-du-Bois as much as any other faithful servant).

While Thérèse might accept the modern business venture of the sawmill, she does not accept much else that changes her life. Nor need she:

she gains a loving marriage to the conveniently bereft Hosmer, and they are supremely unbothered by any scandal or gossip the union may have caused among their neighbors: they "heard little and would have cared less, so absorbed were they in the overmastering happiness" (166). Although Thérèse acknowledges the titular fault in encouraging Hosmer to remarry Fanny out of moral obligation, it is hard to truly see this as a fault, given that this ultimately dispatched Fanny and allowed true love to be joined. When Thérèse asks Hosmer if "it's right we should find our happiness out of that past of pain and sin and trouble?" she could just as well be speaking for the Lost Causist view of antebellum life (165). For all that critics have tended to read *At Fault* as either ahead of its time or firmly of it, the rewards of "Miss T'rèse's system" draw the narrative further into the past than the future.

NOTES

1. For a concise summary of the fad for plantation fiction as an assertion of white supremacy at the end of the nineteenth century, see Gunning, "Kate Chopin's Local Color Fiction and the Politics of White Supremacy." For a brief overview of Civil War references in Chopin's short fiction, see Toth 70; and Taylor 24–25.

2. The Union army won occupation of New Orleans by May 1862, and with the exception of the battles for Port Hudson, on the Mississippi River, and a few other outposts, most of the warfare in Louisiana was categorized as minor skirmishes. See the National Park Service's useful guide "Louisiana Civil War Battles" for a comprehensive list: https://www.nps.gov/civilwar/louisiana.htm.

3. See also Peggy Skaggs, who observes that "Thérèse combines a preference for the quiet, settled life-style of the past with an astute business sense that recognizes, even if grudgingly, the inevitability of change" (75). Skaggs quotes the same passage about the architectural design of the plantation and concludes that "her housing style matches her personal style" (75).

4. Notably, Beauregard also designed the battle flag that is popularly recognized as the Confederate flag (McPherson 342).

5. Critics have paid attention to how well Thérèse dresses to ride (a trait she apparently shared with Chopin herself) (see Toth 141–42; and Skaggs 75).

6. Displays of dashing horsemanship are welcome, as well, but they can still carry implications of good horsemanship: "after all, Southerners were known for their equestrian abilities" (Rubin 22). Grégoire rides "in the reckless fashion peculiar to Southern youth," but it leaves only himself breathless, and no mention is made of his horse (Chopin, *At Fault* 7).

7. As most critics note, the narrative pays no heed to Marie Louise's death beyond a single sentence declaring that she, too, died. As Helen Taylor observes, "the white woman

whose closest and most loyal black servant and friend has disappeared makes no further reference to her existence" and thinks only of Fanny's demise when she is reminded of the accident (Taylor 169; see also Russell 18).

8. Further, horsemanship represents the keenest division between the Grégoire's remaining chivalry and the morally reprehensible and abusive Bud Aiken. Grégoire uses the need to rest his horse as the pretense for staying over at the Aiken household when he sees 'Tite Reine's unhappiness. That night, as Bud Aiken tells of how "it had amused him to witness her distress and terror [as his wife] was thrown to the ground" by the nasty Texas horse (Chopin, "In Sabine" 330), Grégoire resolves to assist 'Tite Reine by giving her the means of escape on a well-trained horse and depriving Aiken of the means of pursuit by stealing his mustang.

WORKS CITED

Anderson, Maureen. "Unraveling the Southern Pastoral Tradition: A New Look at Kate Chopin's *At Fault*." *Southern Literary Journal* 34, no. 1 (2001): 1–13.

Bonner, Thomas, Jr. "Kate Chopin: Tradition and the Moment." In *Southern Literature in Transition: Heritage and Promise,* edited by Philip Castille and William Osborne, 141–49. Memphis, TN: Memphis State University Press, 1983.

Campbell, Donna. "*At Fault:* A Reappraisal of Chopin's Other Novel." In *The Cambridge Companion to Kate Chopin,* edited by Janet Beer, 27–43. Cambridge: Cambridge University Press, 2008.

Castillo, Susan. "'Race' and Ethnicity in Kate Chopin's Fiction." In *The Cambridge Companion to Kate Chopin,* edited by Janet Beer, 59–72. Cambridge: Cambridge University Press, 2008.

Chopin, Kate. *At Fault.* 1890. Edited with an introduction and notes by Bernard Koloski. London: Penguin, 2002.

———. "In Sabine." In *The Complete Works of Kate Chopin,* edited by Per Seyersted, 325–32. Baton Rouge: Louisiana State University Press, 2006.

Gunning, Sandra. "Kate Chopin's Local Color Fiction and the Politics of White Supremacy." *Arizona Quarterly* 51, no. 3 (1995): 61–86.

———. *Race, Rape, and Lynching: The Red Record of American Literature, 1890–1912.* Oxford: Oxford University Press, 1996.

Koloski, Bernard J. "The Structure of Kate Chopin's *At Fault*." *Studies in American Fiction* 3, no. 1 (Spring 1975): 89–95.

"Louisiana Civil War Battles." National Park Service, U.S. Department of the Interior. October 3, 2014. https://www.nps.gov/civilwar/louisiana.htm.

McPherson, James. *Battle Cry of Freedom: The Civil War Era.* Oxford: Oxford University Press, 1988.

Ringe, Donald A. "Cane River World: Kate Chopin's *At Fault* and Related Stories." *Studies in American Fiction* 3, no. 1 (Autumn 1975): 157–66.

Rubin, Anne Sarah. *A Shattered Nation: The Rise and Fall of the Confederacy, 1861–1868*. Chapel Hill: University of North Carolina Press, 2005.

Russell, David. "A Vision of Reunion: Kate Chopin's *At Fault*." *Southern Quarterly* 46, no. 1 (2008): 8–25.

Seyersted, Per. *Kate Chopin: A Critical Biography*. Baton Rouge: Louisiana State University Press, 1980.

Silber, Nina. *The Romance of Reunion: Northerners and the South, 1865–1900*. Chapel Hill: University of North Carolina Press, 1993.

Skaggs, Peggy. *Kate Chopin*. Woodbridge, CT: Twayne, 1985.

Taylor, Helen. *Gender, Race, and Region in the Writings of Grace King, Ruth Mc-Enery Stuart, and Kate Chopin*. Baton Rouge: Louisiana State University Press, 1989.

Toth, Emily. *Kate Chopin*. New York: William Morrow, 1990.

Walker, Nancy A. *Kate Chopin: A Literary Life*. London: Palgrave, 2001.

So Melicent Is a Unitarian
Who's At Fault?

EMILY TOTH

Maybe It Happened This Way

> *Dramatis Personae: Kate O'Flaherty, The Mother Superior*

Kate: Hello, Mudda! I have sinned!

Mother: Oh, yeah, whadja do?

Kate: Hard to explain.

Mother: Aw, come on. Smoked weed: Got knocked up?

Kate: Er . . . uh . . .

Mother: Bought a term paper? Lied about your age and drank yourself shit-faced?

Kate: I think I'm a Unitarian.

Mother: You're gonna burn in hell, for sure.

At Fault is an odd duck of a book. What the hell—or who the hell—is it about? There's the humorless Yankee businessman—I imagine him looking like Ichabod Crane. There's the lovely but iron-stubborn Catholic widow—maybe played by Meryl Streep. There are rebellious sons and silly social climbers. And there are plantation workers ("darkies"—hard to read their parts without cringing).

And then there are tacky "secondary characters" (lower-class, party animals, white trash). One has a ridiculously self-righteous daughter who's a parody of a good Catholic. There are poor excuses for husbands and slimy boyfriends.

There's the hapless wife Fanny, one of the first female alcoholics in American fiction—who does really drink herself shit-faced.

But what about Melicent, the impertinent young flirt from St. Louis?

She seems to have a show-stopping number about halfway through the book; I almost expected her to burst out into "O-o-o-o-klahoma!" Instead, she declares, "I'm a Unitarian!" *(At Fault* 44).

And then the show goes on, leaving me befuddled. As a Unitarian myself, I'd like to know how Melicent got there. Sure, she's a love-interest, an important and somewhat odd second banana. But why did Kate Chopin make her a Unitarian? She's even one of the first in American literature. What was Kate Chopin up to?

Melicent in *At Fault* is a classic second lead. The lead, the heroine, is typically beautiful and blonde, irresistible to men, and usually friendly, though sometimes atrociously catty, to women (see *Mean Girls*). Most often, the lead doesn't have much individuality, and it's up to the second lead to provide the humor, the zest, or sometimes the tragedy. She could be played by Reese Witherspoon or Bette Midler.

She isn't usually responsible for the religion, though.

In American fiction, especially in Kate Chopin's nineteenth century, religious differences weren't a major plot point. Sometimes a romance got derailed because one of the characters turned out to be secretly Black, as in "tragic mulatto" stories like Lydia Maria Child's "The Quadroons" or Chopin's own "Desiree's Baby." Sometimes, rarely, a conflict turned on a character's being Jewish, as in Martha Wolfenstein's "Chaya." But that was treated as a cultural difference much more than a religious one.

Nineteenth-century publishers, the gatekeepers, were mostly East Coast Protestant men who—to judge by their choices—didn't cotton to Catholics or Jews as characters. If they knew about Muslims at all, editors were apt to dismiss them as "Mohammedans" in strange clothes. Native Americans were mostly shown as undifferentiated savages, though one exception is the native girl adopted by church ladies in Kate Chopin's story "Loka." She runs away.

And of course, there are no stories of warring female theologians—because there were hardly any in the United States until the twentieth century. Women weren't allowed to be ministers until 1863, when Olympia Brown became the first—a Unitarian. There were no women rabbis until 1972.

There are still no women Catholic priests.

So why, I continue to wonder, did Kate Chopin create her second banana as a Unitarian?

The second banana, or soubrette, is usually a shadow of or a variation on the main character. Bianca in *The Taming of the Shrew* is the nice, obedient girl that Kate is supposed to be but isn't. Joan in Sylvia Plath's *The Bell Jar* takes the risks that the main character Esther does not—and Esther even thinks about Joan as her double ("Sometimes I wondered if I had made Joan up," she muses [Plath 179]). Lydia in *Pride and Prejudice* is a risk taker, fleeing from the world where other young women are stuck hobnobbing with vicars and curates.

Melanie in *Gone with the Wind* is a serious second banana, the number-two heroine, relentlessly nice and kind. You know she's gonna die. Sometimes, if you're in the kind of snarky mood that Melicent displays in *At Fault,* you kinda wish for—bad things to happen.

Which makes Melicent interesting. But why a Unitarian?

The second banana is often the nice girl who finishes last. Or who doesn't quite understand the plot of the story. In *The Awakening,* Madame Ratignolle does have an intuitive understanding of Edna's psyche—as someone who wants more than she can have as a standard-issue wife and mother. Mademoiselle Reisz, the less conventional female character, might be considered the third banana, an opposite who really doesn't understand Edna at all. (Wants her to get together with a *grand esprit*—the kind of superstar who'd love her and leave her. In my opinion.)

But none of these women cares much, if at all, about religion. In her first novel, why did Kate Chopin?

And why, in the middle of a lazily southern romantic scene, does Melicent burst out with the announcement that she's not afraid of ghosts or scared of hell because "I'm a Unitarian."

I would write it as "Unitarian!!" because she's the first Unitarian lady of American literature. She's bursting out of a shell that most readers don't even know she's in. She is the kind of young woman who'd be a flapper in Zelda Fitzgerald's day. She's been engaged several times ("a fact that ought not to be mentioned," tut-tutted one reviewer), and she's curious and energetic.

Not so the heroine. Thérèse, in my opinion, is Kate Chopin's attempt to be conventional, acceptable. Chopin draws on her own experience, some years back, with a philanderer in Louisiana—but now, in the fictional version, Thérèse has to conjure up some serious guilt and judgmental religion. Kate Chopin, though she'd been reading amoral French literature as a matter of course, knew she couldn't publish anything bordering on out-and-out French-style adultery—the operatic kind with searing passions and tragic stabbings. That wouldn't do in America in 1890. It wouldn't pass muster even if the frisky characters were Unitarian. There was not—and still isn't—a body of stereotypes about Unitarians as free lovers—though some of them always have been. The Transcendentalists, according to Susan Cheever's imaginative rendering in *American Bloomsbury,* were hot bodies who did a lot of social sharing. Does Melicent's "I'm a Unitarian" mean "I'm too hot for this sleepy Louisiana village?"

Like many first novelists, Chopin in *At Fault* throws in everything that's excited or troubled her up to that point in her life. She was forty when she published *At Fault* at her own expense—which makes it her only publication that is exactly the way she wanted it to be, without editorial intervention.

The world of *At Fault* also has quarreling young dudes, Grégoire and Joçint. Chopin, who raised five sons (and a daughter) knew all about hotheaded young men. Her son Jean was nineteen when *At Fault* appeared, and later led a sad, short life as a traveling salesman, dying of typhoid at forty. Her son Fred went through a notorious divorce, reported in a press conference after a night of "jollification." Her son Felix had intriguing memories of her friends, who wore "unconventional clothing" and were a "pink-red group of intellectuals." Her son George was a medical doctor who studied diabetes in cats and raised goats on his roof. And her son Oscar was the *Weather Bird* cartoonist for the St. Louis newspaper.

Young Oscar was conceived in 1872, during the year that the painter Edgar Degas was living in New Orleans. Degas's uncle worked with the adult Oscar Chopin, and some of the juiciest French gossip that Degas knew, even real names, turns up in *The Awakening* twenty-seven years later. Clearly Kate Chopin shared stories with Degas, who was planning to stay in New Orleans for a year. But he left, vamoosed abruptly, after a few months, around the time Kate would have discovered she was pregnant. Young Oscar turned out to be the only Chopin child with artistic talent.

No one involved was Unitarian.

The doings of young men interested Kate Chopin very much in 1889, when she began writing *At Fault.* She drew on what she'd seen in the Chopins' nearly five years in Cloutierville, Louisiana (1879–1884), including the folkways of the people of color. Sometimes her portrayals seem gratingly racist. But she does recognize when Melicent is being an ignorant Yankee, showing gobs of white privilege.

She's also a smart-mouth.

But why is Melicent a Unitarian?

It has to do with her creator, of course. Just as girls today are sometimes called Karens or Beckys (usually with snide intent), I think Kate O'Flaherty Chopin in her day was a bit of a—Melicent, a girl who had the answers. She was raised Catholic, of course.

But there were many bumps and quirks in Kate O'Flaherty's life. Pious souls might call them opportunities for sin to slip in. I would call them what any writer calls a sin or an error: it's material.

Often it's an opportunity.

Kate O'Flaherty, born in 1850, grew up among outsiders and exceptions. Her female ancestors, in early St. Louis, were rebels. A great-great-grandmother, stuck in a violent marriage, got the first legal separation in the territory. (Divorce was forbidden for Catholics). A great-grandmother taught young Kate to speak French, play the piano, and revel in colorful stories of real-life wayward women—things Americans weren't supposed to know about.

Kate's mother, Eliza, was married at sixteen to a man who was thirty-nine, an Irish immigrant who'd made a fortune and wanted a woman with some social status. Kate O'Flaherty grew up among women who were widowed young, did not remarry, and controlled their own lives and money. They owned property and sued powerful men.

They were salty and practical, and when Kate Chopin wrote about romance, it was usually the men who were fools for love. Edna, in *The Awakening,* doesn't need more communication with her husband, she says. Whatever would we talk about? she wonders.

Catholics were more apt to talk about marital duties, if they talked about marriage at all. It was a spiritual state, a surrender of the woman to creating new life and serving others.

Meanwhile heretics, or at least outsiders, said and wrote, in effect, "Yeah, yeah. Yeah. But what about me?" Abigail Adams, wife of the second president of the United States, wrote urging him to "Remember the ladies," and threatening to foment a revolution if their wishes were ignored.

Abigail and the Adams family called themselves deists—but they were Unitarians.

This may sound like the spirits of Unitarians hovering around the helpless Catholic baby Katie O'Flaherty.

She did seem to have bad luck. The two little sisters after her died young, maybe in the yellow fever epidemic of 1853. When Kate was five, her father died in a train accident. When she was thirteen, her half brother and great-grandmother died. When she was twenty-five, her remaining brother was killed in an impulsive buggy race. When she was thirty-two, her husband died.

Her lifelong friend Kitty Garesché said that Kate had "rather a sad nature" because of her many losses.

That could turn a girl against traditional religion.

Unitarians—people who refuse to believe in the Holy Trinity—have been around since early Christianity. They've had congregations and theological disputes all over Europe, including Transylvania. At least one vocal supporter, Michael Servetus, tangled with John Calvin and wound up being burned at the stake. Joseph Priestley, the discoverer of oxygen, was driven out of England for his Unitarian beliefs. And then a knot of New Englanders in the 1700s started building churches for their peculiar ideas of worship.

They weren't scorched-earth heretics; they didn't fight wars about religion. They just quietly said no to some of Christianity's biggest ideas, such as predestination, original sin, and going to hell if you were bad.

They took the fear out of Catholicism, and also the regimentation. If you were a Unitarian—which meant, most likely, you lived in New England in the nineteenth century—you didn't have to grow up scared.

The Transcendentalists, who might be abolitionists, vegetarians, and freethinkers, were the most famous Unitarians: Ralph Waldo Emerson, Margaret Fuller, Louisa May Alcott, Henry David Thoreau. They wrote about wise women, alternative communities, living in the woods, not paying taxes, and otherwise being a creative community of cranks and nuisances.

When a colony of Unitarians moved west, their destination was St. Louis—where they met a lot of interested people.

St. Louis by then was peopled by fiery abolitionists, socialist rebels who'd fled Germany after the failed revolutions of 1848. They weren't interested in traditional Christianity. They wanted social justice.

Then the Civil War tested anyone's faith in God and just rewards. There were bloody skirmishes in the streets of St. Louis. Kate's best friend's family, Confederate supporters, were banished. Kate's household—all women except for slaves—was attacked by soldiers who forced Kate's mother to raise a flag. A neighbor called the home invasion an "outrage"—a term that often had sexual overtones. Teenaged Kate O'Flaherty spent a year after that mostly alone in the attic, self-healing.

She kept being out of step. At the Sacred Heart Academy, she was an honors student but satirized her own clumsiness at a school celebration: "Katie O'F, poor unfortunate lass, broke implements stoutest as though they were glass." In her diary she wrote about hating the debutante social ritual ("I dance with people I despise, amuse myself with men whose only talent lies in their feet" [*Kate Chopin's Private Papers* 82]).

That stuck. When Melicent, in *At Fault*, examines Grégoire as something of an anthropological specimen, she particularly notices his show-offy boots. Several years later, in the story "Athénaïse," the heroine loathes her husband's feet.

But did Kate O'Flaherty settle down and become a good Catholic mom?

No. She married a Louisiana man with a French playboy past and a casual European attitude about religion. On their honeymoon, they gleefully skipped mass and refused to worry about the state of their souls. Of their six children, most born in Louisiana, at least one is missing a baptismal certificate. Especially when they lived in Cloutierville, the tiny village in northwest Louisiana, Kate scandalized the neighbors by lifting her skirts too high, smoking cigarettes, and riding bareback. When an uncle scolded her in the middle of the town's one street, she took out her little whip and whipped him.

Before she was thirty, it was clear that Madame Chopin would not be an obedient, sweet, Catholic matron. Villagers hated her big-city colorful fashions, just as the neighbors in *At Fault,* Black and white, mock Melicent's flamboyant decorations. There were neighbors who said, decades later, that "That Kate Chopin was a dirty lady."

She and Oscar were not invited to be godparents—another snub from her Catholic roots.

Unitarians don't have baptism. No one is left out.

When Oscar Chopin died of "swamp fever" in Louisiana at age thirty-eight, Kate took up with someone else's husband, a man who liked to console widows. He appears in her stories with the name Alcée—and without any guilt or remorse or Hail Marys for forgiveness.

When Alcée Arobin in *The Awakening* says goodnight to Edna after their first time, she wishes there were love—but lust is fine. After Alcée Laballiere leaves their afternoon delight in "The Storm," Calixta laughs aloud. Neither party is going to tell a priest.

Unitarians don't have confession, or guilt.

When Kate Chopin moved back to St. Louis after two years as a widow, she moved to a newer part of town, enrolled her children in the public schools, and started meeting Unitarians and Hegelians, the brainy gang whose members included Denton Snider. He was at work on a grandiose, many-volumed study of the history of all knowledge—very like Mr. Worthington's project, gently satirized in *At Fault.*

Soon the critics, suffragists, and debunkers began gathering at Kate Chopin's weekly salon, the first in St. Louis. There were writers, artists, journalists. They met to pontificate, create, laugh, and emote (one could say "Woe is me!" in fourteen languages). They liked to argue about religion, and Kate Chopin liked to listen and make pithy judgments in her diary.

Her salon regulars took their cultural cues from local characters like William Marion Reedy, a onetime Catholic choir boy who became a fierce, hard-drinking newspaperman who married a madam, inveighed against religion, and published some of Kate Chopin's most daring stories.

The salon also drew news and clues from Dr. Frederick Kolbenheyer, an Austrian-born revolutionary who ranted about poverty and oppression at the salon. He was a gynecologist and a distant friend of Sigmund Freud's.

A Chopin son used to claim that Kolbenheyer was a "borderline bomb thrower" at least in his mind, and also had a little crush on the lady of the house: "Kolby had eyes for Mom."

Kolby was another critic of traditional religion and wrote a novel about anti-Semitism, called *Jewish Blood*. In Russia, it was now the era of pogroms, random massacres of Jews—by some Christians.

But Unitarians, almost unique in the world, have no history of patriarchal violence. They do not have a fighting side, and a movement toward "muscular Unitarianism" in the late 1890s did not make the men more macho—although it did result in kicking out women ministers for a while. (They are now the majority.)

Unitarians have even changed the words to "Onward Christian Soldiers" and other militaristic songs—something a mother of five sons would notice. As she wrote a new script for her own independent life, Kate Chopin noticed other women who were changing the words.

She did, however, keep paying dues to her sodality. Maybe she was hedging her bets.

She also got to know Rosa Sonneschein, the scandalous former wife of a St. Louis rabbi. He had balked at paying her alimony—until Rosa threatened to tell the world about his inadequacies. The settlement gave Rosa the money to start *The American Jewess,* the first American magazine for Jewish women. Kate Chopin's story "Cavanelle" was in the first issue.

But much of this was after she published *At Fault* in 1890. Even then she had figured out, among other things, that a Unitarian character might be more appealing than a traditional Catholic one.

The big appeal of Unitarianism, especially to Catholics, was that there were no rules. No doctrine, no things you have to believe, no ways you can sin and go to hell. It was all washed away in a world of think-for-yourself and do-the-right-thing.

Kate Chopin knew that you're supposed to "write about what you know." When she sat down to write her first chapters of *At Fault* in 1889, she was thirty-nine. What did she know?

She knew a good bit about what sells in the literary world. It wasn't St. Louis, where she lived. The editors and publishers and the reading public favored local color—the portrayal of quaint folklorish ways, very different from the wise and prudent people in the Northeast. They liked dialect writing and colorful Black characters (many cringeworthy now). They liked behavior that was more exotic than their own norm. They liked gossip, humor, and new information.

At Fault appeared and was not a particular success, but Kate Chopin kept writing.

She also joined a literary club—and that's where we know, for sure, that she came face-to-face with Unitarians.

Evidently they faced off with each other—about books. Charlotte Stearns Eliot was a teacher, social worker, and poet, and she came to St. Louis from Massachusetts, the center of Unitarian life and thought. She was angry all her life that women weren't allowed to go to college. When she did write a book, it was the biography of a man, her father-in-law, William Greenleaf Eliot—the founder of Unitarianism in St. Louis. Theirs was a very accomplished family, and her son, Tom, grew up to be T. S. Eliot.

Charlotte Eliot liked literary companionship, but there was some kind of enmity between the women and men in the St. Louis reading community—and so the women split off and formed their own group, the Shelley Club.

The men objected, because the poet Percy Bysshe Shelley, some eighty years earlier, had been an atheist (and an adulterer). The women either shrugged or (I hope) laughed—but they did change the name to the Wednesday Club. And they did not meet with the men.

But here, finally, we have proof that Kate Chopin knew Unitarians.

She was a charter member of the Wednesday Club, along with Charlotte Eliot. Chopin also presented two club meeting papers on German music, a lifelong appreciation.

Later, nine years after *At Fault*, Kate Chopin got in bad odor with St. Louisans who thought her second novel, *The Awakening,* was improper, with things that should not be mentioned (adultery). It also has, mostly unnoticed, a heroine who goes to the church of Lourdes and becomes sick instead of well.

Were the objectors the same bluenoses who objected to the Shelley Club?

We can't know, but Charlotte Eliot did rally the supporters of a beleaguered, gifted woman writer. She arranged a Wednesday Club celebration honoring Kate Chopin, six months after *The Awakening*. Three hundred people attended the celebration.

Kate Chopin and Charlotte Eliot were part of a sisterhood.

And could that be why Melicent was written as a Unitarian? Was Kate Chopin looking ahead to a time when she might need allies?

So, really, what was Kate Chopin doing with an enthusiastic, tactless, dark-haired, flirtatious Unitarian in *At Fault?* Her brother David is a thoughtful Unitarian, but he follows where he's led by the women in his life and by his mysterious alter ego, Homeyer. What did Kate Chopin learn from writing about him?

Or about Thérèse Lafirme, a follower of rules handed down by the fathers of the Catholic Church, who in 1890 didn't much listen to women?

Kate Chopin knew what was expected of a nineteenth-century fictional heroine. She could not have a mother to advise her; she had to be resilient on her own, but not too much. At the end she usually died or capitulated ("Reader, I married him").

The second banana, though, didn't have to follow the script. She could refuse to act girly (no "Oh, poor me" when an alligator seems to be chasing Melicent and Grégoire). She can take it matter-of-factly when her suitor calls her a know-it-all. She admires Thérèse but does not learn from her.

In the center of the book, Melicent and Grégoire have their major scene. It's light-toned but firm. He wants her to be afraid of hell. She says she's not: "I'm a Unitarian" *(At Fault* 44*).*

There's no thread, no rumbling of the earth right then to break them up—but it's clear that they're hopelessly mismatched (and not just because he's too short and his voice is too high). To her he's a hopeless hick, and she's wanting to dump him. It doesn't help that he also shoots and kills the arsonist Joçint.

Melicent is the only one repelled and appalled. The others talk about self-defense or responsibility for others—but Melicent sees murder. In the interconnected web of human existence, Grégoire has taken a human life.

Melicent is the only character who, like a good Unitarian, looks at all sides and seeks knowledge. The others in effect vote yes or no on blaming Grégoire. If Melicent were a totally committed Unitarian, she would no doubt insist on a four-hour coffee hour to discuss the killing; then appoint a committee; convene a book club; make it a yearlong study project. Years after Grégoire had gotten himself killed in a barroom brawl, a report might be issued.

Yet the long pursuit of justice, the unwillingness to condemn immediately, seems to be much more what Kate Chopin wanted to see in the world. She didn't want priests to tell women what to think, or do, or be. She was more in tune with Emerson's "Over-Soul" or with the Unitarian minister Theodore Parker's 1853 declaration that "the arc of the moral universe is long, but it bends towards justice."

That was also true with Kate Chopin's career. Once a forgotten writer, a woman who'd churned out a novel that her critics considered adulterous trash, she is now a star—with Melicent still an undernoticed second banana. But she does speak quite a lot at the end, in a letter full of delicious gossip.

Melicent is the storyteller who gets the last word. She is the independent young woman who takes some time to figure it out, and then reports back.

So why is she a Unitarian?

Why not?

Or Maybe This Happened

Dramatis Personae: Kate Chopin, the Mother Superior

Kate Chopin: Hello Mudda Superior! I wrote it anyway. I created a frisky, immoral, tactless Unitarian and plunked her down in Louisiana, where she turned out to be the only character who was able to tell right from wrong.

Mother Superior: Hmmph.

Kate Chopin: Will I be appreciated in my own time?

Mother Superior: No way in hell.

WORKS CONSULTED

Chopin, Kate. *At Fault.* 1890. Edited with an introduction and notes by Bernard Koloski. London: Penguin, 2002.

———. *Kate Chopin's Private Papers.* Edited by Emily Toth, Per Seyersted, and Cheyenne Bonnell. Bloomington: Indiana University Press, 1998.

Koloski, Bernard, ed. *Awakenings: The Story of the Kate Chopin Revival.* Baton Rouge: Louisiana State University Press, 2012.

Ostman, Heather. *Kate Chopin and Catholicism.* London: Palgrave Macmillan, 2020.

Plath, Sylvia. *The Bell Jar.* New York: Bantam, 1978.

Seyersted, Per. *Kate Chopin: A Critical Biography.* Baton Rouge: Louisiana State University Press, 1969.

Toth, Emily. *Kate Chopin: A Life of the Author of "The Awakening."* New York: William Morrow, 1990.

———. *Unveiling Kate Chopin.* Jackson: University Press of Mississippi, 1999.

What Hosmer Wants

Male Aspirations in At Fault

BERNARD KOLOSKI

At Fault shows that Kate Chopin's celebrated women are not alone in their striving for a fulfilling life. Men in Chopin's early novel, as well as in her short stories, articulate the yearnings that drive many of her women characters. David Hosmer's desires in *At Fault* are much like those of women in Chopin's short stories and of Edna Pontellier in *The Awakening.* Hosmer wants autonomy—self-determination, to live independently, to judge for himself the rightness of his words and actions. He wants freedom more than security, to disregard the protective social and ethical restraints of his times. And he wants fulfillment—to pursue satisfaction and happiness through his work and through a relationship with the person he loves.

Hosmer is Chopin's most thoroughly developed male character. Certainly *At Fault* is about Thérèse Lafirme and the events she sets in motion at her Place-du-Bois plantation. But from the early pages of the novel, we follow Hosmer—a businessman not attuned to the world of human relationships—as he runs the sawmill Thérèse gives him permission to build on her land. We see him as he welcomes his sister Melicent to Louisiana and Place-du-Bois. We are with him as he deals with Thérèse's nephew Grégoire—who is hopelessly in love with Melicent—and with mixed-blood Joçint—who is furious about being forced to work at the sawmill. And we follow him as he declares his love for Thérèse. Later we see him as, out of respect for Thérèse's wishes, he visits St. Louis, where he remarries his alcoholic former wife, Fanny, and brings her to Place-du-Bois. Finally, we follow him as he futilely tries to rescue Fanny from drowning when the cabin she is staying in collapses and is swept away by the raging Cane River.

Scholars have understood Hosmer in different ways. Daniel S. Rankin dismisses him, saying he "falls just short of being more than a figure in a frame" (128). Linda Wagner-Martin sees him as "taciturn and embittered" and speaks of his "comparative woodenness" (197, 202). Peggy Skaggs mentions him only when he interacts with women (74–87). And Helen Taylor describes him as "wretched with frustrated love for Thérèse and with his inability to prevent Fanny drinking" (167).

Donald A. Ringe notes that "by acting upon the moral judgment of another [Thérèse]," Hosmer "becomes false to his own inner nature" (32). Jane Hotchkiss goes further, arguing that Hosmer operates in a "moral vacuum," and she complains about his "nonposition" and "his evasions of a moral stance in favor of self-sacrificing devotion" (35). Barbara C. Ewell considers that Hosmer's "error" is one of "the short-comings of American male individualism generally," the result of "the increasingly specialized functions of male and female. . . . Neither the inner life nor society holds much interest for him. These are the province of women." Hosmer's "dulled emotional life," she adds, "represents a defection from his moral responsibility to participate fully in the human community" (38–39).

And Emily Toth in *Unveiling Kate Chopin,* the shorter, more women-centric biography you are likely to be familiar with, describes David Hosmer as "a sallow, earnest, humorless Yankee" and does not discuss him further (113). But in *Kate Chopin,* her longer, earlier biography, Toth writes that Hosmer "has greater emotional depth than either of the women [Fanny or Thérèse]" and becomes "the sensitive and empathetic man who can understand a woman's feelings." Kate Chopin, she adds, "evidently believed that men could make that empathetic leap" (195).

Chopin shows Hosmer explaining to Thérèse that, having given little thought to anything except business, he fell into a foolish marriage with Fanny. Now, he says, he works hard to earn money to give Melicent the support she needs (their parents are dead, and she has no one else to help her) and to pay Fanny the doubled alimony payments he promised her. But a man of action though he may be, he is also a contemplative person. He wants a better life for himself. Again and again in the novel he quotes the thoughts, the "philosophic stand-points," of an alter ego he calls Homeyer (108).[1] We learn from those thoughts that his aspirations—and, if you read more of Chopin's works, the aspirations of other men—are those we have come to associate with Kate Chopin's women characters in her short stories and *The Awakening*. Those men, like Chopin's women, want autonomy, freedom, and fulfilment.[2]

Autonomy: Hosmer and Grégoire Santien

Concerned about his autonomy, Hosmer cites Homeyer the first time he speaks in the book. When Thérèse complains that he has been working too much, he answers that "you are not what my friend Homeyer would call an individualist since you don't grant a man the right to follow the promptings of his character" (11).

The widowed Thérèse is an intelligent, sensitive, affectionate person, in many ways a wonderful woman. But, driven in part by her aspirations for peace and security on her plantation, she practices "constant interference in the concerns of other people" (89). She agrees with Hosmer that she's "no individualist, if to be one is to permit men to fall into hurtful habits without offering protest against it" (11).

Kate Chopin herself has little patience with an attitude like Thérèse's. In the short story "Miss McEnders" she shows us the wrongheadedness of a woman who has "a burning desire to do good—to elevate the human race, and start the world over again on a comfortable footing for everybody" (205). And in an essay she wrote after publishing *At Fault* but before writing *The Awakening*, Chopin quotes a "wise" man who speaks of an eleventh commandment—"Thou shalt not preach . . . Thou shalt not instruct thy neighbor" on what to do (702).

Per Seyersted writes that Kate Chopin's "irritation with moral reformers was so strong that she had to get it out of her system before she could turn to what really interested her" (91). And Helen Taylor adds that Chopin's "upbringing and education within a Catholic French, then Louisiana-French family had instilled in her a horror of women's participation in social reform and public life" (147).

Thérèse Lafirme, like Miss McEnders, has an ardent desire to do good. And she violates that eleventh commandment. She preaches and instructs throughout much of *At Fault*. When she learns that Hosmer is divorced, she insists that he acted as a coward in leaving his former wife, Fanny, after the death of their child contributed to her withdrawal into alcoholism. He should, Thérèse tells him, remarry Fanny and bring her to Place-du-Bois.

"Do you think that a man owes nothing to himself?" Hosmer asks (39). "Yes," Thérèse says. "A man owes to his manhood . . . to face the consequences of his own actions" (39), which forces Hosmer to consider the possibility that she may be right, although his doubts remain strong. Chopin makes clear that Hosmer will return to Fanny only because of his affection for Thérèse. He will sacrifice the autonomy he yearns for in the service of love.

The Creole Grégoire Santien in *At Fault* is willing to make the same sacrifice. Grégoire, Thérèse's nephew, has been brought by Thérèse to Place-du-Bois from Texas where he has been recklessly acting out his pain because he could not stop their family plantation's loss to creditors.[3] The "irresponsible but charming" Grégoire, as Donna Campbell phrases it (28), loves Hosmer's sister Melicent, and their tangled relationship is the major subplot in the novel. Melicent is attracted to Grégoire, even loves him, but she doesn't like his eccentric way of speaking, and she cannot deal with what she has seen and heard about what Patricia Hopkins Lattin calls his "hot-blooded and arrogant side" (22) and what Joyce Coyne Dyer and Robert Emmett Monroe refer to as his "dominance, his violence, and his indifference" (8).

And Nina Baym explains how a Creole like Grégoire would be difficult for an outsider like Melicent to bond with. Chopin's Creoles and Acadians, Baym writes, "combine a highly developed self-dramatizing ability with a remarkable lack of self-consciousness. . . . They seem to lack guilt and the tendency toward self-analysis. . . . [some of them] move from one moral position to its opposite without suffering guilt feelings over their inconsistency. They are more attuned to the natural flow of their own emotions; they are more trusting of themselves than the typical representative of the American moral code" (xxv, xxvi). Grégoire cannot offer Melicent what she needs. Some of his values, ones he thinks are normal, even admirable, are unacceptable. Melicent refuses to speak to him on learning that he has killed a man. But Grégoire knows no other way, and the hopelessness of his love for her drives him to despair.

You might argue that Grégoire maintains his autonomy after Melicent leaves Place-du-Bois. If anything, he is more like himself than before, as Aunt Belindy points out (119). But his self-destructive actions, first in a nearby town—where he tells the Roman Catholic priest that there is no such place as hell because that is what Unitarian Melicent has convinced him of—and then back in Texas, where he is killed in a brawl, show that his Creole identity is of no interest for him without the fulfillment that a relationship with Melicent would bring him. "He felt himself regenerated through love," Chopin writes, "and as having no part in that other Grégoire whom he only thought of to dismiss with unrecognition" (80). Being loved by Melicent, he believes, would let him become something different from himself. He doesn't want autonomy if it means being without Melicent.

In Chopin's "The Story of an Hour," we can see a woman who briefly stumbles upon autonomy. When she is told—incorrectly, it turns out—that her husband has died in an accident, Louise Mallard reacts first with grief and then with a joyful recognition that she is now on her own. "There would be no one to live for her during those coming years," she thinks, "she would live for herself. There would be no powerful will bending hers in that blind persistence with which men and women believe they have a right to impose a private will upon a fellow-creature" (353).

Today, people reading those sentences understand them mostly in feminist terms, as a recognition that in her marriage Louise Mallard has lacked agency, has not been self-sufficient, because she does not have the same cultural power that her husband has. But we should notice that, as Chopin points out, it is not only men who sometimes "impose a private will upon a fellow-creature." It is "men and women"—at times, women like Thérèse Lafirme.

In *The Awakening*, Edna Pontellier seeks autonomy. "I don't want anything but my own way," she says, although recognizing "that is wanting a good deal, of course, when you have to trample upon the lives, the hearts, the prejudices of others" (996). Earlier she has famously insisted,

"I would give up the unessential; I would give my money, I would give my life for my children; but I wouldn't give myself" (929).

However, as Heather Ostman points out, sometimes Chopin's women, too, are willing to sacrifice having their own way. Mamzelle Aurélie in "Regret," Ostman shows, "exchanges her autonomy for the interconnectedness offered by the presence of children" ("Maternity" 107).

In her novels and short stories Chopin shows us both women and men who, although not always successfully, seek to have their own way, to live for themselves, to follow the promptings of their characters, to be self-sufficient—and to be free.

Freedom: Hosmer, Joçint, and Gouvernail

In *At Fault,* freedom is crucial for David Hosmer. His Homeyer is outraged by Thérèse's acceptance of received ethical norms in arguing that Hosmer must remarry his former wife. He objects to "the submission of a human destiny to the exacting and ignorant rule of what he termed moral conventionalities" (49). Hosmer wants not only freedom from such conventions but freedom to begin a happy life with the woman he loves. He wants to "let the individual man hold on to his personality." And, he insists, if Fanny "must be redeemed," then "let the redemption come by different ways than those of sacrifice: let it be an outcome from the capability of their [Hosmer's and Thérèse's] united happiness" (50).

But in spite of what he believes, Hosmer carries through with what Thérèse has asked him to do, and the result is, as he had expected, dreadful. Alone with Thérèse for the first time back at Place-du-Bois, Hosmer tells her (directly this time, not quoting Homeyer), "it's one of those things to drive a man mad, the sweet complaisance with which women accept situations, or inflict situations that it takes the utmost of a man's strength to endure" (99). But the two then have a quiet moment together in which Thérèse confesses to him that it would make her miserable if he were to leave Place-du-Bois. Hosmer revels in that moment because it has "left his mind free to return to the delicious consciousness, that he had needed to be reminded of, that Thérèse loved him after all" (102). It's the only touch of freedom he feels.

Also in *At Fault,* Chopin shows us mixed-blood Joçint, who wants the freedom to once again hunt in his beloved forests. He hates the way Hosmer's new sawmill has deprived him of the happiness his gun and his dog used to bring him. He is suffering from what Suzanne Disheroon Green and David J. Caudle call "the regimentation of his formerly carefree lifestyle because of the demands of industrial labor" (xxiii). He doesn't care about the wages he receives. He wants to be free. And, Donald A. Ringe adds, "there is irony in the fact that Joçint is not only prevented from living his carefree life but is even forced to cut into lumber the very woods where he loves to hunt, in effect destroying the thing that means the most to him" (28). Nevertheless, as Robert D. Arner points out, "the wish to adhere to a primitive and anarchic way of life destroys Joçint, who can oppose the moral chaos of an industrial society only with his own chaotic violence" (152). There can be no freedom from social constraints—from changing economic demands—for Joçint.

Throughout her fiction, a yearning for freedom is one of Kate Chopin's major subjects. You can see it in Louise Mallard's response upon learning that her husband has died. "Free, free, free!" Mrs. Mallard says to herself in "The Story of an Hour." "Free! Body and soul free!" she repeats (353, 354). You can, in fact, see the theme of freedom appear in Chopin's thoughts well before she became a professional writer, in the little sketch "Emancipation. A Life Fable," that she—Kate O'Flaherty at the time—wrote when she was nineteen or twenty years old.

She describes an animal living happily in a cage where his needs for food, water, and rest are met. He considers that his life is good. One day he discovers that the door to his cage is left open. He hesitates to leave, afraid of the unaccustomed, and again and again retreats to a corner. Then, drawn by the broad sky and intense light, he takes a breath and darts out into a new world, one, to be sure, where he is sometimes hungry, thirsty, and tired. But, the sketch concludes: "So does he live, seeking, finding, joying and suffering. The door which accident had opened is open still, but the cage remains forever empty!" (38). Early in her life, Chopin comes down on the side of freedom rather than security. The animal's cage is a striking metaphor for the way a society offers safety and comfort in return for accepting restrictions.

Twenty years later, now a published author, Kate Chopin shows us a different understanding of what freedom can mean. She creates a journalist of "advanced" opinions (444) named Gouvernail and includes him in three works. Gouvernail in French (Chopin was bilingual, functioning comfortably in French as well as in English) means a rudder, a blade that guides the movement of a boat, suggesting that the journalist understands the direction in which events are moving. In *The Awakening* at Edna Pontellier's dinner party he mutters lines of a Swinburne sonnet about the presence of death in the room (973). In "A Respectable Woman" he quotes Whitman's "Song of Myself," showing that he is aware of the sexual tension flowing between himself and the wife of his friend (335). And in the lovely short story "Athénaïse" he reveals himself as a man who responds not to an external restraint but to an internal one. For him, freedom exists only in relation to other people's desires.

He is living in a New Orleans boardinghouse when young Athénaïse arrives there, having fled an unhappy marriage. Gouvernail is wrapped up in his work and does not seek her out, but he responds politely when she asks him for help in mailing letters, and—although he has forgotten her name—he joins her one evening, recognizing that she is lonely and needs a friend. He listens to her for an hour, concluding that she probably adores her husband without knowing it and that she is "self-willed, impulsive, innocent, ignorant, unsatisfied, dissatisfied" (446).

She is also exquisitely beautiful, he discovers, as he spends more and more time showing her around the city, and he finds himself falling in love with her. When he sees her crying one evening—feeling sick and depressed, longing for her childhood home (she has not yet discovered she is pregnant)—he reaches for her hands, and she throws herself sobbing into his arms. He aches to pull her tightly to himself, to kiss her. But he doesn't. He understands that he is a substitute for her family. He must wait. "He hoped some day to hold her with a lover's arms," Kate Chopin writes: "That she was married made no particle of difference to Gouvernail. He could not conceive or dream of it making a difference. When the time came that she wanted him,—as he hoped and believed it would come,—he felt he would have a right to her. So long as she did not want him, he had no right to her,—no more than her husband had"

(450). Gouvernail's freedom to pursue something beyond friendship with Athénaïse, he believes, depends not upon moral conventions but upon her wanting what he does.

By the end of the story, Athénaïse, having found that "her whole passionate nature was aroused as if by a miracle" on learning she is carrying a child, forgets about Gouvernail and wants nothing more than her husband (451). When she rushes back to him it is not in response to traditional expectations about marriage but, like Gouvernail, to something internal—to her awakened desires, her passions.

Edna Pontellier in *The Awakening* achieves extraordinary freedom. Although she is married and has two young children, she falls in love with Robert Lebrun, a man she has met on her summer vacation. She abandons the reception days that her position as a leisure-class wife demands of her. She does not go with her husband on a business trip to New York and allows her children to vacation with their grandparents. She moves from what she sees as her husband's house to a little house of her own, using money that she has won at horse races and has earned from selling her paintings. And she takes a lover. Since Robert, the man whom she loves and who loves her, has been hiding from her in Mexico, she has sex with a well-known womanizer. "I am no longer one of Mr. Pontellier's possessions," she later tells Robert. "I give myself where I choose" (992).

Edna achieves a degree of autonomy and freedom from traditional restraints remarkable for a married woman in nineteenth-century American fiction. But it is not enough. She dies because she cannot find fulfillment. It is worth noting that at his low point in *At Fault*, when he is in St. Louis having just remarried Fanny, David Hosmer contemplates suicide.

Fulfilment: Hosmer, Lorenzo Worthington, and Wallace Offdean

Hosmer struggles with finding fulfillment. He wants to be like us—or, at least, like many of us living in twenty-first-century Western countries. He wants to be what we think of as a modern person. The word "modern" rarely shows up in Kate Chopin's writing. But in an 1897 essay, she uses it in a discussion of recent books in which readers might find "surprises" and "innovation." Many such books, she notes, "are worth knowing. They come from the new land where 'the modern' holds sway. If we keep them company for awhile we may find ourselves a little blown and dizzy from the unaccustomed pace, but, on the whole, invigorated" (718).

We don't know exactly what Chopin had in mind in writing about "the modern," and modern has a host of meanings today in different fields ranging from architecture to zoology. But Steven B. Smith's twenty-first-century description captures a good part of what Kate Chopin shows us in her 1890s fiction. Modern people, Smith writes, share "the desire for autonomy and self-direction, the aspiration to live independently of the dictates of habit, custom, and tradition, to accept moral institutions and practices only if they pass the bar of one's critical intellect, and to accept ultimate responsibility for one's life and actions" (x).

David Hosmer's "critical intellect" demands autonomy and freedom. Hosmer also wants fulfillment, but he cannot accept what many people believe—that the received wisdom in religion is a pathway to fulfillment. When he visits St. Louis, Chopin introduces us to Lorenzo Worthington, who tries his best to persuade Hosmer of religion's importance. Religions, Mr. Worthington argues, are central to preserving social stability. But Hosmer—who is not at this point in the novel much focused on social stability—argues that, according to Homeyer, religions are "mythological creations" that "satisfy a species of sentimentality—a morbid craving in man for the unknown and undemonstrable" (68).

No, Mr. Worthington says, "the religious sentiment is implanted, a true and legitimate attribute of the human soul—with peremptory right to its existence." Your Homeyer, he adds, is "an Iconoclast, who would tear down and leave devastation behind him; building up nothing. He would deprive a clinging humanity of the supports about which she twines herself, and leave her helpless and sprawling upon the earth" (68). People, Mr. Worthington concludes, are not prepared to face the challenges of life without religious faith.

Kate Chopin had abandoned her Roman Catholicism by the time she began her writing career.[4] She feels no sympathy, she writes in one of her essays, with midwestern writers who have "no doubt in their souls, no unrest: apparently an abiding faith in God as he manifests himself through the sectional church" (691). She complains in another essay about a person who wants her to "cultivate" her faith, "as though it were to be acquired like a foreign language!" But, Chopin adds, "I have discovered my limitations and I have saved myself much worry and torment by recognizing and accepting them as final. I can gain nothing by cultivating faculties that are not my own" (702).

In *At Fault* Kate Chopin explores a fundamental concern that she was grappling with as she began her writing career. She is without question convinced that people's needs for autonomy and freedom must be met. But she is struggling—as she would continue to struggle throughout the 1890s as she wrote her stories, her essays and poems, and *The Awakening*—with how people are to obtain happiness at a time when in western Europe and the United States philosophers, scientists, artists, and others have abandoned their trust in traditions and religions and are reaching for new ways, modern ways, to find fulfillment.

You can get a glimpse of what Chopin thinks could replace religion by focusing on the yearnings of young Wallace Offdean in "A No-Account Creole." Chopin had drafted that story in 1888, before she wrote *At Fault* in 1889 and 1890, and then finished it in 1891, after publishing the novel. Offdean is a commission merchant making a decent living at his position. The opening pages of the story show him rejecting an offer to invest his modest inheritance in a business that could make him far wealthier than he is likely to become in his present job.

Offdean wants instead to "get his feet well planted on solid ground," to "keep clear of the maelstroms of sordid work and senseless pleasure in which the average American business man may be said alternately to exist, and which reduce him, naturally, to a rather ragged condition of soul" (81).

In "A No-Account Creole" we follow Offdean investigating the run-down condition of a plantation on which his firm has foreclosed and, in the process, meeting the charming Euphrasie Manton, whose father manages the plantation. He slowly comes to see that his future could be on the plantation "bought and embellished with his inheritance; and

Euphrasie, whom he loved, his wife and companion throughout a life such as he knew now he had craved for,—a life that, imposing bodily activity, admits the intellectual repose in which thought unfolds" (97). Offdean's aspiration for loving companionship and a work/life balance should ring true for many people in the twenty-first century.

A yearning for satisfying sex should also ring true for many people today, and sex can be an element of fulfillment in Chopin's work. If you are used to explicit sexuality in today's print and mass media, you might wonder—as many readers wonder—if Edna Pontellier actually has sex with Alcée Arobin in *The Awakening*. And in reading *At Fault*, you may need to recall Victorian or Puritan norms about what should be written or shown, and you may need to keep in mind that although many magazines and newspapers existed in the United States by the 1890s, and books were widely available, most were not so specialized in their intended audiences as they are today. Children were likely to have access to them. And editors needed to keep in mind the values of the people who bought the publications they sought to sell, as well as pay attention to the 1873 Comstock Laws governing the circulation of what could be thought of as obscene literature through the mails.

At Fault may come across as an erotic-free novel. But the signs of sex are clear in the book's closing moments when Hosmer notes that his sister has asked him to give his wife Thérèse many kisses and then whispers in Thérèse's ear something that makes her "turn very rosy in the moonlight" (170). And they are obvious earlier when Thérèse watches in dismay as Fanny glows on Hosmer's return to their cottage at the end of the day, as well as when Grégoire kisses Melicent—a kiss that later "brought the hot color to her cheek" (147)—and when Hosmer and Thérèse kiss "in utter blindness to everything but love for each other" (40).

In *The Awakening*, among Edna Pontellier's aspirations is a need for satisfying sex. Edna has borne two children, but she has not experienced with her husband what Chopin calls "this cup of life" as she does with Alcée Arobin. Edna feels irresponsible after having sex with Arobin, along with feeling shock and the rebuke of her husband and Robert. But she does not feel shame or remorse because she has been "inflamed" by sex outside of marriage, by sex without love: "Above all," we learn, "there was understanding. She felt as if a mist had been lifted from her eyes, enabling her to look upon and comprehend the significance of life, that monster made up of beauty and brutality" (967).

Yet for Edna Pontellier, good sex does not lead to fulfillment, as it does, at least momentarily, for Calixta and Alcée Laballière in Chopin's "The Storm." Those two, Chopin shows us in the earlier "At the 'Cadian Ball," have been yearning for each other, perhaps loving each other, well before they yielded to the pressures of their communities by marrying someone within their social group—Alcée a Creole woman, Calixta an Acadian man. Now, when a violent thunderstorm finds the two together and alone, Calixta is free to unleash "the generous abundance of her passion" and Alcée "his own sensuous nature." Calixta's body, Chopin writes, "was knowing for the first time its birthright" (595). In sex with Alcée Arobin, Edna Pontellier's body is also knowing its birthright, although not through union with the man Edna loves.

Autonomy, Freedom, Fulfillment—and the Community

In Kate Chopin's work, autonomy, freedom, and fulfillment are individual yearnings. Chopin presents David Hosmer as correct in his conviction that the well-being of the individual must take precedence over the well-being of the group. But in spite of her finding Thérèse at fault for behaving as she does, Chopin emphasizes that Thérèse's conservatism—her concern for the security of the Place-du-Bois community—is not misguided.

She begins *At Fault* by showing us the dangers Thérèse faced when her husband died. Thérèse is a courageous nineteenth-century woman who assumed the management of a large plantation by herself rather than turn it over to a male relative or a supervisor. Consumed by her grief, Thérèse is shocked in recognizing a breakdown in social order and its resulting lawlessness, with her workers stealing the plantation's essential cotton seed. She comes to accept her responsibility for the land and for the people who depend on it for their living. It's that sense of responsibility that draws her out of mourning for her husband and motivates her actions throughout the novel. She has on her shoulders major responsibilities for the common good, for other human beings as well as for property. She does not act out of groundless fears.

Scholars have acknowledged that truth. Nina Baym writes that Chopin stresses the importance of "the interaction between a person's sense of himself (or herself) and the recognized obligations to community" (xxii–xxiii). And Mary E. Papke writes that *At Fault* is about "the individual's search for a moral, socially responsible, and self-fulfilling existence" (45). "Self-fulfillment," she says, "is not presented as a finished product, a commodity that one can purchase cheaply, but as a process one must effect" (50).

Thérèse is in the process of challenging her beliefs in the second half of the novel. Her convictions at the end of the book are close to those of Hosmer. The two are ideal life partners for each other. Neither ignores the importance of social stability. Neither would tolerate workers stealing the plantation's cotton seed. They find happiness together through balance, through attention to their own needs—as Hosmer has articulated them—as well as to the needs of their community, as Thérèse has shown through her actions.

Kate Chopin thoroughly understands the importance of community. It's helpful to keep in mind that she grew up during the American Civil War and spent her entire adult life in the defeated American South, experiencing firsthand the economic and cultural devastation people face when their traditional ways of life are destroyed by sudden social change. She is fully aware of conditions in her post-Reconstruction community—of poverty, especially, of racial and social inequality, and of the cultural power that men have over women (consistent motifs in her short stories). But there is little in her work to suggest that she is eager for another upheaval. She does not advocate reordering society.

In her fiction, instead of promoting social change, she seeks to tell the truth about what she has seen and experienced in Louisiana and St. Louis. She seeks to show what she calls "human existence in its subtle, complex, true meaning, stripped of the veil with which ethical and conventional standards have draped it" (691). And truth, she writes, "rests upon a shifting basis and is apt to be kaleidoscopic" (697). At the end of *At Fault* Thérèse confesses that "I have seen myself at fault in following what seemed the only right. I feel as if there were no way to turn for the truth. Old supports appear to be giving way beneath me. They were so secure before" (165).

Hosmer responds, "The truth in its entirety isn't given to man to know.... But we make a step towards it, when we learn that there is rottenness and evil in the world, masquerading as right and morality—when we learn to know the living spirit from the dead letter" (165). The violence in the novel—the raging river, the sudden deaths of Joçint, Grégoire, Fanny, and others—have allowed Hosmer and Thérèse to openly embrace each other. Earlier, declaring his love for her, Hosmer is stunned by Thérèse saying, "Love isn't everything in life; there is something higher" (40).

"God in heaven," Hosmer exclaims—it's an unusual phrase for him—"there shouldn't be!" (40).

Pamela Glenn Menke, drawing on the feminist work of Hélène Cixous, Julia Kristeva, and Joanne Dobson, finds it "surprising . . . the degree to which Chopin invests agency in David Hosmer" and makes him "the agent of change" in *At Fault,* "the instrument of the 'living spirit,' the purveyor of insight, and the champion of action based on genuine, spontaneous feeling" (48–49).

It's true that since Kate Chopin was suddenly rediscovered in the 1970s, since her work emerged like a burst of sunlight on a cloudy day, she has been celebrated for her women characters in "The Story of an Hour," *The Awakening,* and other works that bring to classic American fiction a long-overdue and compelling emphasis on ways that women are damaged by patriarchal societies. But it is not especially surprising that Chopin describes fulfillment as a human need, that she creates a male character like David Hosmer. We can find—as others have found—sympathetic men as well as sympathetic women at many places in her fiction.

Half a century ago, in 1970, Lewis Leary, reviewing Per Seyersted's just-published *Complete Works of Kate Chopin*—the volume that launched Chopin into the literary canons—writes that he is delighted with the new book. "Mrs. Chopin is here at last," he begins, "and welcome to her." He expects she will become "a spokeswoman for liberation" (138).

Her unifying theme, he says, asks "to what extent and at what sacrifice can people (women usually) pursue the freedoms which society (men) denies them?" (141). "What sustained her," he writes, "was her comic sense, her winsome skepticism, her riotously nimble insight." However, he adds, "neither male nor female has sole right to the domain which she explored with humor and compassion" (143–44).

Leary ends his review by citing Chopin's poem "The Haunted Chamber." He notes that "there was a twinkle in [Chopin's] words which guaranteed that the nouns could as well be interchanged, one for the other, when she closes the poem by writing that 'women forever will whine and cry / And men forever must listen—and sigh—'" (144).

Kate Chopin would not again create such a highly detailed male character as David Hosmer. But in spite of the agency with which she has endowed him, Hosmer is not by himself able to find happiness with the woman he loves. It is rather Thérèse whose actions shape what happens on her plantation. By asking Hosmer to bring Fanny to Place-du-Bois, Thérèse sets up an inevitable conflict. Then the natural forces of heavy rain and the Cane River—a motif throughout the novel—bring closure to Hosmer and Fanny's failed remarriage.

By the end of *At Fault* Hosmer fulfills his aspirations and Thérèse fulfills hers. Together they find some of what Gouvernail, Offdean, Athénaïse, and Calixta need, what Grégoire, Joçint, Louise Mallard, and Edna Pontellier cannot grasp. They find the right human relationship for themselves, the right life partner. They find autonomy and freedom. And they find fulfillment through balancing their concern for other people and the community with their individual needs for work, sex, companionship, and love.

NOTES

1. Textual citations to *At Fault* refer to *At Fault,* edited by Bernard Koloski, and citations to all other Chopin writings refer to *The Complete Works of Kate Chopin,* edited by Per Seyersted.

2. Some ideas included here I have presented in different ways in the introduction to the Penguin Classics edition of *At Fault* and in chapter 2 of *The Historian's Awakening: Reading Kate Chopin's Classic Novel as Social and Cultural History.*

3. Grégoire and his brothers appear in Chopin's short stories. You can find a thorough guide to which Chopin's characters appear in which stories in Thomas Bonner's *Kate Chopin Companion.*

4. Heather Ostman discusses religion in detail in *Kate Chopin and Catholicism.*

WORKS CITED

Arner, Robert D. "Landscape Symbolism in Kate Chopin's *At Fault.*" *Louisiana Studies* 9 (1970): 142–53.

Baym, Nina. Introduction to *The Awakening and Selected Stories of Kate Chopin,* edited by Baym, vii–xl. New York: Modern Library, 1981.

Bonner, Thomas, Jr. *The Kate Chopin Companion with Chopin's Translations from French Fiction.* Westport, CT: Greenwood, 1988.

Campbell, Donna. "At Fault: A Reappraisal of Kate Chopin's Other Novel." In *The Cambridge Companion to Kate Chopin,* edited by Janet Beer, 27–43. Cambridge: Cambridge University Press, 2008.

Chopin, Kate. *At Fault.* 1890. Edited with an introduction and notes by Bernard Koloski. London: Penguin, 2002.

———. *Complete Works of Kate Chopin.* Edited by Per Seyersted. Baton Rouge: Louisiana State University Press, 1969.

Dyer, Joyce Coyne, and Robert Emmett Monroe. "Texas and Texans in the Fiction of Kate Chopin." *Western American Literature* 20, no. 1 (1985): 3–15.

Ewell, Barbara C. *Kate Chopin.* New York: Frederick Ungar, 1986.

Green, Suzanne Disheroon, and David J. Caudle. Introduction to *At Fault: A Scholarly Edition with Background Readings,* edited by Green and Caudle, xix–xxxii. Knoxville: University of Tennessee Press, 2001.

Hotchkiss, Jane. "Confusing the Issue: Who's 'At Fault'?" *Louisiana Literature* 11, no. 1 (1994): 31–43.

Koloski, Bernard, ed. *The Historian's Awakening: Reading Kate Chopin's Classic Novel as Social and Cultural History.* Westport, CT: Praeger, 2019.

———. Introduction to *At Fault,* by Kate Chopin, edited by Koloski, vii–xxii. London: Penguin, 2002.

Lattin, Patricia Hopkins. "Kate Chopin's Repeating Characters." *Mississippi Quarterly* 33, no. 1 (1979): 19–37.

Leary, Lewis. "Kate Chopin, Liberationist?" *Southern Literary Journal* 3, no. 1 (1970): 138–44.

Menke, Pamela Glenn. "Fissure as Art in Kate Chopin's *At Fault.*" *Louisiana Literature* 11, no. 1 (1994): 44–58.

Ostman, Heather. *Kate Chopin and Catholicism.* London: Palgrave Macmillan, 2020.

———. "Maternity vs. Autonomy in Chopin's 'Regret.'" In *Kate Chopin in Context: New Approaches,* edited by Ostman and Kate O'Donoghue, 101–15. London: Palgrave Macmillan, 2015.

Papke, Mary E. *Verging on the Abyss: The Social Fiction of Kate Chopin and Edith Wharton.* Westport, CT: Greenwood, 1990.

Rankin, Daniel S. *Kate Chopin and Her Creole Stories.* Philadelphia: University of Pennsylvania Press, 1932.

Ringe, Donald A. "Cane River World: *At Fault* and Related Stories." In *Kate Chopin,* edited by Harold Bloom, 25–33. New York: Chelsea House, 1987.

Seyersted, Per. *Kate Chopin: A Critical Biography.* Baton Rouge: Louisiana State University Press, 1969.

Skaggs, Peggy. *Kate Chopin.* Woodbridge, CT: Twayne, 1985.

Smith, Steven B. *Modernity and Its Discontents: Making and Unmaking the Bourgeois from Machiavelli to Bellow.* New Haven, CT: Yale University Press, 2016.

Taylor, Helen. *Gender, Race, and Region in the Writings of Grace King, Ruth McEnery Stuart, and Kate Chopin.* Baton Rouge: Louisiana State University Press, 1989.

Toth, Emily. *Kate Chopin.* New York: William Morrow, 1990.

———. *Unveiling Kate Chopin.* Jackson: University Press of Mississippi, 1999.

Wagner-Martin, Linda. "Kate Chopin's Fascination with Young Men." In *Critical Essays on Kate Chopin,* edited by Alice Hall Petry, 197–206. Boston: G. K. Hall, 1996.

Kate Chopin's Queer Etiologies

What's At Fault *in the History of Sexuality*

MICHAEL P. BIBLER

In many ways, Kate Chopin is a writer of sex more than sexuality: of erotic impulses and sensual experiences of pleasure, desire, amativeness, and attraction, as well as aversion, revulsion, and even duty, but not so much how these things settle on an individual to create something like a coherent sexual identity. This dynamic creates a unique challenge for locating Chopin's fiction within the history of sexuality. At a time when sexologists and other writers were defining the outlines of our modern sexual categories, does her work swim against the tide by avoiding fixed taxonomies? Or does her work already prefigure those categories in order to subvert them, putting her ahead of her time? I propose that a better way to understand Chopin's work is to shift our understanding of the history of sexuality itself. Using her novel *At Fault* (1890), I show how Chopin asks different kinds of questions about the nature of sexuality than scholars working in the history of sexuality usually consider. *At Fault* is unquestionably modern in its treatment of divorce, and I argue that it is also thoroughly modern in its treatment of sexuality, including what we might loosely call queer sexualities. However, rather than simply showing us nascent forms of gay or lesbian subjectivities that look something like we do now, *At Fault* explores another aspect of sexuality that scholars have only recently begun to give more attention: namely, questions about what *causes* different kinds of sexuality, or what Benjamin Kahan calls the etiologies of sexuality.

As Kahan argues, the history of sexuality has focused primarily on "the effects of sexuality" (6)—the desires expressed, the acts committed—that allow us to glimpse "fully formed subjects" behind them (7). The figures that loom largest within this history are those who, in one way or another, appear to possess a sexuality similar to how we think about sexuality now: as an innate, even inborn part of our individual being that shapes and steers the acts we prefer and the bodies and objects we cathect, as well as things like gender expression and even social and cultural attachments. This interest in sexual subjectivities emphasizes the "congenital model" of sexuality (Kahan 4)—the notion that homosexuals are "born this way," for example. However, Kahan demonstrates that this question about the congenital nature of sexuality was far from settled in the late nineteenth and early twentieth centuries, as most sexologists gave equal consideration to the idea that sexuality was something people "acquired" (4). Sexologists pointed toward a dizzying array of causes—from climate and temperature to alcoholism to occupation of single-gender environments and even to types of industrial labor—to show how homosexuality could be "mutable, voluntary, learned, and environmental" (1). And, beyond homosexuality, they argued that environmental factors also produced an infinite array of other "acquired sexual practices and minor perversions that have not crystalized into varieties of personhood or come to be understood as congenital and biologized" (7–8). In our own time, shifting the methodological focus of the history of sexuality from the effects of sexuality to "representations of its causes" does not mean, of course, insisting on the truth of any particular etiological model (Kahan 3). Rather, mapping historical etiologies of sexuality helps bring into sharper relief the "discourses that forged sexual personhood" over time (7). It charts a messier evolutionary trajectory in which competing models of sexuality emerged and fell away—Kahan's "minor perversions" (à la Foucault)—as the congenital model gained precedence and the gender of object choice became the defining characteristic of sexuality in the form of the homo/hetero binary.

A history of sexuality that focuses on representations of the causes of sexuality is one that Chopin, an ardent reader of Charles Darwin, would have loved. Her canonical works *The Awakening* (1899) and "The Story of an Hour" (1894) track infinitesimal changes in their protagonists' sexualities—their desires, object choices, expressions of gender, and so on—in response to changes in their circumstances. And, as I argue here, *At Fault* charts a wide collection of causes and effects as her characters adapt, or fail to adapt, to the changing environments and events in their lives. This focus on etiologies suggests new avenues for understanding Chopin's interest in literary naturalism and its emphasis on determinism; but an etiological reading does not mean treating sexuality as fatalistically determined. Rather, mapping sexual etiologies in *At Fault* reveals the complex interplay and overlap of multiple models of sexuality at the crossroads between environment and subjectivity, culture and biology, sex and identity. To make this argument, I examine the surprisingly long list of etiological forces that shape each character's sexuality, including Thérèse's indominable will, Hosmer's almost obsessive interest in work, Fanny's alcoholism, Grégoire's racism and violence, and Melicent's capriciousness and, at the end of the novel, interest in natural history. These etiological variations, I argue, expose new levels of sophistication in Chopin's emphatically feminist *and queer* response to Darwin's theory of sexual selection. And, by presenting sexuality as something that is not immutable but can change over time, these etiologies add further power to her broader rejection of the hetero-patriarchal constraints placed on femininity, sensual pleasure, and women's self-empowerment. For if sexuality is not necessarily fixed and absolute, as the novel suggests, then the variable elements of sexual and gender difference cannot be used to rationalize *social* inequalities between men and women and between what we would call straight and queer.

Situational Lesbianism

It is impossible that Chopin would not have known the work of sexologists and other contemporary writings about queer sexualities. She was deeply interested in the latest research in philosophy, science, and natural history, especially Darwin, and she certainly would have encountered early sexological theories of the 1870s and 1880s. She also could not have missed the 1892 English translation of Richard von Krafft-Ebing's *Psychopathia Sexualis,* one of the most influential works of sexology. In fact, the book had already gone through an astounding seven editions in German in the six years since its first publication in 1886, and we know that Chopin also read German. If she did not read Krafft-Ebing in the original language, there is no doubt she would have encountered summaries or reviews of the book before she began writing *At Fault* in 1889. Furthermore, Chopin was a devotee of Walt Whitman, Guy de Maupassant, Émile Zola, and Alphonse Daudet, all of whom offered clear representations of homoeroticism and what we would call homosexuality. And there is no question that she knew of the romantic friendships between women that came to be known as "Boston marriages" thanks, in large part, to Henry James's depiction of such a relationship in *The Bostonians* (1886)—a novel that has received a great deal of attention in the history of sexuality, to say the least.[1] What if we began recognizing Chopin's novel as being as important to the history of sexuality as that more canonical work by a male writer from the industrialized North?

Not surprisingly, most of the critical attention devoted to Chopin's representations of homoerotic, homosexual, and other queer sexualities focuses on *The Awakening*. Without going so far as to claim that Edna Pontellier is exclusively attracted to other women, Kathryn Lee Seidel, Elizabeth LeBlanc, Mary Biggs, and others have shown how her sensual attachments to Mademoiselle Reisz and Adèle Ratignolle make it "possible to see a lesbian identity as one potential fulfillment of Edna's search for meaning in her life" and, thus, to imagine "strategies . . . for reconstructing a (lesbian) identity both within and apart from the heterosexual economy" (LeBlanc 289, 290). Critics have also argued that Mademoiselle Reisz and Robert LeBrun can be read as prototypes of lesbian and gay identities. And some have shown how Chopin's stories "Fedora" (1895) and "Lilacs" (1896) offer fairly explicit representations of lesbian attraction and love, even as their ambiguities continue to resist easy sexual categorization. Finally, the 2020 Ripe Figs film adaptation of Chopin's story "Regret" (1895) explicitly represents the protagonist Mamzelle (in the story she is Mamzelle Aurélie) as a lesbian who "came out" as a teenager and now "begins to realize what this choice has cost her."[2] In *At Fault*, I argue that the character of Melicent similarly embodies an ambiguous form of lesbian identity. However, *At Fault* engages in a much more direct conversation with the theories and debates of sexology than do those other works. In doing so, the novel reveals a more complex consideration of the intersections and overlaps between congenital and etiological models of subjectivity.

Melicent's thoughts about her suitor Grégoire offer the most explicit articulation of sexological discourse in the novel. We learn at the end of the text that Melicent develops an interest in natural history, but the novel foreshadows that interest in part 1, when the narrator claims that Melicent "was not then awake to certain fine psychological differences distinguishing man from man; precluding the possibility of naming and classifying [Grégoire] in the moral as one might in the animal kingdom" (44). Although Melicent has no available taxonomies to name and classify Grégoire as a particular type of man, the impulse to do so remains. She studies him through a "pathological aspect" and determines that while the "short-comings" of his manner of speaking do not "detract from a definite inheritance of good breeding," they still "touched his personality as a physical deformation might," presenting him as "a species of fascination, for a certain order of misregulated mind" (44). Melicent also turns this interest in pathological differences on herself, "making a diagnosis of various symptoms, indicative by no means of a deep-seated malady," to "decide" that she must be in love with Grégoire. By studying the "symptoms" of her own thoughts and behavior—what we would call the effects of sexuality—she comically deduces that they must evidence a particular form of emotional attraction to Grégoire and, thus, a particular form of sexual subjectivity within herself.

By pathologizing both Grégoire and, implicitly, herself as belonging to certain "species" of human "personality," Melicent invokes the congenital model of sexuality. Indeed, the "eccentricity of speech" that makes it impossible for Grégoire to "adapt . . . to the requirements of polite society" reveals an innate difference in spite of his "inheritance of good breeding" (44). Yet the novel also satirizes Melicent's invocation of the congenital model through what appears to be her *misdiagnosis* of her own sexuality. As if it weren't comic enough that she has to measure her own "symptoms" to decide whether she loves Grégoire, her behavior more consistently suggests that she does not love men at all and that her own psychological difference might be a sign of lesbianism. Melicent has accepted and broken several engagements before coming to Place-du-Bois, and in almost every case, she finds that kissing "was not to her liking" (44). Thus, she forbids Grégoire to "ever repeat" his kiss "under pain of losing her affection," just as when, in most of her previous engagements, "kissing had been excluded as superfluous to the relationship" (44). Although the novel describes Melicent as "capricious" (41), her antipathy to physical intimacy with men suggests that she is not the terrible "flirt" Fanny accuses her of being (111). Rather, she appears to be a woman who does not yet recognize that she is not attracted to men in the first place.

The end of the novel supports this lesbian reading when Melicent writes to Hosmer about her enthusiastic friendship with Mrs. Griesmann. As the two women prepare to go out west to study "Natural History and all that" (168), they exemplify the "New Women" of the time—women who "rejected being defined by men," as Emily Toth writes, and instead pursued their own professions outside of the domestic sphere and often either remained single or entered into romantic friendships with other women (Toth 111). Carroll Smith-Rosenberg has argued that by the turn of the twentieth century, misogynist stereotypes of the New Woman conflated her with the "Mannish Lesbian" (268), and Chopin draws a similar association, albeit in a funnier, less phobic way. Quoting Mrs. Griesmann's philosophy that one must push beyond appearances and pursue "a true knowledge of life as it is" by "studying certain fundamental truths and things" (*At Fault* 168), Melicent invites us to consider that their intense connection rests on a deeper, more erotic foundation than just friendship. Couched in the context of their shared interest in the "true knowledge" of natural history, the text also invites us to regard that underlying homoerotic attraction as entirely natural, not deviant or bad. As with Melicent's earlier investigation of her own feelings for Grégoire, the scene suggests that her attachment to Mrs. Griesmann is "indicative by no means of a deep-seated malady" (44). Indeed, Hosmer and Thérèse react to Melicent's news with nothing more than a light-hearted joke when Hosmer puns on the figure of the New Woman and asks, "Is Melicent ever anything else than new?" (168).

However, while Melicent's potential lesbianism invokes the congenital model of sexuality, the novel does not treat that model as the absolute truth of "life as it is." Instead, *At Fault* also invokes an etiological model of lesbian sexuality as something possibly acquired through her contact with Mrs. Griesmann, for Melicent develops these new interests (in natural history but also, the novel implies, in women) exactly when Mrs. Griesmann introduces her to them. Melicent writes that Mrs. Griesmann thinks she has "a quick comprehensive intellectualism (she calls it) that has been misdirected," implying that Mrs. Griesmann has found the right way to "direct" her by bringing her into this romantic friendship (168). She further writes that "Mrs. Griesmann thinks I ought to wear glasses during the trip. Says we often require them without knowing it ourselves. . . . I'm trying a pair, and see a great deal better through them than I expected to" (168–69). The irony here is that Melicent sees things better—physically and metaphorically—only because Mrs. Griesmann has given her the means to do so, which suggests that Melicent doesn't actually see unbiased, natural "truths" but rather the *adjusted* truths that Mrs. Griesmann helps her to see. I do not mean that Mrs. Griesmann is predatory. Well into the twentieth century, sexologists continued to argue that acquired homosexuality was more common for women than for men, and in this case, we should recognize Melicent's queer etiology as partly the product of her capricious love for "novelty" and the situational context of her new intimacy with Mrs. Griesmann (14).[3] Melicent's letter underscores this suggestion of situational homosexuality when she tells Hosmer about an extramarital affair between Fanny's friend Lou Dawson and Bert Rodney in St. Louis when the pair thought Lou's husband was out of town on business. In the stories of both couples, the situation might elicit the desire, or the desire might precede the situation. The novel raises the possibility for reading Melicent's lesbianism as both innate *and* acquired without insisting that one model is more "true" than the other.

Failure to Adapt

The novel invokes other etiological models of sexuality, as well. When debating philosophy with Mr. Worthington in St. Louis, Hosmer quotes his friend Homeyer as believing in "a natural adjustment," which he defines as "an innate reserve force of accommodation" (68). Hosmer explains: "What we commonly call laws in nature, he styles accidents—in society, only arbitrary methods of expediency, which, when they outlive their usefulness to an advancing and exacting civilization, should be set aside" (68). This Darwinian philosophy insists that as a "civilization" evolves, it should "set aside" its previous, "arbitrary" way of doing things. The principles it once took for granted as "laws in nature" turn out to be not immutable, transhistorical truths but only "methods of expediency" adapted to their time. Each new evolution thus requires a "natural adjustment," proving that the only "innate" force is the force of "accommodation," of adaptation itself. Chopin has filled the novel with stark examples of forces that necessitate such "natural adjustment": the railroad's incursion into the natural landscape of farm and forest; the fire at the lumber mill that must burn itself out; the river that washes away the land and everything on it. But she also offers subtler examples, as in her description of Fanny's slow accommodation to life at Place-du-Bois: "Outside influences meeting half-way the workings of unconscious inward forces, were the agents that by degrees were gently ridding her of the acute pressure of dissatisfaction" (82). Here, as with Melicent's relationship with Mrs. Griesmann, we see the confluence of Fanny's congenital "inward" nature as it meets the etiological "outward" forces" of her environment.

Ultimately, however, Fanny loses this struggle to adapt, for she once again succumbs to alcoholism and eventually gets swept into the river by the raging current as she tries to distance herself from her husband. And there are other characters who similarly fail to make a "natural adjustment" to the forces that assail them, including Grégoire and Joçint. We can understand the etiologies that prohibit these characters' ability to adapt as examples of what Kahan calls "volitional etiologies" (101). As sexologists described them, volitional etiologies are acquired, but they confuse the narrative sequencing of cause and effect because they "occupy the paradoxical space between choice and compulsion, between voluntarity and involuntarity, and between active and unconscious action" (102). These volitional etiologies include all kinds of behaviors, including "gambling, smoking, celibacy, criminality, donning 'excessive' or opposite-gender clothes, opium and hashish indulgence, or overin-dulgence in food"; and, in every case, the "errancy and unruliness" of these etiologies keeps individuals "from obeying . . . the logics of sexual orientation and narrative subjectivity whereby congenital desire leads to sexual object choice" (101–2). In Chopin, such "errancy and unrul-iness," or what she repeatedly calls "disorder" (121), drives these three characters to self-destructive actions, and it is impossible to untangle whether the causes of those actions are matters of conscious choice or unconscious compulsion, because they are both.

The volitional etiology that Kahan focuses on is alcohol consump-tion, which many sexologists argued "might lead to immoderate het-erosexual sex" or even homosexuality, but might also be *caused by* "an innate queerness, which exists prior to the consumption of alcohol," even in the very same person (104). Such confusion between cause and effect is obvious with Fanny. In her first marriage to Hosmer in St. Louis, it seems she turned to alcohol to compensate for the death of her child and the neglect she felt at Hosmer's prolonged absences at work. At Place-du-Bois, it is still fairly clear that Hosmer does not love her, but he is careful to give her more attention. Nevertheless, Fanny quickly turns to alcohol again when given the opportunity. Here the novel leaves us asking, Does Fanny turn to alcohol because she feels unfulfilled in her marriage, because she wants to spite her husband, because she simply has a "weak character," as Thérèse suggests, or because Hosmer's ne-glect "furnishe[s] her with every means to increase that weakness" (*At Fault* 39)? The answer seems to be all of the above, for her alcoholism is clearly the result of a combination of internal impulses and environmen-tal conditions. Volitional etiologies multiply the question of what is "At Fault" in this novel. But, whatever the reason for Fanny's "weak" return to alcohol, drink ultimately becomes "her dominant passion [that] had been leading and now controlled her" (155); it becomes a "stronger feeling" than even her hatred for Hosmer, "moving and possessing her; crowding out every other" feeling (152). Thus, Fanny takes the compul-sive risk of crossing the swollen river in a heavy storm to get another bottle in Marie Louise's cabin; and, when she refuses to return with Hosmer, the force of the river destroys the bank and sweeps both her and Marie Louise to their deaths. Because Fanny cannot adapt to the conditions of her new marriage with Hosmer and to her new environment, she resorts to old habits that ultimately get her killed.

We see similar etiological forces at work with Grégoire. As in Melicent's attempt to classify him, the novel emphasizes Grégoire's innate character by describing him as an "intelligent animal" (15, 108) and naturally "hot-blooded" (80, 140). After he kills the unarmed Joçint for starting the mill fire, Hosmer and others cite "heredity" to explain his rashness, claiming that "it was a deed characteristic of any one of the Santien boys" (108). But the novel also suggests the "pathology" of more environmental causes linked to his upbringing (108), for Grégoire admits to Melicent that he and his brothers "all'ays done putty much like we wanted" and were never disciplined (45). And his life of white, masculine privilege makes him quick to anger whenever his sense of the "aristocracy of blood" is challenged, either by the necessity of "undue toil" or by an animal or African American (he uses the N-word) who refuses to do the work for him (80, 15). The extent to which his "desires" are "undisciplined" is also evident in his tendency to "raise Cain" drinking, gambling, dancing, and fighting (80, 80, 45)—volitional etiologies that again confuse cause and effect because we cannot know if they are the *product* or the *source* of his unbridled passions. Importantly, these etiologies are directly linked to his sexuality. His peacockish delight in his clothes and his "misregulated" need for constant stimulation complement the same features in the extravagantly dressed and "misdirected" Melicent (48, 168), while his ability to dance makes him "keenly" attractive to "certain belles of upper Red River" (15, 15).

The extremity of his passions also queers Grégoire by making him appear too "feminine" at times, not just in the "shapeliness" of his "close fitting high-heeled boots" and the "note of pleading or pathos" in his voice (15, 15, 15), but also in the difficulty he has "concealing" those passions when they overwhelm him, as when he "sobbed and wept" when Thérèse tells him that Melicent does not love him (80, 81). Even his rambling journey west after Melicent rejects him is a sign of his queerness (as it also is for Melicent), for as Kahan notes, many sexologists defined "wanderlust" as a sexual "perversion in and of itself" (Kahan 56). And, as Grégoire drinks to excess and picks fights with anyone who will respond, his reckless behavior puts him into erotically charged physical contests with other men. Nevertheless, unlike Melicent, Grégoire is not able to change and adapt as his circumstances change. Instead, he completely succumbs to his volitional etiologies until finally he is killed "out there in some disorderly settlement" that matches his disorderly pathology (140). Most importantly, Thérèse gives Grégoire the chance to adapt by facing up to the crime of shooting Joçint, but he either cannot or will not do so, prompting Melicent's final rejection of him and, thus, his own self-destruction: Thérèse "could not move [him] even to an avowal of regret. He could not understand that he should receive anything but praise for having rid the community of so offensive and dangerous a personage as Joçint; and seemed utterly blind to the moral aspect of his deed" (108). That Grégoire cannot settle his passions or adhere to changing social codes signals his inability to adapt and evolve in response to the environmental forces around him.[4]

Grégoire's inability to recognize the "moral aspect of his deed" makes the interesting suggestion that racism can also be an etiological force that shapes subjectivity. In Joçint, the response to racism is similarly a determining force. Like Grégoire, Joçint is characterized as an innately "unruly subject" with "an impulse of defiance" (22, 24), although in this case his Black and Indian heritage give him an "ugly countenance" (24). But Joçint is also the product of his social environment in that he constantly resents and reacts to the structures of white power that marginalize him, "rebelling against the power of the industrial world that Hosmer represents" and rejecting "complicity in the post-colonial fiction of racial harmony in Louisiana," as Donna Campbell writes (8). As Campbell explains, Chopin "takes pains to make Joçint a villain as well as a victim" by blurring the forces that drive him to get in fights with white men (especially Grégoire) and to sabotage and then destroy the mill, for his act of hanging his own dog prior to the fire suggests an innate villainy that mitigates any political sympathy the reader might have for him (8). Chopin further confuses any effort to identify what causes his behavior by showing Joçint deliberately eating poor-quality food and drinking water with "wiggles" in it, which are presumably worms (24). Nevertheless, whether Joçint's violence is congenitally or environmentally determined, his fate is obviously tied to Grégoire's, because they are both the products of Louisiana's systemic racism and because they both perpetuate the cycles of violence that define that system instead of learning to adapt into something different.

The ambiguous causes of Joçint's behavior showcase the troubling ambiguity of Chopin's treatment of race throughout the novel. Joçint's father, Morico, voices a searing criticism of the white power system as he drags Joçint's body from the flames of the mill and calls all the whites around him "Murderers!" (106). But he then dies as a result of the effort. Meanwhile, Chopin demeans the "elfish and ape like" Sampson (75), while her most romanticized figure, the grotesquely large mammy-figure Marie Louise, also dies as a result of her inability to adapt. Although Thérèse had Marie Louise's cabin moved several times to avoid being washed away as the river erodes the land, and although the river is again posing a threat, Marie Louise refuses any further relocations, saying that she "will die here with all her belongings if it must be" (91). Of course, this is exactly what happens when she, Fanny, and the house fall into the river during the storm. In the context of Chopin's engagement with Darwin, it is hard not to read Joçint's, Morico's, and Marie Louise's deaths as suggestions that African Americans collectively occupy a lower place on the evolutionary scale and cannot survive the test of natural selection. I have no interest in trying to sidestep or excuse the novel's racism, but it is important to recognize how Chopin also makes these deaths primarily matters of *individual,* rather than broadly *racial,* character. Joçint is killed because he replicates the same violence against which he rebels. Morico dies because he is blinded by wholly justifiable grief and rage. And Marie Louise dies because she does not want to suffer further upheaval in her old age. (Or maybe it is also her refusal to let Thérèse continue to dominate her life.) Just as Chopin deliberately confuses congenital and etiological causes of sexuality, her treatment of race tries to have it both ways. As what Campbell calls a "social-problem novel," *At Fault* recognizes the need to confront the racist social structures that destroy Joçint and Morico (1); but it also clings to notions of essential racial differences and even racial primitivism as the Black characters either remain partially dependent on whites or die. At the same time, however, while none of these characters undergo the "natural adjustment" needed for survival, Chopin also never ties their deaths to larger questions of reproduction and survival of the species. By asking us simultaneously to acknowledge and ignore the structural, environmental forces of racism, Chopin dodges the question of "social Darwinism" that inspired many of her contemporaries, including Charlotte Perkins Gilman, and turns the reader's gaze back to the question of how to understand the nature of the "solitary individual" (Bender 203).

Sexual Selection

We see how Chopin turns from the social to the individual in Melicent's final thought about Grégoire's death: "The crime for which she had scorned him, was wiped out now by expiation" (147). In this logic, Grégoire's death balances out Joçint's and Morico's deaths, making a broader response to the structures of racism unnecessary. However, while this move underscores Chopin's racial conservatism, at least in this novel, it also reveals the extent of her feminist response to Darwin. For by focusing her attention on the individual, she sets aside the theory of natural selection and ties her study of sexual etiologies strictly to the theory of *sexual* selection. Natural selection is primarily a matter of survival through reproduction of the species, whereas sexual selection is a more complicated matter of variation for the sake of attaining sexual partners, which may *or may not* result in reproduction. In *Descent of Man,* Darwin gave far more consideration to the theory of sexual selection; and, as Bert Bender and other critics have shown, Chopin also gave far more attention to this theory in her fiction. Although Bender strangely dismisses *At Fault* as "artless and amateurish" (199), he notes that Chopin "questioned [Darwin's] interpretation of the female's role in sexual selection—especially his views on the inferiority of women and . . . the female's modesty: her passivity in the sex drama as a creature without desire" (197–98). However, by focusing on the question of women's choice of sexual partners, Bender omits a large component of both Chopin's novel and Darwin's theory, for both *At Fault* and *Descent of Man* are interested in the possibilities of etiological and sexual variation far beyond matters of choice.

Instead, Elizabeth Grosz offers a more useful way to understand Chopin's feminist response to Darwin. Grosz argues that while natural selection "regulates the operations of birth and death" through competition for reproduction (124), "sexual selection regulates the operations of beauty, appeal, and attraction" (124). Sexual selection is part of "the processes that lead to reproduction, as well as those that may not lead to reproduction, those activities which intensify the bodies and organs of living things, which excite and enervate the body for the sake of pleasure, display, and performance"—no matter how "illogical, nonfunctional, [and] nonadaptive" those "operations" may be (128). Inasmuch as sexual selection is about choice, its function is "to maximize difference or variation, and it succeeds in doing this by maximizing sexual interests as much as bodily types or forms" (130). Importantly, as Grosz sees it, this maximization of sexual forms even includes homosexuality, because all "sexual attractions of various kinds are part of the production of variation for its own sake" (130). Chopin's depiction of Melicent supports this idea, for her implied lesbianism is a form of sexual variation that corresponds directly with her love of unusual and exaggerated clothing—even at the level of wearing eyeglasses whether she needs them or not. Campbell writes that Chopin uses different body types in this novel to explore "the correlation between physical and emotional attributes, a Darwinian typology of gesture, self-adornment and sexual attraction" (6). And Katherine Joslin similarly writes that Chopin's heroines use fashion to "experiment with the limits of individual freedom to gratify ambitions, tastes, likings, even caprices" (78). Melicent's lesbianism exemplifies this exploration of individual variation as the basis for greater freedom, both bodily and socially. So does Grégoire's queerness, except that he fails to seize the opportunity for freedom and clings, instead, to the most fatal forms of white masculinity.

We might say that Melicent's love of novelty helps her adapt more than others. But the central characters, Hosmer and Thérèse, also learn to adapt by making natural adjustments to the etiological forces that shape their sexualities rather than totally suppressing or succumbing to them. Hosmer's key etiology is his tendency to overcommit to his work. He tells Thérèse that it wasn't long into his first marriage to Fanny that he quickly tired of the "rounds of amusement that had no sort of attraction whatever for me" in the "society" of "Fanny's associates," who "were not of the best social rank" (37). Because he was not inclined to the style of those amusements, and because he was also somewhat snobbish, he instead turned to the alibi of work: "my business connections were extending, and they claimed the greater part of my time and thoughts" (37). Fanny confirms that his interest in his work caused him to neglect his wife more and more. Because he constantly read "that everlasting newspaper in his pocket," she tried also to read the paper and "talk to him about what I read" (83). But it turned out "he'd never even looked at the same things," giving the two no common ground to communicate (83). She explains: "here'd be the edges all covered over with figuring. I believe it's the only thing he ever thought of dreamt about; that eternal figuring on every bit of paper he could lay hold of" (83). Hosmer's single-minded attention to business stifles his ability to take emotional or sexual pleasure in his partner, and Thérèse also recognizes this fault early in the novel when she tells him: "there is an unsuspected selfishness in your inclinations that works harm to yourself and to those around you" (12). Focusing singly on "money getting," she explains, "deprives [a person] of a charm which any man's society loses, when pursuing one object in life, he grows insensible to every other" (12). The word "insensible" is crucial here, for it means not only that he is unaware of other pleasures but also that he is unable to sense them— that the erotic possibilities of his life have been lost to his meager love of working to increase his wealth.

Nevertheless, Hosmer does adapt as he falls in love with Thérèse and falls under the influence of her will. First, she convinces him to remarry Fanny and bring her back to live at Place-du-Bois. His attempt to re-kindle something good and pleasurable in that relationship produces a strained attempt to give more attention to Fanny and less to his work at the mill: "Hosmer sat beside her, curiously inattentive to his newspaper; observant of her small needs, and anticipating her timid half expressed wishes" (73). But he only becomes more and more despondent and confesses to Thérèse "the torture of it; the loathsomeness of it" (99). Thus, when the mill burns down, he happily returns to it "with a zest—an absorption that for the time excluded everything else" (109). Because he has found love with Thérèse but cannot be close to her, he dives back into being a workaholic and gives full rein to the same volitional etiology that pulled him away from his wife the first time. However, in the moment of crisis, when Fanny rebukes him for loving Thérèse instead of her, he realizes that his neglect and his faithless remarriage have "wounded her nature cruelly" (153). He plans to make "reparation" by making "an open and manly apology" (153), and he begins to take new interest in Fanny as a person: "Fanny was not now the wife whom he hated; his own act of the morning had changed her into the human being, the weak creature whom he had wronged" (154). This realization does not change the fact that he loves Thérèse more than her, but it does push him to make the natural adjustment to become a more sympathetic and honest husband. Ultimately, this adaptation comes far too late, because it comes immediately before her death in the river. But it does prepare Hosmer to make a more meaningful natural adjustment in his marriage to Thérèse a year later, as I will discuss.

The etiology associated with Thérèse is her overpowering will. She comes out of her grief for the death of her first husband when she learns that the poor management of the farm amounts to "a tangible abuse and defiance of authority" (5). She thus takes charge of the farm to set it in order and protect it against any modern changes that might come with the railroad: "There was hardly a soul at Place-du-Bois who had not felt the force of her will and yielded to its gentle influence" (22). Grégoire praises his aunt for the care she gives everything around her, but he acknowledges that her will is a fault: "they ain't no betta woman in the worl' then Aunt Thérèse, w'en you do like she wants" (18). When she learns that Hosmer has been married before, she even uses her will to suppress her own natural inclinations and convinces him to remarry and take better care of Fanny. She does so out of fidelity to "the prejudices of her Catholic education" (34), and Hosmer tries to appeal to the power of her will to get her to change her mind, saying: "Prejudices may be set aside by an effort of the will" (36). Nevertheless, Thérèse continues to insist on doing what she believes is "right" according to those religious and social conventions (11), and it is only later, when she sees how the situation is a source of torment for Hosmer, Fanny, and herself, that she begins to question the willfulness of her actions: "Were Fanny, and her own prejudices, worth the sacrifice which she and Hosmer had made? This was the doubt that bade fair to unsettle her; that called for a sharp, strong out-putting of the will before she could bring herself to face the situation without its accessions of personalities" (90). Like Hosmer's devotion to his work, Thérèse's will comes to act as an etiological force that stifles her erotic life. She recognizes that she must make the natural adjustment to shed those prejudices and allow herself to become more flexible and open to change, as she confesses to Hosmer when they meet in the year after Fanny's death: "I have seen myself at fault in following what seemed the only right. . . . Old supports appear to be giving way beneath me. They were so secure before. . . . But do you think, David, that it's right we should find our happiness out of that past of pain and sin and trouble?" (165). The answer, of course, is that it is "right" because adapting to those etiological forces allows them to experience their sexuality fully. But, as Hosmer advises, acting on these natural adjustments will be easier when they try to do so "together" as a couple (165).

Thus, as Hosmer learns how to create a better balance between work and marriage, and as Thérèse learns to ignore social convention and embrace her own pleasures by softening her willfulness, they achieve a much more fulfilling and sexually liberated union together. Importantly, this union does not replicate conventional patriarchal power structures because it is profoundly mutual and not defined by dominance and submission: "Through love they had sought each other, and now the fulfillment of that love had brought more than tenfold its promise to both" (166). This mutuality also extends to their work in the mill and on the farm. Hosmer continues to manage the mill, but he also contracts some of the work to investors, giving him more time to spend with his wife. When Thérèse asks if working with partners will give him "more to do," he says, "it will give me less: division of labor" (167). And when Thérèse asks if he will then help with the plantation, he says no: "I'll not rob you of your occupation" (167). Skewing traditional associations of gender and labor, Hosmer relinquishes some influence while Thérèse maintains her separate authority. In this context, both characters become more feminine and more masculine together. Indeed, the novel further underscores the nonheteropatriarchal queerness of their partnership when Thérèse jokes that Hosmer's devotion to their modern "division of labor" as a married couple "remind[s] me sometimes of Melicent" (167).

Work, will, novelty, situational intimacy, alcohol, gambling, violence, racism, and bad food: all of these are etiologies that help determine the subjectivities of Chopin's characters in *At Fault*. While it is possible to read Melicent's ambiguous lesbianism and, to a certain extent, Grégoire's queerness as evidence of congenital sexual queerness, Chopin does not embrace the rigidity of such taxonomies. Rather, she complicates them by foregrounding the debates among sexologists about how environmental and other factors might be "at fault" for queering sexualities at the same time. This emphasis on sexual variation goes beyond an exploration of what Emily Toth describes as "the different ways that people handle sexual attraction" because the novel asks how various causes create different *kinds* of sexual attraction that people must then "handle" (120). And this variation helps us recognize that the existence of what one early critic called "entirely too many plots" is not a flaw of a writer in her apprenticeship (Toth 116), for an etiological study of sexuality works best when considering *multiple* etiologies. Finally, Chopin's focus on the etiologies of sexual variation adds to her feminist response to Darwin's theory of sexual selection. Not only do sexual etiologies reveal how forms of sexual variation, including homosexuality, count as what Elizabeth Grosz calls "excess" within the processes of natural selection, but they also reveal how sexualities can change over time (118). Just as Melicent seems to change with each new encounter in her life, Thérèse and Hosmer also make "natural adjustments" as their environments change. And, by implication, if such natural adjustments are possible in terms of sexuality, then we have to recognize that gender differences are also not entirely innate and immutable. In Chopin's hands, the deterministic factors of sexual etiologies actually can be liberating instead of constraining. (Indeed, it is congenital sexuality that looks much more constraining.) For if it is possible to imagine that people are not necessarily limited to the taxonomic classifications that appear to fit them, then there is no reason to believe in absolute divisions of sexual and gender difference—let alone the social inequalities connected to those divisions. As circumstances change, the varieties of sexual and gender possibility also change, opening space for more feminist and equitable forms of love and partnership, such as we see in Thérèse and Hosmer at the end.

NOTES

1. For a more detailed account of Chopin's familiarity with queer literature and ideas, see Biggs 148–52.

2. See Utsu; Dyer; and Joslin.

3. See Kahan 17, 26–44.

4. It would seem that Chopin softens her depiction of Grégoire in the later story "In Sabine" (1894). In this story, Grégoire is riding west into Texas, perhaps in his exile from Place-du-Bois. Stopping in Sabine Parish, he encounters an old acquaintance, the young woman 'Tite Reine, with her abusive, alcoholic husband, Bud Aiken, and a Black man who helps on the farm, Uncle Mortimer. Grégoire ultimately rescues the woman by helping her ride away on his horse while Bud is passed out drunk; Grégoire takes Bud's horse to Texas, thus preventing the man from pursuing either of them. Grégoire's actions are kind and sympathetic, but ultimately they are not out of character with the chivalric attitudes we see in *At Fault.* Moreover, the story also references the same etiological concerns entwined with his identity as those raised in *At Fault,* suggesting that Chopin has not rethought or redeemed him as a character so much as she has simply given us further evidence of his complexity. For example, Grégoire happens to be in Sabine only because of his "erratic fancy," which is leading him "by circuitous paths" instead of setting him on "the regular Texas road" (325). Later, when Grégoire hears of Bud's abuse, he barely holds his temper in check and wonders "if it would really be a criminal act to go then and there and shoot the top of Bud Aiken's head off. He himself would hardly have considered it a crime, but he was not sure of how others might regard the act," recalling exactly the same circumstances he has just fled in *At Fault* (330). Finally, when he decides to lull—perhaps even seduce— Bud Aiken into a comfortable sense of trust and companionship so that he can help 'Tite Reine, Grégoire supplies the alcoholic with his own whiskey, "saying that he himself had no further use for it, as he had 'sworn off' since day before yesterday, when he had made a fool of himself in Cloutierville," referencing the pattern of excessive behavior alluded to in *At Fault* (331). We might ask here, did he make a fool of himself by fighting while drunk, or by doing something less violent, yet equally intimate, with another man? Grégoire is a hero in this story, but Chopin makes sure the complexities of his character remain consistent with those presented in her earlier novel by reminding us of his wanderlust, propensity for violence, troubled relationship to alcohol, and even queer intimacies with other men.

MICHAEL P. BIBLER

WORKS CITED

Bender, Bert. *The Descent of Love: Darwin and the Theory of Sexual Selection in American Fiction, 1871–1926*. Philadelphia: University of Pennsylvania Press, 1996.

Biggs, Mary. "'*Si tu savais*': The Gay/Transgendered Sensibility of Kate Chopin's *The Awakening*." *Women's Studies* 33 (2004): 145–81.

Campbell, Donna. "*At Fault*: A Reappraisal of Kate Chopin's Other Novel." In *The Cambridge Companion to Kate Chopin*, edited by Janet Beer, 27–43. Cambridge: Cambridge University Press, 2008.

Chopin, Kate. *At Fault*. 1890. Edited with an introduction and notes by Bernard Koloski. London: Penguin, 2002.

———. "In Sabine." In *The Complete Works of Kate Chopin*, edited by Per Seyersted, 325–32. Baton Rouge: Louisiana State University Press, 1969.

Dyer, Joyce Coyne. "The Restive Brute: The Symbolic Presentation of Repression and Sublimation in Kate Chopin's 'Fedora.'" *Studies in Short Fiction* 18, no. 3 (1981): 261–65.

Grosz, Elizabeth. *Becoming Undone: Darwinian Reflections on Life, Politics, and Art*. Durham, NC: Duke University Press, 2011.

Joslin, Katherine. "Kate Chopin on Fashion in a Darwinian World." In *The Cambridge Companion to Kate Chopin*, edited by Janet Beer, 73–86. Cambridge: Cambridge University Press, 2008.

Kahan, Benjamin. *The Book of Minor Perverts: Sexology, Etiology, and the Emergences of Sexuality*. Chicago: University of Chicago Press, 2019.

LeBlanc, Elizabeth. "The Metaphorical Lesbian: Edna Pontellier in *The Awakening*." *Tulsa Studies in Women's Literature* 15, no. 2 (1996): 289–307.

Regret. Directed by Rachel Grissom. Ripe Figs, 2020. www.fiiff.org/.

Seidel, Kathryn Lee. "Art Is an Unnatural Act: Mademoiselle Reisz in *The Awakening*." *Mississippi Quarterly* 46 (1993): 199–214.

Smith-Rosenberg, Carroll. "Discourses of Sexuality and Subjectivity: The New Woman, 1870–1936." In *Hidden from History: Reclaiming the Gay and Lesbian Past*, edited by Martin Duberman, Martha Vicinus, and George Chauncey Jr., 264–80. New York: New American Library, 1989.

Toth, Emily. *Unveiling Kate Chopin*. Jackson: University Press of Mississippi, 2009.

Utsu, Mariko. "Lesbian and Heterosexual Duality in Kate Chopin's 'Lilacs.'" *Mississippi Quarterly* 63, nos. 1–2 (2010): 299–312.

Quick, Dead, and Widowed

Failed Reading of "Unwholesome Intellectual Sweets" and
the Importance of Knowing Whose Story You're In

JOHN A. STAUNTON

'Twixt Hope and Fear—Reading Nineteenth-Century Texts
with Twenty-First-Century Students

> Nameless voices—weird sounds that awake in a Southern forest at twilight's
> approach,—were crying a sinister welcome to the setting gloom.
>
> —KATE CHOPIN, *At Fault*

Kate Chopin's *At Fault* is in many ways an impossible text for twenty-
first-century readers and teachers to encounter without sifting through
layers of literary and cultural history, narrative and publishing trends of
the late nineteenth century, and the changing representations of race,
class, and gender. Indeed, despite the task of the present volume, it's
hard to imagine anyone who is not *already* interested in Chopin finding
their way to the novel at all. But that is exactly the point of entry I encourage my own students to adopt through "time travel" readings of the
"nameless voices" of nineteenth-century women's writing, a sustained
critical engagement designed to resituate key works in a (re-)serialized
context to see how those texts participated in and challenged the literary and cultural discourses of their time.

The invitation goes something like this: forget for a moment that
these are texts that have *already* been selected for your edification, and
imagine the context for late nineteenth-century readers hearing for the
first time the "sinister welcome" of these texts. Take on that critical
and historicizing view, and consider what readers would be looking
for between the pages of their magazines and journals. What sort of

characters and plots might they expect to see, what nameless voices to hear? What would seem safe and familiar, and what would be unsettling and entirely new? Adopting some of the scientific adventuring spirit of the era (but with a decidedly more feminist framing), student groups chart cultural expeditions through full volumes of a journal or magazine—chosen for actual serializations, such as Jewett's *Country of the Pointed Firs* or Phelps's *Doctor Zay*, or to provide strategic "what-if" venues for works like Chopin's two novels—to see just how texts behave in their own times and to consider how they might manage to break out of their own historical moments and enter later ones.

Chopin's *At Fault* is well-suited for this "what-if" treatment, especially when surrounded by the serialized texts of her fellow southern women writers, offering from her own edge of the southern literary landscape strange accounts of women's romantic, aesthetic, and domestic lives. What might at first seem contrived to twenty-first-century readers—Thérèse Lafirme's insistence that David Hosmer remarry Fanny Hosmer as a testament of his devotion to *Thérèse* and *her* virtue seems needlessly and capriciously complicated; "Why not *ghost* her?" students might well ask—ends up sharing a *remarkable* similarity of theme and axes of triangular desire to several novels contemporary to Chopin's early efforts as an author. For instance, a single 1888 volume of the popular *Lippincott's Magazine* includes *three* novels, all written by southern women (two Virginians and a fellow Louisianan), that feature widows as matchmakers, panderers, and predatory lovers: Julia Magruder's *Honored in the Breach* (March 1888), Amélie Rives's notorious *The Quick or the Dead?* (April 1888), and Grace King's *Earthling* (November 1888). These tales sit between selections on the advances in technology, the temperance movement, and right conduct and contemporary morality for women—all topics featured in *At Fault*—and they each showcase what seems to be an impossible love triangle that needs a radical solution to reconcile what is and what might be for late nineteenth-century women.

Six months before starting in earnest on the manuscript that would become *At Fault*, Kate Chopin began her career as a published writer with the short poem "If It Might Be" (*America*, January 1889). In two

short stanzas, Chopin imagines alternating views of constancy in love—
one in death, the other in life, though neither vision fully realizes a
successful union of two souls without some kind of self-sacrifice or submission of one will to another. The poem stands in contrast to the ideal
of the uncompromising, solitary soul we know from *The Awakening*
(published a decade later), and so as a way to introduce Chopin's work
to students, "If It Might Be" quickly invites them to see an early inflec-
tion point on the arc of her career. What would become characteristic
economy of language and aesthetic ambiguity, here operates to unite
life/death/love in a triangular bond within the space of eight lines. With
its dual subjunctive clauses framing each stanza, the poem holds these
terms in suspension—life/death in stanza 1; love/live in stanza 2—allowing all three to be resolved only with some reciprocal engagement of
"thou"—both the absent lover(s) addressed in the poem and the *reader*
staring down at the page:

> If it might be that thou didst need my life;
> Now on the instant would I end this strife
> Twixt hope and fear, and glad the end I'd meet
> With wonder only, to find death so sweet.
> If it might be that thou didst need my love;
> To love thee dear, my life's fond work would prove.
> All time, to tender watchfulness I'd give;
> And count it happiness, indeed, to live.
>   (Quoted in Toth, *Unveiling* 107)

As Emily Toth notes, the poem also holds two possible biographical readings linked to a love triangle between a widow, the lingering
memory of a dead husband, and a present lover more or less straight out
of Chopin's own 1880s history in Louisiana. In this biographical light,
stanza 1 captures her mourning of her late husband, Oscar, who died in
1882, while stanza 2 engages in wistful fantasy of a possible/impossible
life with the married and mercurial Albert Sampite (*Unveiling* 107), with
whom Chopin carried on a romance after her husband's death. Sampite
was, Toth notes, "the image of the wealthy creole planter in popular

novels . . . a violent, angry man who gambled and drank too much—
but he was also dangerously attractive" (*Kate Chopin* 165–66). This biographical either/or has been fertile ground for investigating Chopin's
work as a whole, particularly the Cane River stories and *At Fault,* for
"the memory of Albert Sampite lurks everywhere in her fiction" (*Unveiling* 97). The principal lover's triangle of *At Fault* has its correspond-
ing analogues in Chopin's relationship with Albert, for instance: the
widow Thérèse Lafirme a more pious stand-in for Chopin herself, and
David and Fanny Hosmer as refigurations of Albert and Loca Sampite.

To be sure, delving into the off-the-page lives of the authors we encounter in our time-travel excavations can motivate students to seek out
other historical and cultural touchstones of nineteenth-century texts.
But such one-to-one correlations also risk merely resolving the subjunctive possibilities of the texts into discrete points on an interpretive grid,
and they limit Chopin's artistic achievement to particular biographical
instances rather than a more widely envisioned and culturally situated
aesthetic exploration of desire, loss, and human connection. It is perhaps
notable that Chopin's career as a writer begins in earnest only once she
has returned to St. Louis in the trappings of a respectable widow, leaving
the intrigues and romances of Louisiana behind her. The poetic rendering of this love triangle in "If It Might Be" enlists the cooperation of the
reader—we can choose to realize or forestall the union, but either choice
makes us complicit in holding the lovers in separation, like the gap between stanzas that limits and divides, forever cleaving them together.

I linger on this brief reading of the poem to highlight some key aspects of Chopin's writing in 1889 and to acknowledge that Chopin's
particular combination of theme, biography, and form in *At Fault* is
certainly personal, though not thematically unique in the literary marketplace of the era. Indeed, as strange as the widow-deceased-lover triad
might be to contemporary readers, when my students and I immerse
ourselves in our "time-travel" reading, our imagined "what-if" (re-)
serializations of a text such as Chopin's (which as a self-published novel
was most decidedly *not* serialized in its own time) reveals this particular
marriage trope as a highly successful literary discourse. As Chopin was
starting to write *At Fault,* it would have saturated her reading. In the

pages of magazines as wide-ranging in audience and aesthetic style as *Lippincott's,* the *Century,* the *Atlantic,* and *Scribner's,* tales of widows, divorcees, and reluctant brides—and all manner of love triangles—are not just common but seemingly ubiquitous, as late nineteenth-century women writers in particular attempted to reimagine the traditional marriage plot in light of changing ideas of what the temporal conditions of the marriage vows—"'til death do us part"—could really mean.

Love's New Refrain—We Call Each Other "Husband—Wife"

'O wife, wife, wife! As if the sacred name
Could weary one with saying! Once again
Laying against my brow your lips' soft flame,
Join with me, Sweetest, in love's new refrain,
Since the whole music of my late-found-life
Is that we call each other "husband—wife."
    (Edith Wharton, "The Last Giustiniani" [*Scribner's Magazine,* October 1889])

It is with more fear than hope that Fanny Hosmer, the ill-fated "third leg" in the strange love triangle at the center of *At Fault,* enters into this well-cultivated literary marriage discourse for a second time. Fanny operates both as the backstory for Thérèse's love-interest David, and as the vehicle for David and Thérèse's eventual union. David has divorced Fanny because of her alcoholism and her crippling despair over their lost child—"the act of coward" (60), Thérèse chides him. Now, at Thérèse's moralistic bidding, David must take up the "self-imposed burden" of remarriage. Not surprisingly, then, the reluctantly remarried Fanny almost immediately finds herself overcome again by dread and confusion upon her arrival in the rain to Place-Du-Bois. "I don't believe I can stand it," she tells David through her tears (64). And she's right, of course. Fanny won't long survive her remarriage to David under the strangely smothering, though outwardly beneficent, conditions orchestrated by Thérèse Lafirme. The second half of the novel in which Fanny mostly appears is filled with death and violence (Joçint, Grégoire, and Fanny herself all come to grief), with Fanny's end keeping time for the plot. Her tragic exit finally clears a path to marriage for David and Thérèse. But Fanny's seeming prescience is muted throughout the narrative by the repeated descriptions of Fanny as "uncomprehending," "speechless," and "at a loss" before the slowly unfolding events and competing discourses of her new life.

Fanny's expression of doubt and dismay also captures something of the thematic challenge of the text, for David and Fanny themselves are stuck in a marriage plot not of their own design, but they must see it through to her tragic end before it is fulfilled. There is perhaps hope for them that their remarriage will succeed, but there is also fear (for David in particular), that it will *not* fail. In fact, this sense of dread enters almost immediately upon their remarriage. Still in St. Louis, David considers "the problem of his new existence.... He hated this woman of whom he must be careful, to whom he must be tender, and loyal, and generous" (60). For a successful re-union means the dissolution of the romantic bond between David and Thérèse, and a lifelong submission to what "Must be" (61). Now, far from St. Louis, and surrounded by reminders of Thérèse, the Hosmers stand in fearful tableau: the chapter ends with Fanny's discovery of her husband "seated and bowed like a man who has been stricken. *Uncomprehending,* she stood a moment speechless, then crept back noiselessly to bed" (77, emphasis added). Fanny's confusion here heightens the narrative irony for the reader, for we already know about David's devotion and feeling for Thérèse, his hatred for Fanny, and his resignation somehow to endure in this new marriage for the sake of his honor. And we know that Fanny herself warns that it will simply end as before. By the end of their time in the South, David will have put aside these "must be's," physically assaulted her, and angrily told her he would kill her. In short, anyone following the narrative should understand that of course this experiment will fail; the question, then, is not so much why, as how and when.

The narrator's gratuitous insistence on *Fanny's* inability to read this moment for herself or to feel grateful to her husband for taking her back (rather than, say, appreciative of Fanny's dumbstruck realization that the man who insisted on remarriage now seems entirely devastated by the prospect of continued life with her), perhaps lends itself to a biographical reading of the novel, in which Chopin enacts revenge against her real-life rival in the fictional analogue of Fanny. But as I discovered with my students when we immersed ourselves in the periodical discourse of the 1880s and 1890s, it is not just Chopin's personal history with Albert Sampite lurking in the narrative shadows. *At Fault* also seems deliberately to engage a particularly widespread literary discourse of marriage, divorce, and widowhood. It puts the readerly refiguration of that "husband—wife" discourse at the heart of the encounters between Fanny, David, and Thérèse, as they seek to understand what it means to *read* or *enact* a design for one's own life.

Honest Studies and Unwholesome Sweets—Or, You Find What You Look For

> Books well meant, strongly written, and from a clean heart resemble mirrors, wherein every one who reads sees his own reflection. The pure will see purity,—the foul-minded, foulness.
>
> —AMÉLIE RIVES, preface to *The Quick or the Dead?*
> (*Lippincott's Magazine,* April 1888)

David's chiding response to Fanny's dread reinforces the narrative sense of Fanny as a poor reader of her own experience and feelings. "Come now," he cajoles, "don't be a baby—take courage," suggesting the insufficiency of her interpretation of her situation: "It will all seem quite different by and by, when the sun shines" (74). David's forecast could not be more off; instead, the rain *remains* for several days, and Fanny occupies her time by sitting before the fire and *"reading the latest novel of one of those prolific female writers who turn out their unwholesome intellectual sweets so tirelessly, to be devoured by the girls and women of the age"* (78, emphasis added). Emily Toth notes that Fanny Hosmer is singular among Chopin's many characters as a reader of "sentimental," "domestic novels" (*Kate Chopin* 53). Indeed, Toth claims, Fanny is apparently the *only* character called out in this way, suggesting she lacks the skeptical eye and the lesson Chopin herself acquired in her formative years and "carried through the rest of her life: not to believe everything she read" (53). The characterization allows Chopin to mark her narrative enterprise in her first novel as both distinct from and in dialogue with the work of other women writers.

Chopin does not name Fanny's latest "unwholesome literary sweet"—perhaps a strategic, even shrewd, omission from a new author, keen to find a home for her work in the literary marketplace. But the narrative implication is clearly that late nineteenth-century readers can readily fill in their own titles from among the many examples of this "morbid" genre serialized in the magazines of the day. For *twenty-first*-century readers, though, it is worth examining more closely the popular literature Fanny—or even Chopin herself—would have had at hand so that we might discover just what sort of reader Fanny is—or *ought to have been*—of the story she is in. If she is to adopt the skeptical eye and not believe everything she reads, how is she also to escape the warnings of the very script she seems to be in? We know from Chopin's own record keeping and the excellent biographical and historical work of Emily Toth that Chopin began writing *At Fault* in July 1889; what then were contemporary treatments of her theme before the novel's publication in October 1890?

In addition to the three 1888 *Lippincott's* novels by Grace King, Julia Magruder, and Amélie Rives that I will examine in more detail below, other popular journals of the day were no less preoccupied by marriage, divorce, sectional unions, and racial, ethnic, and class divisions as ways to figure the prospects for women in late nineteenth-century American life. For instance, throughout the late nineteenth-century volumes of the *Atlantic,* the *Century, Harper's,* and *Scribner's* (and especially in the 1880s), the focus on divorce easily operates as a trope for the reunification of the country *after* the Civil War and Reconstruction. Tales of southern widows and northern bachelors lie beside the memoirs and histories of "Battles of the Late War" and enthusiastic articles on the advances of science and industry. As Green and Caudle note in their introduction to the critical edition of *At Fault,* "Thérèse's marriage to Hosmer becomes not only a love match but a symbolic representation of the shotgun wedding between agriculture and industry that was occurring all over the post-Reconstruction South" (xxiii). The literary effort to smooth it all over in the interest of restoring a dominant order would require the whitewashing of the past and the disappearing of communities, histories, and people. Chopin seems less interested in defending the southern past than in tracing the ill-effects of any imposition on individual will, and seeking an artistic outlet for realizing one's autonomy.

That more aesthetic vision appeared in the 1889 volumes of the *Atlantic,* which carried the serialization of Henry James's *The Tragic Muse* (which sees a displacement of conventional marriage by artistic pursuit) and Sarah Orne Jewett's "A Winter Courtship" (a story of a shrewd widow landing her romantic quarry). The 1889 volumes of *Scribner's* again saw the pairing of James and Jewett serializations; as well as Jacob Riis's *How the Other Half Lives* (in December 1889); and Edith Wharton's poem of arranged marriage, "The Last Giustiniani" (in October 1889). Where these pieces might take a sustained or aesthetically complex perspective on marriage, the end pages, miscellany, and occasional poems by a host of women writers offered lighter renderings, frequently deploying racial and gender stereotypes of the day for comedic or sentimental effect.

Whatever "unwholesome intellectual sweets" might be at hand for Fanny in her chambers as she waits out the rain, then, seem exactly the kind of story line she finds herself living in *At Fault.* As a reader of just such popular fictions, in which the romantic rival almost always dies, why doesn't Fanny see it coming? How is it that the "skeptical eye" Chopin cultivates in her youth is unavailable to Fanny? Or, at the very least, why doesn't Fanny, who understands she is a rival to Thérèse for David's attention, come to recognize herself as the *expendable* third element in the love triangle, the one whose eventual demise brings about the final union of hero and heroine and the happy resolution of the plot?

These are not just whimsical or anachronistic student queries prompted by some very odd texts, but critical and pedagogical provocations—what Nancy Miller described as "arachnologies" and more recently Melissa Jones characterizes as "errant readings": prodigious over-/mis-readings that nonetheless can be generative of further insight into the text or period, letting inquiry emerge from "failed reading[s] failed" (Jones 128). Jones observes that "taking seriously, at least provisionally, these superficial or digressive readings students learn to try on 'ways of reading' that foster inquiry stances on both text and period" (125). At the very least, such queries imagine what Fanny might encounter as the singular reader Toth identifies—whether practiced and with skeptical eye, or forever the unwitting naïf, reading her own life slowly erased before her very eyes.

In centering Fanny's "uncomprehending" in this way, I am mindful of the error "Flora," the pseudonymous early local reviewer of the novel, makes in misreading Fanny as the heroine of the novel—"which if accepted by the reader," Chopin rebukes in "At Fault: A Correction," would "throw the story out of perspective" (Toth, *Unveiling* 118–19). Perhaps it is my own skeptical eye calling me to resist Chopin's authorial correction, but I confess I am drawn to Fanny *precisely* for her very predictable demise, as the necessary cog in the machinery of Chopin's first novel. When my students and I sift through the titles of the magazines and journals from the era, we look closely at the myriad texts that start to line up as possibilities for the book in Fanny's hand. We are also engaged in an act of creative refiguration—putting ourselves into positions to consider the *initial* narrative or aesthetic encounter and then bring those forward into conversation with our present moment. It is likewise an interpretive act, a mirroring quite different from that which Amélie Rives suggests in her defense of *The Quick or the Dead?* Perhaps neither entirely foul-minded nor pure of heart, we put ourselves in Fanny's shoes, imagining what someone like her is doing, newly arrived in a dismal place with a feckless husband who clearly regrets having married her again. We see that it is still raining. She feels isolated and alone. She takes up the nearest "unwholesome sweet," begins to read, and perhaps sees *her* experience reflected back to her.

Strange True Stories of Quick, Dead Earthlings—All at Fault

> True stories are not often good art. The relations and experiences of real men and women rarely fall in such symmetrical order to make an artistic whole.
> —GEORGE W. CABLE, "Strange True Stories of Louisiana"
> (*Century Magazine,* November 1888)

The three *Lippincott's* novels are certainly very strange from a twenty-first-century perspective, but their openings bear strong corollaries to features of *At Fault,* particularly with Fanny's experiences. Consider the three different openings of these novels. Amélie Rives's *The Quick or the Dead?* begins with an eerie mood and rainstorm much like what surrounds Fanny early on at Place-Du-Bois: "There was a soughing rain asweep that night, with no wind to drive it, yet it ceased and fell, sighed and was hushed incessantly, as by some changing gale. . . . Barbara [Pomfret, the heroine of the novel] was a good deal unnerved by the lanternless drive from the station. . . . [I]n the glimpsing light she saw scurrying trees against a suave [*sic*] autumn sky, like etchings on bluish paper" (1). The description is both evocative and impossible—there is no wind, and yet the effect is gale-like; light glimpses; trees scurry. This atmospheric opening is of course not meant to be realistic; it is an affective, protofilmic description of something otherworldly or extratextual at play. A practiced reader of 1880s journals might see here Edison and Dickson's "kinetoscopic" view of the landscape, captured in rapid succession through the windows of an advancing carriage. But a reader such as Fanny, stuck in a large southern manor house in a gloomy downpour, might feel something a bit more ominous, trapped within someone else's story in which affective images tumble relentlessly toward impending doom.

The opening scene of Grace King's *Earthlings* offers a similar ironic contrast to Fanny's arrival. In King's novel, the men and women of society in a Louisiana town await the train carrying Aglaé Middleton, the heiress whose sizable inheritance sets in motion the rekindling of a past romance between her and the executor of her estate, George Feltus: "The evening train was due. Encircled by a refreshing bit of woodland, a fantastic gaudy little station-house awaited the arrival of it, with its platform full of people in summer gala toilet. . . . The event of the month, week, day, was indeed about to take place" (601, 603). Fanny's appearance in Place-Du-Bois heralds no such excitement or buzz, heir to nothing more than her previous, unhappy marriage. Even David receives a lukewarm welcome, as a "rather mystified agent who had not known of his absence" (73) perfunctorily shakes David's hand. The only folks greeting the Hosmers at *their* final stop are Henry, the clerk, "a great many negroes loitering about," and Thérèse's nephew Grégoire, there to drive them over to the house (74). All, save Grégoire, solely address Mr. Hosmer, ignoring Fanny entirely.

Finally, the opening chapter of Julia Magruder's *Honored in the Breach* (March 1888) stages a strangely affecting encounter at a summer resort between a beautiful young heiress, Gladys Montaveril, and a graceful young widow, Constance Acland. Gladys would like to maintain the happy and gay life of ease she enjoys after her wealthy father's death, and she insists on choosing the sort of marriage she would make. Constance appears almost literally out of the morning mist (or out of the very narrative machinery of the nineteenth-century marriage discourse) to convince her otherwise. The narrative describes Gladys's uncanny waking each morning and the melancholy mood that overtakes her: "She was possessed by that worst kind of longing, which is ignorant of its own object. The tears welled up in her eyes, and before the mist had cleared away, she saw, coming slowly along the lane that bordered her grounds a figure clad in deep black. It was a woman, and she was evidently young, though her face was hid behind a thick black veil" (290). Eventually, of course, Gladys meets Constance, they become confidants, and Constance seeks to convince her of the impossibility of having any choice whatsoever in matters of finding true love. True to her name, Constance prevails in her counsel to Gladys, and orchestrates her marriage to Constance's brother David Leigh. Gladys's unknown longing becomes Fanny's uncomprehending stare, and Fanny Hosmer's remarriage to her own David comes at the abandonment of her life of diversion in St. Louis society in exchange for the marriage script devised by the widow Thérèse Lafirme.

In any one of these opening gambits, Fanny would almost certainly be able to see herself and her condition laid bare, but the resolution of each of those stories requires significant sacrifice and—in two instances—the death of the rival, more minor character. Thus, *as* a minor character in the plot being fashioned by Thérèse Lafirme for David Hosmer's redemption, Fanny would have to be on guard, acquire not just a skeptical, but a self-critical, eye to see herself as the extraneous party in the triangle. And the narrative repeatedly implies that such insight is beyond Fanny's powers of discernment. But by reimagining *what* Fanny is reading, and seeking out some likely texts among the literature of Chopin's day, we begin to discover traces of early literary and discursive influences on Chopin as she herself begins her career as a writer. That comparative look invites us to consider *how* Chopin thinks about what it means for women to read and write their world at all.

Like Champagne with the Sparkles Out—Or, How to Write Your Way out of a Bad Marriage

> Ilva did not care for toilets, and had startlingly precocious ideas concerning love and matrimony. On the eve of her tenth birthday she had begun [to write] a romance in the following manner: 'Married love is like champagne with the sparkles out.' . . . She was very moderate in her ambitions. She only desired to become a painter more great than Sanzio, a poet more original than Dante, and a novelist more striking than Alessandro Manzoni.
>
> —AMÉLIE RIVES, *The Witness of the Sun* (*Lippincott's Magazine*, April 1889)

Of the three *Lippincott's* novels above, Amélie Rives's *The Quick or the Dead?* is by far the most notorious and odd. Selling more than three hundred thousand copies, Rives's debut novel was first serialized in April 1888 and immediately became a sensation—it was morbid, sentimental, filled with thinly veiled scenes of erotic desire. By comparison, Chopin's *At Fault* "was not profitable," according to Toth, earning "only $51 over the next two years" (*Unveiling* 120). On the surface, *The Quick or the Dead?* is the story of a young widow, Barbara Pomfret, reconciling her enduring, and still highly affective, love for her dead husband, Val (whose ghostly presence seems to hover everywhere Barbara goes in their old house), with her physical and passionate attraction to Jock Dering, Val's cousin and veritable doppelgänger. That's right: they're cousins; identical cousins. But instead of a plucky Patty Duke, we might imagine a mashup of *Ghost, Twilight,* and *The Prisoner of Zenda,* with a carriage ride to shame Emma Bovary—all seen through the lens of a film-school cinematographer with a sentimental streak. The sort of thing, in short, that Chopin's narrator suggests Fanny Hosmer would readily snatch up.

Upon Rives's death in 1944, the *Charlottesville Progress* still puzzled over the staggering success of *The Quick or the Dead?* a half century before: "it immediately aroused a *furore* of criticism because of its frank treatment of subject matter which today would occasion no comment" (quoted in Moore 486). Rives's friend Virginia Moore counters that dismissal in her bemused review of the novel in the *Georgia Review* (1954): "'Subject matter which today would occasion no comment?' Well, no more than dynamite" (486). Given the novel's notoriety, it seems unlikely that any emerging writer in the late 1880s, let alone Kate Chopin, would have been unaware of Rives's novel or uninterested in the success of the young author who seemed to appear suddenly out of the publishing ether.

The connection between the novels is not, however, at the level of simple copycat publishing, which Toth describes as having facilitated some of Chopin's early publishing successes. Despite the opening description of Thérèse as a "handsome, inconsolable, childless Creole widow of thirty," she is hardly the morbid obsessive that the younger Barbara Pomfret is. Thérèse does have some days of grief, when she "wanted to die with her Jérôme, feeling that life without him held nothing that could reconcile her to its future endurance" (5). But she quickly is brought out of "her lethargy of grief" by the news of things "goin' wrong" on the plantation, and by a fear of any disregard for the authority of her race and class (5). In this role, she manages to take on agency for the growth of the community and attempts to shape the moral development of the cast of characters who surround her. She wears the cloak of widowhood comfortably.

Barbara's widowhood, on the other hand, alternately plunges her into eddies of despair and raises her to transcendent moments of spiritual ecstasy. Her return to the country house marks, to the day, the customary period of mourning for a widow after her husband's death. Two years on, Barbara still struggles with the imagined obligation a widow ought to have to her dead husband, even if (as in her case) the period of mourning *doubles* the length of the marriage itself. As Lady Constance Howard instructs in *Etiquette: What to Do, and How to Do It* (1885): "Widows do not, as a rule, mourn for less than two years. . . . Where widows have lost all this world holds for them of love and happiness, by the death of their husbands, they very often mourn and wear 'widows' weeds' to the end of their lives, and quite right that it should be so" (quoted in Green and Caudle 275). Though Barbara knows the vows of marriage clearly release partners from their bond through death, Val's profession on their wedding night of a love *beyond* death haunts Barbara and prevents her from embracing a future with anyone else. It is morbid—everyone tells her so—but it is also the working through of romantic love over against the expectations of etiquette and social convention, attempting to reconcile the notion of soulmates matched for eternity with the more earthly aspects of married love ("champagne with the sparkles out," as Rives's precocious Ilva imagines in *The Witness of the Sun*).

Seeking solace from her grief, Barbara finds herself alone in the room she once (and only briefly) shared with her husband, Val. Improbably, and not just a little symbolically, she finds his spent pipe still beside the bed, plucking up a bit of tobacco that remains in the bowl, "kissing it again and again" (9). Rives allows the reader and Barbara herself to step back from this intense emotional act, explaining: "She was a woman with an almost terrible sense of humor, and presently she began to laugh, not hysterically, but quietly, appreciatively. *She saw how ridiculous a thing that act of hers would seem to an on-looker*" (9). For the briefest of moments, Barbara manages to read herself as overwrought, but without the external sense of obligation Thérèse enjoys, Barbara quickly falls back into a "shuddering passion of sobs, tearless, noiseless, and terrible" (9). Again Rives interjects, this time with an editorial gloss: "All this will not seem overstrained when one knows its origin" (9). In the descriptive moment that follows, we see Barbara allowing the vision of the room and the memories it evokes to likewise conjure the haunting, almost physical sense of her dead husband, Val: "His arms held her, his breath warmed her, his voice was in her ear, vibrating, actual. . . . The room was full of his voice, of his sighing, of his laughter. . . . There again! His laughter, about her, above her, and his lips at her ear. . . . 'Barbara!

Barbara! Your curled lips are a cup, and your breath is wine. You make me drunk!—drunk!'" (10). The use of the indicative mood here creates the reverse effect of the subjunctive in Chopin's poem "If It Might Be," with past and present measured as part of the same line. Comforted by her maid, Barbara eventually recovers enough to sleep but soon seems to dream or magically summon Val back to life:

> The pressure of a warm, curly head against her breast was with her as an actuality.
>
> "Oh, Val," she whispered,—"oh, Val! Oh, darling,—mine!—mine!—mine! Touch me, come to me, here in the darkness,—here where you used to love me. . . . She flung herself . . . upon the large [bed] . . . of carved mahogany . . . , sobbing, shuddering, kissing wildly the silken coverlet and pillows that rose softly through the thick firelight, so finally slept, worn out, desolate, chilled to the very core of soul and body. (18–19)

After this intense and clearly sensual end to her period of formal mourning, Barbara slowly begins the task of restoring herself to some path forward. The identical cousin, Jock Dering, soon appears, holding some of these haunting whispers at bay while Barbara lingers upon Jock's physical likeness to Val. Their romance grows through fits and starts, with furtive glimpses of flesh (necks, gloveless hands, bare arms), and even more sensuous re-veilings (fingers and hands slowly *re*-gloved), and the taking up and letting down of flowing tresses. There are even late-night exchanges of books (usually something by Browning), pages meaningfully turned down to capture exactly the height of feeling or image they have for each other. Throughout these elaborate narrative *toilets* come the periodic hauntings of Val's memory, which reset the process again, until finally Barbara rejects Jock and embraces fully her widowhood to achieve, she imagines, her perpetual union with Val. It is a breathless, maddening, and exhausting plot—for reader and character, alike. The extended deferrals and delays in the romance between Barbara and Jock have much more in common with Edna and Robert in *The Awakening* than Thérèse and David in *At Fault*. But the on-again, off-again cycle of love generated by the powerful vision of a widow is also very much present in *At Fault*. And looking at the two novels together reveals the vectors of desire that inform and constrain nineteenth-century women's lives.

Marriage of Convenience as Escape from the Hideous Commonplace

"I *want* to marry him! . . . I want to escape from this hideous commonplace life with my stepmother, who often drives me to the verge of madness with her stupidity and frivolity. It may be simply a marriage of convenience. Well, I won't deny it . . . is the custom with girls of my station in life."

"Then let it be a custom honored in the breach instead of the observance!" exclaimed Constance, fervently. "Oh Gladys, *you* have something in you too high for this."

— JULIA MAGRUDER, *Honored in the Breach* (*Lippincott's Magazine*, March 1888)

Despite the violence of *At Fault* and the steamy passions in *The Quick or the Dead?* each is more properly the sustained study of a woman's agency and struggles against mere convention. Those are the same struggles for the principal women characters in King's *Earthlings* and Magruder's *Honored in the Breach*. Each of these novels—including Chopin's—is not without its sense of scandal among the love triangles linking the characters. Indeed, if we were to chart them together, we'd see that the narratives of King and Chopin have to engineer the death of one woman (the young, artistic Misette, in *Earthlings;* the dreary alcoholic Fanny in *At Fault*) in order to bring about the happiness of another woman. The narratives of Magruder and Rives require their heroines to reject a principal suitor (Jock in *the Quick or the Dead?* and Reginald in *Honored in the Breach*) to find themselves a more fitting match arranged by the strong will of a widow. Barbara gives in to the voices in her head and embraces her dead Val, and Constance wins over Gladys and brings her into proper union with her brother. (Magruder uses a similar resolution in *The Princess Sonia,* published in the same

1895 issue of the *Century Magazine* as Chopin's "Regret"). Perhaps the differences are evidence of regional cultural sensibilities: the Louisiana characters of Chopin and King ultimately find resolution when *external* factors bring the death or elimination of the rivals—removing some of the agonizing ethical choice from the characters; the Virginian and East Coast society sensibilities of Magruder's and Rives's heroines leave their fates more precariously resolved. Nonetheless, the endings of all four novels suggest these resolutions are a restoration of a natural order and that all is finally (if perhaps only provisionally) well.

The repeated insistence on such endings is striking, but the critical readings afforded by our time-travel excursions resist such returns to convention. Rather than lead us to the same unwholesome intellectual sweets that Fanny turns to in her misery, a focus on Fanny as the readerly touchstone or entry point for contemporary readers underscores the difficulty nineteenth-century women writers had dealing frankly with desire and subjectivity. What results, as both Virginia Moore and Emily Toth note, is a series of transferences, deflections, substitutions, and sublimations to get around what Gladys calls the hideous, commonplace life available for women of a certain station. And, as others in this collection have noted, among the most obvious and repeated deflections twenty-first-century readers face from these nineteenth-century tales of the struggles of southern women of a certain class, is the unsettling and pervasive traces of a racist underpinning of their privilege, hideously commonplace or not.

From the perspective of the twenty-first-century reader Chopin's *At Fault* is all a little too easy, too resigned, and perhaps even a bit glib on issues of race and class, even as it remains strange and fascinating and compelling in its exploration of the struggles of privileged white women. We might note that Chopin mostly leans away from an overuse of racial stereotypes in her work, but that is only to evade that here in *At Fault* she deploys them readily: for comedic effect; to establish setting and mood; and for shorthand references to draw contrasting characterizations of the principal white women in the novel. Consider again Fanny's first night in Place-Du-Bois, which showcases all those uses in quick succession. Sampson, the young servant who will eventually supply Fanny with the liquor that will send her back down the path to alcoholism, comes to tend the fire: "He was *intensely black,* and if Fanny had been a woman with the slightest sense of humor, she could not but have been amused at the picture which he presented in the revealing fire-light with his *elfish* and *ape-like* body much too small to fill out the tattered and ill-fitting garments that hung about it. *But she only wondered at him and his rags, and at his motive for addressing her*" (75, emphasis added). The narrator would like us to see in this encounter evidence of Fanny as a dreary, humorless northerner—just as she is presented as uncomprehending of her own position within the marriage plot. Indeed, the two views are yoked together by Fanny's inability to understand how *place* in the postwar South operates at all. The narrative clearly casts this as a deficiency, but in centering Fanny's experience we allow for a still unarticulated critique of these representations: in the language of a twenty-first-century reader, why *shouldn't* Fanny wonder at the strangeness of the system that makes Sampson an object of mirth rather than a fully formed subject of his own?

But as we have pursued Fanny down the pages of the "unwholesome intellectual sweets," we see that even if she could give voice to this feeling or have seen her own end coming, the narrative framework doesn't yet exist for her to be the character she needs to be to speak out or escape her fate. We might say Kate Chopin hasn't yet written that story at this point, which would still be an evasion. As immersive as the time-travel reading my students and I pursue may be, it is worth reminding ourselves that even as we seek to understand something about Chopin, her contemporaries, or the condition of women in the late nineteenth century, we risk becoming complicit in perpetuating other toxic representations if we are not already positioned as critical, careful, and perhaps even skeptical readers. Here in this first novel, read against the time traveling discourses, we witness Chopin experimenting seriously with voices, settings, representations, themes—some drawn from models in the literary marketplace, others from experiences closer to home. But like Fanny's failure as reader to recognize the story she is in, perhaps Chopin as writer also fails here to use her nascent talents to escape the discourses of race that trap her characters and contemporaries

JOHN A. STAUNTON

into blindly overlooking the lives they push to the margins of their own interests.[1] That does not have to be the case, and my hope is that this pedagogical and critical immersion in those discourses won't dismiss them as minor or wash them away but will eventually help surface them for our consideration and struggle against our own "uncomprehending."

NOTES

1. For further, more in-depth discussions of race, American imperialism, and *At Fault,* please see, in this volume, "Reconciling the (Post)Plantation in *At Fault:* Reunion Romance, Western Expansionism, and the (Neo)Liberal Turn" by Natalie Aikens; and "'Miss T'rese's System': *At Fault* and Antebellum Nostalgia" by Nadine M. Knight.

WORKS CITED

Cable, George W. "Strange True Stories of Louisiana. Introduction." *Century Magazine* 37 (November 1888): 110–16.

Chopin, Kate. *At Fault.* 1890. Edited with an introduction and notes by Bernard Koloski. London: Penguin, 2002.

———. "If It Might Be." In *Unveiling Kate Chopin,* by Emily Toth, 107. Jackson: University Press of Mississippi, 1999. Originally published in *America,* January 1889.

Green, Suzanne Disheroon, and David J. Caudle. "A New Generation Reads *At Fault.*" Introduction to *At Fault,* by Kate Chopin (1890), edited by Green and Caudle, xix–xxxii. Knoxville: University of Tennessee Press, 2001.

Howard, Lady Constance. *Etiquette: What to Do, and How to Do It.* 1885. Quoted in *At Fault,* by Kate Chopin [1890], edited by Suzanne Disheroon Green and David J. Caudle, 275–76. Knoxville: University of Tennessee Press, 2001.

Jones, Melissa J. "Errant Pedagogy in the Early Modern Classroom, or Prodigious Misreadings in and of the Renaissance." In *Teaching the Literature Survey Course: New Approaches for College Faculty,* edited by Gwynn Dujardin, James Lang, and John Staunton, 120–32. Morgantown: West Virginia University Press, 2018.

King, Grace. *Earthlings.* Published in *Lippincott's Magazine* 42 (November 1888): 599–679.

Magruder, Julia. *Honored in the Breach.* Published in *Lippincott's Magazine* 41 (March 1888): 287–389.

Miller, Nancy K. *Subject to Change: Reading Feminist Writing.* Cambridge: Cambridge University Press, 1990.

Moore, Virginia. Review of *The Quick or the Dead?*, by Amélie Rives. *Georgia Review* 8, no. 4 (Winter 1954): 485–88.

Rives, Amélie. *The Quick or the Dead? A Study.* Published in *Lippincott's Magazine* 41 (April 1888): 481–522.

———. *The Witness of the Sun.* Published in *Lippincott's Magazine* 42 (April 1889): 461–570.

Toth, Emily. *Kate Chopin.* New York: William Morrow, 1990.

———. *Unveiling Kate Chopin.* Jackson: University Press of Mississippi, 1999.

Wharton, Edith. "The Last Giustiniani." *Scribner's Magazine,* October 1889, 405–6.

Divorce and the New Woman

Precedents to Modernism in At Fault

HEATHER OSTMAN

Over the years, scholars and literary historians have often categorized Kate Chopin as a local-color author—a designation she resisted, although not an entirely inaccurate identification. *At Fault* (1890) certainly draws from some of the recognizable conventions of local color, such as the southern landscape, the local community, its inhabitants' occupations and patterns of speech. However, "local color" does not sufficiently characterize the novel. The view from this Cane River plantation—idyllic as it may be—betrays a world of fragmentation and loss. Indeed, such dissonant elements look more to the modernist era of the next century than to the nostalgia of late nineteenth-century local color. The notion of protomodernist elements in Chopin's fiction has been introduced by a handful of scholars. A few have noted the protomodernist features in Chopin's later work *The Awakening* (1899), including Michael T. Gilmore, who compares the novel to impressionist painting, and Emily Riser Smith, who points to the novel's inherent discontentment with late nineteenth-century culture. Others have identified protomodernist elements in the author's short fiction. For instance, in her examination of selected short stories, Susan Lohafer has examined Chopin's use of "preclosure points," which designate metanarratives that move the narrative toward an emphatic ending, and Alice Horner has suggested that several Chopin stories demonstrate contradictions and ambivalence, pointing to a pervasive, underlying disillusion. For the purposes of this study, Lohafer's and Horner's analyses of the protomodernist components in other Chopin texts are especially useful to an examination of *At Fault.* Their work enables a deeper understanding of Chopin's appreciation for the shifts in American and European literature and her anticipation of the modernist era, and the focus on the novel's narrative strategies shows how divorce and the emergence of the New Woman signify the dawn of the modernist era in *At Fault.*

By all accounts, *At Fault* is a complex novel. It presents a local-color story with the usual elements: the southern plantation landscape, quaint local characters, and representative dialects. The characters on Place-du-Bois, Thérèse Lafirme's plantation, express little to no memory of the recent Civil War or slavery. The novel also presents a dense narrative that wrestles with complex social issues. Aligned with the post–Civil War effort to reconcile the southern loss of the war, local color offered an acceptably realistic picture of the American South to its northern readers, who identified redemption and reconciliation in its stories. It also portrayed a familiar authenticity to its southern readers, who would have recognized the complexity of the southern lives it represented. Coined originally in French, *la couleur locale* developed in the United States: "But whether import or native, the hallmarks of local color were manifestly realistic: an accurate attention to detail, an emphasis on landscape, carefully created characters, provincial customs, and the peculiarities of local speech (dialect). But what also characterized local color was its interest in difference: not simply 'realistic' portraits but portraits of some 'other' places and experience, a role that the South— with its lively frontier humor traditions, racialized family structures, slaveholding rebel past, and renewed attractiveness both to tourists and investors—played like a natural" (Ewell and Menke xxxviii). In spite of its perceived authenticity and representations of "difference," local color's featured elements were superseded by early twentieth-century critics' preferences for modernist sensibilities. The next century's literary critics privileged modernist considerations and dismissed local color, so that even a writer with Chopin's vision and ability could not influence critics' presumptions that linked local color with an "old-fashioned" and decidedly "female" ethos (Ewell 41–42).

As mentioned in the introduction to this volume, *At Fault* received its own mixed critical reviews, but regardless of its early reception, *At Fault* offers a lens for reading the transition from late nineteenth-century sentimentalism, realism, and local color to the next century's literary emphasis on modernist sensibilities. Chopin infused the novel with competing plot exit points and narrative ambiguity that arises from character choices, both strategies that anticipated twentieth-century modernism. These narrative techniques arise in several of Chopin's short stories and help demonstrate the same elements in *At Fault,* as they render narrative outcomes that can be interpreted in multiple ways. For example, Susan Lohafer argues that Chopin's use of preclosure points, such as in "Aunt Lympy's Interference," sets up metanarratives within her stories, and they work to draw the reader toward the intended, emphatic ending (158–67). In "Aunt Lympy's Interference," the main character is presented with three possibilities for the outcome of her life: independent teacher, city socialite, or a man's wife. Lohafer notes that the preclosure points that delineate these possibilities tend to be anchored to a scene change and "a leaning toward one future or another" (163). Instead of reading Chopin's short stories only in terms of their "wholeness," as a unified effort toward their own resolution, Lohafer emphasizes that the stories offer "tellable units" that emerge within the broader narrative as individual "stories" (161). Especially where Chopin's fiction appears to be recognizably sentimental and regional is where the preclosure points strategy tends to be most effective: "Where her texts may appear 'artless' in form, or conversely, too neatly wrapped up; where they may appear more sentimental than in her more famous work; where they seem more sketchy and regional than rooted in the global history of storying—even there, *especially* there, we find richer work by looking for preclosure points and following their lead" (Lohafer 171). These preclosure points identify metanarratives that scaffold her stories and present Chopin's main characters with a range of choices but point toward an emphatic ending. In "Aunt Lympy's Interference," "the preclosure points reemphasize the serialized presentation of the alternate futures, but also the larger perspective, unseen by Melitte [the main character], that shades all her options with humor and irony" (Lohafer 164).

Lohafer's study complements Alice Horner's critical examination of another of Chopin's narrative strategies, one in which the characters' choices render ambiguous outcomes. As a result, selected Chopin stories may be read from different perspectives, without privileging one interpretation of the characters' outcomes more than another. This particular narrative technique aligns Chopin with twentieth-century modernists, who dismissed the stability of a character's "ego" and attempted new ways of expressing the ambiguity of modern life. As an example, Horner demonstrates the alignment between Chopin's "A Vocation and a Voice" (1902) and James Joyce's "Araby" (1905). Both stories feature a nameless boy whose adolescence confronts him with competing longings that compel him to run away from the web of everyday life. The two stories end in different ways, but they both refuse to answer several questions that arise within the narratives. Joyce's "Araby" forces the reader to sort out the narrator's understanding of himself and the repercussions of his life, but Chopin's "A Vocation and a Voice" is far more ambivalent about its main character's choices than it appears on the surface. As a result, Chopin's narrative elicits multiple lenses that offer different interpretations but does not prioritize one over another:

> Read from a Catholic perspective, "A Vocation and a Voice" is the story of a fall into temptation, of a man unable to transcend his own physical instincts despite his desire to dedicate himself to God. Read from a Darwinian perspective, the ending is predictable and endorses the notion that the instincts we all share are, for most of us, irresistible. Seen through the lens of romantic love, the tale seems to follow—almost to the point of parody—the plot convention of the happy ending in which true love triumphs over all. It can also be interpreted as a portrait of the artist as a young man who finally chooses sensuality, sexuality, and art rather than religion, asceticism, and the Church. Chopin's closure suggests all of these possibilities but privileges none of them. (Horner 137)

This narrative ambiguity prevents a clear sense of closure to the story. The main character in "A Vocation and a Voice," who grows up to be the man named Brother Ludovic, makes choices that raise additional questions. For example, to what does the title of the story even refer? Whose vocation and whose voice? Brother Ludovic's decision to leap over the wall and follow the singing woman's voice at the story's end seems to reflect the title, but in what regard: as a choice between the call of religious vocation and the voice of a woman? The reader is not even told that the voice is definitively Suzima's, the woman whom Brother Ludovic loved as a younger person.

The preclosure exit points that Lohafer discusses and the characters' choices and resultant narrative ambiguity, such as Horner argues, in these stories present a framework for looking at the narrative technique in *At Fault*. Whereas the main story in *At Fault* centers around Thérèse and David Hosmer's journey toward marital union, the stunted romance between Grégoire and Melicent parallels this narrative with fraught moral dilemmas and ultimate disunion, in opposition to the romance plot that *appears* to shape the novel. Thérèse and Hosmer's romance is predicated on developments from Hosmer's divorce, and Grégoire and Melicent's disunion is predicated on Melicent's embodiment of the figure of the New Woman. A study of Chopin's use of preclosure points and narrative ambiguity shows how the Hosmers' divorce and the figure of the New Woman intersect and anticipate the modern era, even as they were two distinct developments in the late nineteenth and early twentieth centuries.

Divorce in At Fault

At Fault opens with David Hosmer's arrival at Place-du-Bois. Hosmer is a northerner, hailing from St. Louis, and he has come to Thérèse's plantation to request the use of its timber for milling. After she reluctantly agrees, Thérèse and Hosmer grow fond of each other, eventually falling in love. Widowed at thirty, Thérèse is now thirty-five years old, but she recognizes that she is able to love again. Then, Hosmer's sister Melicent tells her that Hosmer is divorced from Fanny, his first wife, a condition that Thérèse had not anticipated and one that changes everything thereafter, when she becomes resolved that he must remarry his first wife (33–40).

The reason behind Thérèse's stance regarding divorce *appears* to be religious—she is a Catholic—but beyond any kind of religious conviction or belief she might have is her lack of experience with real divorce. She even inwardly recognizes that for some couples, divorce might be the best option, but she defaults to presumptions that seem largely based on her inexperience: "With prejudices of her Catholic education coloring her sentiment, she instinctively shrank when the theme confronted her as one having even a remote reference to her own clean existence. There was no question with her of dwelling upon the matter; it was simply a thing to be summarily dismissed and as far as possible effaced from her remembrance" (34). And yet Hosmer's divorce is not something that Thérèse "summarily dismisses." Instead, she hardens her position even after he explains the reasons behind his divorce: the death of his and his wife Fanny's three-year-old son and its disastrous effects on their happiness and Fanny's stability, as she soon after becomes an alcoholic. Hosmer even explains that he doubled Fanny's alimony (38–40), but to no avail: Thérèse insists on his remarriage to Fanny.

Thérèse claims a moral authority in her obstinate insistence, even as her position is somewhat loosely founded on religion. Hosmer has been caught off-guard by her resolute objection to his divorce and admits he had not considered the obstacle her Catholicism presents, to which she responds: "Because you have never seen any outward signs of it. But I can't leave under a false impression: religion doesn't influence my reason in this." Her assertion leads to an exchange between them that reveals their divergent positions on moral absolutes:

> "Do you think then that a man who has had such misfortune, should be debarred the happiness which a second marriage could give him?"
>
> "No, nor a woman either, if it suit her moral principle, which I hold to be something peculiarly one's own."
>
> "That seems to me to be a prejudice," he replied. "Prejudices may be set aside by an effort of the will," catching at a glimmer of hope.
>
> "There are some prejudices which a woman can't afford to part with, Mr. Hosmer," she said a little haughtily, "even at the price of happiness." (36)

While Thérèse intimates some vague relationship with religion, she insists it does not influence her. In fact, she more adamantly claims the prerogative of moral relativism, as she asserts that "moral principle" is something she "hold[s] to be something peculiarly one's own" (36). But one result of Thérèse's clinging to an ambiguously defined moral principle is the unraveling of Hosmer and Fanny's marriage, as it devolves into misery and finally death.

The premise of the couple's divorce and disintegrating second marriage provides Chopin a framework for depicting the cultural world of her characters in transition. By recasting a central social institution such as marriage in terms of fragmentation and loss, Chopin reflects a key characteristic of the modern era. In *At Fault,* divorce is both a literal, real phenomenon of the age, as well as a metaphor for a perception of cultural disintegration and impoverishment. Not only is Hosmer and Fanny's marriage reinstituted under the shadow of their divorce, all other action in the novel, including Hosmer and Thérèse's marriage at the end of the novel, is based on the fragmentation and loss of this marriage as well.

At Fault concludes with the ambiguity that constitutes Thérèse and Hosmer's future, but before the reader arrives at the ending, Chopin offers several plot exit points that stem from Hosmer's divorce. One of these points is the Hosmers' remarriage itself. Resulting from Thérèse's interference in Hosmer's and Fanny's lives, their reunion becomes a "tellable unit" of its own and offers a preclosure point within the narrative. Had the novel ended there, *At Fault* might have affirmed Thérèse's pious morality. But the novel continues to include two murders— Grégoire's murder of Joçint and Grégoire's own murder—and a flood that kills Fanny (and Marie Louise) within the course of her second marriage, each of which complete additional tellable units or metanarratives with their own preclosure points.

However, the novel does not end at any of these points; instead, they provide scaffolding toward the emphatic ending. A year after Hosmer's unsuccessful attempt to save his wife from drowning, he and Thérèse reunite on a train. At this meeting, the reader is presented with yet another possible exit point: Thérèse's and Hosmer's lives might have continued on in their independent directions. Instead, the two characters marry, despite the ambiguity of the future and particularly as Thérèse speaks to the contradiction of their happiness in light of the suffering that preceded it. The ambiguity and contradiction of their reunion echoes the fragmentation of Hosmer's earlier divorce, as well as "the very modern attempt to represent a divided consciousness" that Chopin integrates into other stories, as noted by Horner (133). As a result, the metanarratives and the ambiguous ending of *At Fault* lend themselves to a few different interpretations—none more privileged than the others. For instance, one reading of the novel might compare Hosmer and Thérèse's marital union to a vision of northern and southern reunion and harmony after the Civil War. Through this lens, the characters reflect a union between the encroaching northern economy upon the South's devastation following the war. Hosmer and Thérèse's marriage echoes the death of former labor and socioeconomic practices, and even suggests the dawn of new hope. As Maureen Anderson has noted:

> With the marriage of Thérèse and Hosmer at the conclusion of *At Fault,* Chopin reinforces and promises a future for the South in the novel. Whereas Chopin utilizes the pastoral convention of marriage, their marriage ensures the demise of the old way of life. In *At Fault,* the marriage promises a future for a new way of life, not for a traditional pastoral lifestyle. The springtime atmosphere combined with Hosmer's and Thérèse's parenting-like role to Melicent at the conclusion of the novel implies the possibility of children in their future. . . . Finally, when Hosmer and Thérèse do marry, neither Hosmer nor Thérèse assume the role of a pastoral master of the plantation. Instead, Hosmer and Thérèse create a compromise as to what their roles will be. (11–12)

On one level, Anderson's reading of the conclusion seems plausible: marriage and the suggestion of childrearing signal unity and renewal. But even besides the fraught history behind this couple, both characters embody a deep level of moral ambiguity. Thérèse acknowledges that she has been "at fault" because of her adherence to "what *seemed* the only right" (165, italics mine). She recognizes that the arbitrary application of absolutes was wrong. Hosmer responds with the assurance that absolute truth is unknowable but that together they might try to "make a step towards it" (165). This closing conversation would appear to support

Anderson's reading because the two characters seem to be embarking on a new way of approaching the world: in unity and clarity. But despite Thérèse's new awareness, the appearance of moving forward and renewal is undercut by Hosmer reiterating the notion that absolute truth is ambiguous and possibly elusive.

The ambiguity that surrounds Thérèse and Hosmer's marriage invites, though, another way to read the ending of *At Fault*. Through a different lens, the conclusion shows us how fraught is the long-standing institution of marriage. For one thing, marriage has not gone well for anyone earlier in the novel. Divorce and early widowhood end three of the four marriages in *At Fault*. Hosmer and Thérèse's marriage is not the only union predicated on unsteady ground. For example, even after Hosmer's remarriage to Fanny, doubt and ambivalence cast their shadow over the union; Thérèse doubts her decision to refuse to marry Hosmer and her insistence on his second marriage. She wonders if she has been interfering too much with other people's lives, and she begins to question her own intentions (89–90). Further, she wonders: "Were Fanny, and her own prejudices, worth the sacrifices which she and Hosmer had made? This was the doubt that bade fair to unsettle her" (90). Hosmer, as well, begins to struggle with "moral difficulties" once he is remarried to Fanny. Divorce, then, provides a fragmented, unstable foundation for Hosmer and Fanny's second marriage, and it casts a shadow upon the later marriage of Hosmer and Thérèse.

As a plot device, divorce enabled Chopin to portray the moral relativism and ambiguity that arose with the dawn of the modern era because it too was a distinct feature of the changing social and moral landscape. At the time of Chopin's writing *At Fault,* the divorce rate was soaring in the United States, especially in the northern and western states. As Kimberly Freeman has written, divorce is a notable "American" phenomenon, as it has functioned as "a symbol of American autonomy and citizens' rights" (1). Dating back to the seventeenth century, even Puritans viewed divorce as a "necessary evil," which prevented worse sins from occurring from marital disharmony (Freeman 2). The Declaration of Independence, central to the American political foundation and national identity, asserts "divorce" claims from Britain and affirms the rights of Americans to disconnect themselves from displeasing situations and "seek greater happiness than they experienced within the British Empire" (Riley quoted in Freeman 3). An excerpt from the Declaration of Independence, for example, states: "When, in the course of human events, it becomes necessary for one people to dissolve the political bonds which have connected them with another, and to assume, among the powers of the earth, the separate and equal station to which the laws of nature and of nature's God entitle them, a decent respect to the opinions of mankind requires that they should declare the causes which impel them to the separation" (Jefferson). However, divorce was "no mere metaphor" just before the Civil War, as Adam Goodheart has noted. The question of whether or not a married couple should be allowed to divorce inspired energized arguments on both sides, in fact, by many of the same individuals who publicly argued for or against the dissolution of the Union. Nineteenth-century diarist Mary Boykin Chestnut wrote in 1861: "We separated North and South because of incompatibility of temper. . . . We are divorced because we have hated each other so. If we could only separate, a 'separation à l'agréable,' as the French say it, and not have a horrid fight for divorce" (quoted in Goodheart). But besides the cultural complexity that surrounded actual divorce later in the post–Civil War period, when America was still reeling from the divisive violence, divorce became a familiar trope, seen in William Dean Howells's 1881 novel *A Modern Instance,* for example, where it figures heavily as an extension of contemporary life. Like Chopin, he, too, "casts divorce as American, foreshadowing the worst aspects of the modern American social character may become: fragmented, self-absorbed or self-referential, and nihilistic" (Freeman 26)—and reflective of the modernist narratives to come in the early twentieth century.

Since the marriage of Thérèse and Hosmer is predicated on divorce, a complex phenomenon in post–Civil War American culture, it does not mirror the harmonious unity of the North and South—though it does not preclude the possibility either. Instead, contrary to Anderson's suggestion of a productive future that holds the possibility of bringing children into the world, Thérèse and Hosmer's marriage does not promise a productive future, similar to his first marriage. Thérèse is already thirty-five years old—well past the average childbearing age of her time, as Deborah L. Williams notes in the first essay of this collection—and Hosmer is forty. In any discussion of the possibility of their union, their love, or their marriage in the novel, bringing children into the world is never mentioned. Their marriage only provides superficial closure, and it does not portend any less ambiguity, despite Thérèse's admission of being "at fault." Their future is uncertain, as Hosmer himself essentially states at the end:

> "Thérèse," said Hosmer firmly, "the truth in its entirety isn't given to man to know—such knowledge, no doubt, would be beyond human endurance. But we make a step towards it, when we learn that there is rottenness and evil in the world, masquerading as right and morality—when we learn to know the living spirit from the dead letter. I have not cared to stop in this struggle of life to question. You, perhaps, wouldn't dare to alone. Together, dear one, we will work it out. Be sure there is a way—we may not find it in the end, but we will at least have tried." (165)

Hosmer asserts that while there is a meaning to their existence, they can only hope to find out what it is. He intimates her own moral lesson: only evil may come of moral righteousness. But beyond that knowledge, there is only ambiguity, even as they may face that together. The ambiguity in this final scene follows several preclosure points; as a result, the marriage appears fraught, as easily interpreted as a metaphor for union as it is interpreted an emblem of moral relativism.

The New Woman

The premise of divorce conveys fragmentation and ambiguity, as noted above, but insofar as it was a particularly American phenomenon in the late nineteenth century, as a narrative device it also serves in the text to foreground another cultural development: the New Woman. An additional signifier of the emerging modern era in *At Fault,* Hosmer's sister, Melicent, embodies New Woman sensibilities in the novel. Melicent disappears from the novel after she leaves town but reappears in the final pages of the novel when Thérèse and Hosmer are united in marriage. While it is not clear if they may hope for children of their own or not, Thérèse and Hosmer *appear* as parental figures for Melicent—to Anderson's point. Hosmer had already been her guardian, and once he marries Thérèse, she joins him in an apparent parental role. By that point, though, Melicent is well beyond the need for their care or guidance. Chopin closes *At Fault* with the letter sent by Melicent, who has now befriended Mrs. Griesmann, an independent woman who knows about "natural history" and who will accompany her to Yosemite National Park (168). This final scene imparts Chopin's readers with a vision of female autonomy, situated in the imaginative West, and distinctly separate from the northern-southern struggles. Melicent's letter portrays her as an independent woman, like her companion, as they set out to explore the wilderness.

Notably, Thérèse, too, exhibits a distinctive autonomy, as she manages a business after her husband's death. She is a forceful figure on Place-du-Bois and a powerful influence on the lives of Hosmer and every other character on the plantation, as several contributors to this volume note. In a 2013 study of the New Woman and Chopin's fiction, Ali Khoshnood, Rosli Talif, and Pedram Lalbakhsh make a case for considering Thérèse as a New Woman figure, given her childlessness and independence: "Chopin creates a female character at a time when employment discrimination based on sex still prevailed in Louisianian society. In this sense Thérèse emerges as a version of 'New Woman' who rejects the dominant ideology that insists that men and women are meant to occupy different spheres of activity according to their biological sex. Thérèse is childless and it seems she is unencumbered with motherly duties and domestic upkeep" (1137). The authors continue by asserting the ways Thérèse's widowhood enables her to circumvent traditional gender roles and move into a "masculine space and profession" in charge of Place-du-Bois (1137). In this regard, Khoshnood, Talif, and Lalbakhsh are correct: Thérèse has remained childless so that even as a widow, she is autonomous and able to oversee the operations of her plantation. However, her moral claims appear to align her with more conventional and traditional ideologies, as seen in her adherence to Catholic principles and her resultant insistence on Hosmer's remarriage to Fanny. For those reasons, Thérèse's moral standards do not position her as a progressive or as forward-thinking, and because of her age, she is less externally aligned with the youthful image of the New Woman.

Khoshnood, Talif, and Lalbakhsh make a stronger case for reading Melicent as a figure of the New Woman. As they point out, in addition to her multiple engagements, "her rejection of Grégoire portrays her as a modern woman desiring a perfect union with a man on par with her sociocultural level. She is not a docile and traditional homemaker, rather she travels extensively and wishes to explore and make new scientific discoveries" (1141). Melicent, who has been morally consistent and distinct from every other character in the novel, embodies the characteristics of the New Woman, a cultural figure who emerges prominently at the turn of the twentieth century. Unlike Thérèse, Melicent has been far more consistent in her rejection of traditional gender roles, as seen in her multiple broken engagements. Independent-minded, despite her filial dependence on her older brother at first, Melicent travels across the country through the novel, from St. Louis to Cane River to her anticipated trip to Yosemite. She ultimately rejects the morality of her elders, particularly Thérèse, but even Hosmer, as his reasoning for re-marrying Fanny appears to her to be impaired.

Given her autonomy and freedom, as well as her moral consistency, Melicent develops as a literary prototype for the New Woman. The New Woman was a cultural figure of a young woman who exhibited more independence and expected more independence than her mother's generation. In Gail Finney's words:

One of the primary factors motivating the typical New Woman is rebellion against the "old woman," described by one member of an 1890s women's club as "bounded on the north by servants, on the south by children, on the east by ailments and on the west by clothes." The conventional Victorian woman is accustomed to self-sacrifice; the New Woman pursues self-fulfillment and independence, often choosing to work for a living. She typically strives for equality in her relationships with men, seeking to eliminate the double standard that shaped the sexual mores of the time, and is in general much more frank about sexuality than the old woman. . . . Furthermore, the New

Woman tends to be well-educated and to read a great deal. Although not necessarily a woman suffragist, she is likely to be more interested in politics than the conventional woman. Finally, the New Woman is physically vigorous and energetic, preferring comfortable clothes to the restrictive garb usually worn by women of the era. (195–96)

This "new" construction of womanhood opposed the former Victorian conception of woman as the "inspiration and guardian of civilization" (Dowling 440), the pristine embodiment of domestic authority and purity. But the critics of the New Woman believed she had aligned herself "perversely with the forces of cultural anarchism and decay precisely because she wanted to reinterpret the sexual relationship. Like the decadent, the heroine of the New Woman fiction expressed her quarrel with Victorian culture chiefly through sexual means—by heightening sexual consciousness, candor, and expressiveness" (Dowling 440–41). Regardless of how one viewed the New Woman, she was unquestionably distinct from her predecessor.

Melicent's character embodies several of the more favorable New Woman elements, particularly in her candor and expression of her independent mind and in her expectation of equality. When she first appears at Place-du-Bois, she is a ward of Hosmer's, and she becomes romantically linked to Grégoire, who is in a sense a ward of Thérèse's. He tells Melicent that his aunt, Thérèse, saved him because she did not approve of the way his father had been raising his brothers and him (18). Melicent's and Grégoire's respective dependence on Hosmer and Thérèse effectively casts them as belonging to the next generation.

Yet, unlike Grégoire, Melicent never integrates into the community at Place-du-Bois. As soon as she arrives, she is at odds nearly immediately with the southern "help," whom she seems unable to inspire to attend to her. Like her brother, Melicent is an outsider to this southern community. Thérèse and all other natives in the Cane River region are Catholics, but Hosmer and his sister—in addition to hailing from the North—are also Unitarians. Melicent asserts the reason why she cannot believe in hell or spirits, for example, is because, as she says plainly: "I am a Unitarian" (44). Unlike Hosmer, who presents some resistance to Thérèse's religious claims, Grégoire listens to Melicent and admits that Unitarianism is new to him (44). While he treats her like an equal and professes to love her, she does not, admittedly, love him, and she understands at first, at least, that he is too rough to bring around polite society and therefore not marriageable. Nevertheless, Melicent speaks freely with him, unguardedly sharing her beliefs and ideas with him, which he receives with thoughtfulness and some introspection.

Melicent's independence of mind emerges in the discussion of Hosmer's remarriage to Fanny, to which she vehemently objects. She becomes ill from the knowledge of his second marriage and verbally expresses her dissatisfaction with it (76). She privileges happiness in marriage over doctrine or tradition. Reflective of the New Woman, she rejects past convention if it impinges on the notions of independence and self-fulfillment.

The reader sees further evidence of Melicent's independent mind when she categorically rejects Grégoire for committing murder. Once Joçint has set the mill on fire out of his resentment over working there, Grégoire stalks him that night and shoots him. Later he looks "down indifferently at the dead" (106). While the community of Cane River is appalled on one level, the common consensus decides that Grégoire is still a result of his upbringing, though it offers no such allowance for Joçint, a person of color, who "only" burned down a mill and did not commit murder. Grégoire himself, the narrator explains, "could not understand that he should receive any thing but praise for having rid the community of so offensive and dangerous person as Joçint; and seemed utterly blind to the moral aspect of his deed" (108). In spite of his crime, Grégoire is received by his aunt, and later, after his death, his memory is honored with several masses, requested by Thérèse. Again an outlier, Melicent rejects any sympathetic response to Grégoire. She is offended by Thérèse's request of her to offer him a "friendly word," and she responds with bewilderment and rejection:

> Melicent looked at her horrified. "I don't understand you at all, Mrs. Lafirme. Think what he's done; murdered a defenseless man! How can you have him near you—seated at your table? I don't know what nerves you have

in your bodies, you and David. There's David, hobnobbing with him. Even that Fanny talking to him as if he were blameless. Never! If he were dying I wouldn't go near him."

"Haven't you a spark of humanity in you?" asked Thérèse, flushing violently.

"Oh, this is something physical," she replied, shivering, "let me alone." (112)

Melicent does not stray from her moral position, and she unreservedly speaks her disapproval. Her independence and ideals of self-fulfillment remain constant amid the events of the novel. Melicent executes her decisions with clarity, and her choices result in unambiguous outcomes, unlike Thérèse, whose doubt only increases through the novel: "She had always thought this lesson of right and wrong a very plain one. So easy of interpretation that the simplest minded might solve it if they would. And here had come for the first time in her life a staggering doubt as to its nature. She did not suspect that she was submitting one of those knotty problems to her unpracticed judgment that philosophers and theologians delight in disagreeing upon, and her inability to unravel it staggered her" (127). Thérèse's subsequent uncertainty never relents, even as she admits her "fault" at the end of the novel. She still does not feel certain about her access to happiness in light of the "past of pain and sin and trouble" (165). Thérèse's doubt stands in stark contrast to Melicent's unwavering rejection of Grégoire and her later, happy embarkment on a western adventure. She is bound neither by doctrine nor relativism, but her morality reaffirms her status as an outsider to this southern community that often resists variations from tradition.

Chopin's characterization of Melicent instead aligns her with a new generation, one that resists the habits of the past. Additionally, Melicent's friend Mrs. Griesmann further links her with modernity, as the woman knows about "natural history" (168). This knowledge places Mrs. Griesmann in the Darwinist camp. Several Chopin scholars have noted the author's knowledge of Darwin's nineteenth-century texts and their influence on her thinking, including Bert Bender, who explains that Chopin's close reading of Darwin's *The Descent of Man and Selection in Relation to Sex* (1871) appealed to her logic. Further, he writes, "As she first viewed it, the theory of sexual selection offered a profoundly liberating sense of animal innocence in the realm of human courtship, especially for the Victorian woman" (Bender 459–60). Melicent embodies this aspect of Darwinist theory in the sense that she rejects Grégoire at first because he belongs to a lesser socioeconomic class, but then certainly later when he commits murder. Grégoire, in either instance, is not an acceptable partner/mate for Melicent, so despite her fondness for him, she is able to separate and leave Place-du-Bois without him. Her alliance with Mrs. Griesmann links them both to the new generation that has rejected the religious-based conventions associated with the past and further distances Melicent from Thérèse.

Chopin might have ended Melicent's own subplot with her departure from Place-du-Bois, but she "reappears" at the end of the novel, independent and about to travel with Mrs. Griesmann. Chopin reminds her readers of Melicent by closing *At Fault* with Hosmer reading Melicent's letter to Thérèse (169). The narrative ends with the echo of Melicent's blessings, as Hosmer reads aloud his sister's request: "Give that sweet sister Thérèse as many kisses as she will stand for me" (169). Melicent's reemergence in the narrative, particularly the ending, points the reader toward the moral figure in the novel, the character who portends the promise of the modern period. As much as Melicent is the embodiment of the New Woman, she is also the moral standard-bearer of the novel. Whereas the other protomodernist elements of *At Fault* speak to ambiguity and uncertainty, predicated on the fragmentation of Hosmer's divorce, the New Woman emerges independently as the vision of optimism and innovation, as she eschews the world of Place-du-Bois and heads out west. The preclosure points in the novel direct the reader toward the closing scene, which features the final marital union of Thérèse and Hosmer, but the contrast of this marriage's predication on fragmentation, loss, and doubt to the independence and moral clarity of the New Woman ushers in Chopin's most emphatic point. The closure of *At Fault* is fraught with ambiguity—reflective of Horner's interpretative reading of Chopin's narrative strategy—but it is this ambiguity, as seen in Thérèse and Hosmer's marriage, that engages Lohafer's central point:

the narrative develops through multiple preclosure points, all of which direct the reader toward the emphatic ending. In *At Fault,* the preclosure points foreground the New Woman against the context of a marriage predicated on divorce and death. The irony of Thérèse and Hosmer's marriage echoes the "irony" that surround each of Melitte's possible "exits" in "Aunt Lympy's Interference," as Lohafer notes (164), and it also drives home Chopin's point that the more outstanding phenomenon to emerge at the dawn of modernity was the New Woman.

Melicent's identification as an early New Woman underscored the cultural value of independence, which was also inherent in the American phenomenon of divorce. At its core, divorce permits the dissolution of "bonds," enabling individual autonomy and perhaps personal happiness. Insofar as Melicent and Mrs. Griesmann are headed out west, where divorce was far more acceptable in the nineteenth century, the narrative device of divorce in the novel directly supports and illuminates the figure of the New Woman. Importantly, the New Woman and divorce both offer individualism and detachment from a past moral code in the text. The freedom identified with both phenomena enabled Chopin to explore the ambiguity, fragmentation, and relativism that would later characterize the new age, but it also allowed her to point toward a newly imagined space for women within it.

WORKS CITED

Anderson, Maureen. "Unraveling the Southern Pastoral Tradition: A New Look at Kate Chopin's *At Fault.*" *Southern Literary Journal* 34, no. 1 (Fall 2001): 1–13.

Bender, Bert. "The Teeth of Desire: *The Awakening* and *The Descent of Man.*" *American Literature* 63, no. 3 (September 1991): 459–73.

Chopin, Kate. *At Fault.* 1890. Edited with an introduction and notes by Bernard Koloski. London: Penguin, 2002.

Dowling, Linda. "The Decadent and the New Woman in the 1890's." *Nineteenth-Century Fiction* 33, no. 4 (March 1979): 434–53. https://lib-proxy.sunywcc .edu:2159/stable/2933251?.

Ewell, Barbara C. "Linked Fortunes: Kate Chopin, the Short Story (and Me)." In *Awakenings: The Story of the Kate Chopin Revival,* edited by Bernard Koloski, 32–46. Baton Rouge: Louisiana State University Press, 2009.

Ewell, Barbara C., and Pamela Glenn Menke. Introduction to *Southern Local Color: Stories of Region, Race, and Gender,* edited by Ewell and Menke, xiii–lxvi. Athens: University of Georgia Press, 2002.

Finney, Gail. *Women in Modern Drama: Freud, Feminism, and European Theater at the Turn of the Century.* Ithaca, NY: Cornell University Press, 1989.

Freeman, Kimberly A. *Love American Style: Divorce and the American Novel, 1881–1976.* Abingdon, UK: Routledge, 2003.

Goodheart, Adam. "Divorce, Antebellum Style." *New York Times. Opinionator,* March 18, 2011. https://opinionator.blogs.nytimes.com/2011/03/18/divorce -antebellum-style/.

Horner, Avril. "Kate Chopin, Choice and Modernism." In *The Cambridge Companion to Kate Chopin,* edited by Janet Beer, 132–46. Cambridge: Cambridge University Press, 2008.

Jefferson, Thomas. *The Declaration of Independence.*

Khoshnood, Ali, Rosli Talif, and Pedram Lalbakhsh. "Kate Chopin's Early Fiction as a Prologue to the Emergence of the New Woman. *Social Sciences & Humanities* 21, no. 3 (2013): 1133–47.

Lohafer, Susan. "Kate Chopin and the Future of Short Fiction Studies." In *Awakenings: The Story of the Kate Chopin Revival,* edited by Bernard Koloski, 157–72. Baton Rouge: Louisiana State University Press, 2012.

Personified Matter
Empowered Things in At Fault

SUSAN MOLDOW

First Things First: Commodity Culture in Victorian Studies

For those who study the Victorian era, there is no escape from "things." In fact, the wealth of detail and artifact available is one of the attractions of the era: who could resist the hats, coaches, buttons, newspapers, ribbons, tea, old lace, and pocket watches that clutter the pages of Dickens and crowd among the characters of Thackeray, Trollope, Eliot, and Brontë? The Victorians abroad and in America had a predilection for the careful acquisition and utilization of objects, and this preoccupation has become a focus for research (Sattaur 347). My interest in the presence of objects yields analysis of how the objects in Kate Chopin's 1890 novel *At Fault* change and illuminate of the lives of its nineteenth-century individuals. The objects in the setting—natural and man-made—such as the plantation, woods, river, railroad, and lumber mill both reflect and contribute to the sweeping changes in the region during the novel's time period. Consequently, objects are things that have power in *At Fault*. The application of "thing theory" facilitates not only a lens through which to view the story, but this theoretical approach shows how certain objects in the novel exert power to affect the narrative.

The Victorians were fascinated with objects and things, and recent scholarship has proved equally fascinated with this Victorian obsession (Pykett 1). This scholarly focus can be traced back to a turn in Victorian criticism in the 1980s, beginning with Brigg's *Victorian Things* and based on theories of commodity culture by writers such as Roland Barthes and Walter Benjamin who had "an interdisciplinary interest in material culture and particularly in consumer culture and theories of consumption"

(Briggs 347). More recently, critics have shown a renewed interest in exploring objects, even commodities, in contexts other than the traditionally Marxist nexus of value, production, and consumption.

Beginning with Bill Brown's *A Sense of Things* in 2003, critics have sought additional ways to evaluate an object as a signifier. His book started the critical move away from commodity-based readings of literary objects toward the more complex subject-object relations in literature that comprise thing theory (Sattaur 351). Not only is *A Sense of Things* considered to be the first major critical work to examine the idea of powerful subject-object relationships, Brown utilizes nineteenth-century literature to explore Victorian thing culture. This link between thing theory and literature invites new analyses of stories and novels. Brown is particularly concerned with the "slippage between having (possessing a particular object) and being (the identification of one's self with that object)" (*A Sense* 13). Although Brown starts his argument with Marx's concern with the commodity, he transitions into an analysis of the ways in which American "subjects identify with and through the objects they possess and which come to possess them" (Sattaur 353). Brown's study echoes William Carlos Williams's modernist assertion that there are "no ideas but in things" as he negotiates the nineteenth-century concept of a material identity where subjects and objects are interchangeable and cross-referential.

John Plotz's *Portable Property* (2008) similarly views objects as he traces the identity and investments that imperial subjects placed in the objects that traveled with them. He writes that "when possessions fill Victorian novels, they generally serve not as static deadweights, but as moving messengers who acquire meaning" (1). He asserts that the most important objects in Victorian culture and literature are those in which "tension is caused by an oscillation" between a market value of a commodity item and the item's sentimental value as a nonsaleable item (Sattaur 351). While the commodity may have been a starting point for exploration of the relations between people and things, additional scholarship suggests that the significance of the object extends far beyond consumption processes and that its significance is particularly relevant in nineteenth-century literature.

Notable research in the 1990s and the early 2000s on nineteenth-century consumer culture highlights the interest in the world of objects in Victorian studies and exhibits a connection to thing theory's rising popularity and focus on Victorian literature (Sattaur 348). In 1995, Millar published *Novels behind Glass,* the first critical work on the social impact of the commodity in Victorian culture and literature. In his foundational study, Millar asserts that, for Victorian writers and thinkers, the significance of the object extends beyond economic value (Sattaur 348). Later, in 2003, Christoph Lindner's *Fictions of Commodity Culture* built upon Millar's work to study commodity culture in literature. As Millar did in *Novels behind Glass,* Lindner suggests that objects cannot be read as commodities alone but instead must be read in the context of their wider cultural relations. Gaining obvious theoretical traction from classical Marxism, thing theorists are interested in the way objects sustain economic, cultural, and social relationships, but they tend to be more oriented to the social power rather than the economic power of things.

Study of the object as a commodity and then as a thing originated with evaluation of the complex interactions between people and objects in literature. Critics have been keen to embrace thing theory and what Elaine Freedgood calls "Victorian thing culture" as a richer form of object relations than that suggested by commodity culture (Mills 6). Brown's work aligns with Millar's, Lindner's, and Plotz's assertion that the nineteenth century offers a rich opportunity to explore subject-object relationships. Elaine Freedgood's *The Ideas in Things* and Jane Bennett's *Vibrant Matter* are also essential to this study's consideration of *At Fault.* Freedgood notes that "a host of ideas resided in Victorian things: abstraction, alienation, and spectacularization had to compete for space with other kinds of object relations—ones that we have perhaps yet to appreciate" (7–8). Freedgood's readings of mahogany furniture in *Jane Eyre,* of calico curtains in *Mary Barton,* and tobacco in *Great Expectations* take commodity culture into consideration, and, like Brown, Freedgood is concerned with the histories that reside in these objects and can be read as alternative object relations. A political theorist interested in materiality, although not specific to the Victorian period, Bennett argues that materiality, too often considered as an inert substance, can be reconsidered as assemblages of human and nonhuman actors or actants, to use Bruno Latour's terms. This is a paradigm shift that sees space and energy as the result of how humans and nonhumans associate to form precarious wholes, and, therefore, change how we view the force of objects in our world.

Fiction Writers and Literary Critics Have Had Things on Their Minds

While modernist poets such as Williams may have sought "no ideas but in things," thing theory also seems a natural fit for nineteenth-century fiction (Markovits 593). Consideration of how objects become things and assemblages as well as the nature and impact of their thing power breathes new life and meaning into classic texts such as Chopin's *At Fault,* in which objects in the story become "vibrant matter" and wield power as "things." Bill Brown argues that because things become most visible when objects are used differently or misused, "thingness" can be exemplified in time, and examples are necessarily "narrative" ("Secret Life" 3). For instance, in *A Sense of Things,* Brown evaluates how a physical object, the bowl in Henry James's *The Golden Bowl,* is described and redescribed, "intensely framed, doted upon, and thus becomes a thing, elevated to significance that it hardly possesses on its own, yet a significance that it seems to have autonomously assumed" (172). Additionally, Brown suggests that in *The Country of the Pointed Firs,* Jewett's sketches "attain something of the uncanny arrangement of these life-group exhibits . . . and disclose . . . whereby an object seems to embody a way of life, attaining an aura of culture" ("Regional Artifacts" 205).

This critical notion that things can alter people's identities and change people's lives parallels the subject-object relations in *At Fault.* Things are important and exceed mere object status. By examining the role of things in Chopin's *At Fault,* we can gain insight into the way the forces of things impacted nineteenth-century lives through reinvention or destruction.

The Thing about Mother Nature

Although many critics have offered praise for Kate Chopin's *At Fault,* the idea that objects in the story, such as those in nature and industry, have power and that they can enact change in the characters and their lives has not yet been discussed in research. But objects such as the plantation setting of Place-du-Bois as well as the woods, river, railroad, and lumber mill become powerful catalysts for change in *At Fault.* The setting in *At Fault* has the same power as the smaller objects typically considered to have the ability to become "things." This exploration is unlike a traditional examination of setting. Usually the mood, details, atmosphere, and historical context are evaluated in a discussion of setting; however, an analysis of the power of the objects in *At Fault* offers a new view of the setting as more empowered and central to the novel.

In *At Fault,* Chopin establishes Place-du-Bois as a pastoral setting that seems safely removed from the outside world (Anderson 3): "The short length of this Louisiana plantation stretched along Cane River, meeting the water when that stream was at its highest, with a thick growth of cotton-wood trees; save where a narrow convenient opening had been cut into their midst, and where further down the pine hills started in an abrupt prominence from the water and the dead level of the land on either side of them" (6). Place-du-Bois is separated from the rest of society by deep woods and a rough river—too rough to cross. The woods in *At Fault* are more than mere pretty scenery in the story as might be discussed in a more typical consideration of the effects of setting in the novel; the woods, like much of the setting of Place-du-Bois, play a role of protector for characters who seek their refuge and inspiration. In this regard, the setting becomes a character in the novel whereby it has agency to impact and change lives forever.

Because of the setting, Melicent and Grégoire's impossible connection becomes magical and feasible within the woods, which are an agent of change and therefore "thingness" in the story. Melicent sees Grégoire's bilingual "peculiarities" and speech as "unfamiliar" and having the ability to "remove him at once from the possibility of her consideration" and which "could not adapt itself to the requirements" of her "polite society" (44). Yet, despite the "deformation" of his speech and that she "bores" with him, she decides she is "in love with Grégoire." She also decides that "nothing could come of it" (44). Their attraction is undeniable, however, and it is fueled in the privacy and protection of the woods in which they rendezvous. They row in a boat on a lake amid "rank and clustering vegetation" that has become more "dense as they went on, forming an impenetrable tangle on either side and pressing so closely above that they needed to lower their heads to avoid the blow of some drooping branch." The trees above them form an "impenetrable" and powerful wall between them and the outside world. The lake can "carry" them to the "far spreading waters" and under a "canopy" of open sky (16). The trees and the lake have thing power and seem to protect and transform these individuals.

On the lake and among these trees, Melicent and Grégoire are in danger, but they are also free. The trees are animated and have thingness; a nearby "grim cypress lifted its head above the water" and spread "wide its moss-covered arms inviting refuge to the great black-winged buzzards that circled over and about it in mid-air" (16–17). The cypress is a refuge for Melicent and Grégoire, albeit one that foreshadows an unhappy ending between them. They must "watch carefully to escape the hewn logs that floated in numbers upon the water" (17). The woods and water transform the characters positively, but their thingness also signals the obstacles and differences between them as represented by the logs. Overall, the lake and the woods offer a liberating love potion. Melicent cries out an exclamation of "Oh!" This is a "sigh of relief which comes at the removal of some pressure from body or brain." She is unfettered while on the lake with Grégoire, and the "wildness of the scene" "speeds" her "fancy" into the realms of romance as connected to the thing power of the setting (16).

The woods effect change on the two lovers on and off the lake and are examples of objects that becomes actants and have thing power. Grégoire is no longer sad when he is with Melicent on the lake, and the woods have the power to nearly transform him into another being. In the bayou, Melicent discerns joy and says that she doesn't "suppose he was ever sad." To this observation, Grégoire shares his admission that "Oh my, yes!" he has been sad, but that Melicent "ain't ever seen" when he was "real lonesome." He admits to Melicent "that it tain't so bad" since she arrived on the plantation (17). The bayou and wooded lake enhance the passion between these two characters. Melicent appears with a "veritable armful of flowers, leaves, red berried sprigs, a tangle of richest color." Later, in the woods, she has "bedecked him with garlands and festoons of autumn leaves, till he looked a very Satyr; a character which his flushed, swarthy cheeks, and glittering animal eyes did not belie." They laugh "immoderately" and their "whole bearing" reflects "exuberant gaiety." The "great cedar tree" seems to change Melicent as she sits on a bench that wraps around it. Nature overtakes her, and she embraces a "recklessness of spirit." Entranced with this version of herself, she "guards her treasure of flowers from Thérèse" and "flings" a rose in Grégoire's face (84). Instead of allowing him to sit next to her, Melicent commands Grégoire to "go sit by Fanny and do something to make her laugh" and "flings her flowery wealth" into Thérèse's lap. Melicent's behavior reflects the woods' infectious power to change Fanny and Thérèse into happier beings. Still overtaken by her experience in the woods, Melicent departs to help Grégoire feed the mules. She is changed, as she is suddenly willing to do farmwork, a job beneath her social status, and to follow a man who is outside her "polite society" (44). Melicent's "mischievous and handsome" face has "an unusual animation . . . warmed by a sudden faint glow" (86). The woods are powerful things that transform and unite two people, despite their differences.

The society portrayed in southern pastoral is an archetype that Chopin uses in *At Fault* to reflect the Old South; it contrasts northern influence on post–Civil War Louisiana, but this pastoral setting is unable to shield Place-du-Bois from change. The setting of Place-du-Bois is typical of stories in the southern pastoral genre, which was popular during Reconstruction. Educated and well-read, Chopin would have been familiar with the southern pastoral conventions of her time. She and her readers would have enjoyed this type of fiction written by Sidney Lanier, Nelson Page, and Chandler Harris (Anderson 2). These writers employed a southern pastoral setting that idealized the freedom of a slow, rural environment and an austere code of honor (MacKethan 37). The pastoral setting of Place-du-Bois in *At Fault* has "negro quarters" that "gleam" against the "tender green of the cotton and corn." Hector lies "half awake" under the shade of an umbrella China tree, and Betsy is "youthful ebony" and crosses the field "leisurely" (Chopin 7).

Chopin refers to the plantation as a female, noting "her fair domain" (6). Place-du-Bois is not only peaceful, it is "rich in its exhaustless powers of reproduction" like a mother figure, a giver and protector of life. Newly widowed, Thérèse is at first trapped in her grief, but the necessity of managing the plantation forces her to move forward. Critics have maintained that from the very first page of the novel, Thérèse struggles to maintain stability at Place-du-Bois (Koloski, introduction xiv). However, readers of *At Fault* have yet to explore the plantation's role in inspiring Thérèse to strive to be her best self within the plantation and also with Hosmer. She takes over the plantation to save it from economic ruin and does not ask a male relative or friend to help her with her finances. When she learns that her workers are stealing cotton seed from her, she makes changes in her management of the plantation and no more cotton seed goes missing. Similarly, although she asks her nephew Grégoire to help her supervise the fields, she remains in charge; even Grégoire acknowledges that "they ain't no betta woman in the worl' than Aunt Thérèse when you do like she wants." The plantation provides employment when Thérèse gives her nephew Grégoire work after he loses his own plantation to creditors (18). "Alone" in her "beloved" plantation woods, Thérèse ponders changes that confront her in the form of a new railroad and lumber mill. Here, Chopin no longer describes Thérèse as "inconsolable" (3). Inspired by her new status and bolstered by the protection of Place-du-Bois, Thérèse becomes a "clever enough businesswoman" who exerts control of her life.

Plantation objects inspire Thérèse to make choices about Hosmer that divide as well as unify them. They are not mere objects; they are actants and have thingness, like the woods and the lake. Even though they are in love with one another, Thérèse chooses not to be with Hosmer, to encourage him to do what is "right," and to seek something "higher" than love. He is "blind" and does not share her morality. The powerful plantation bell's chime reminds them of the conflicts between them, which delays their union (40).

Plantation bells have always been a significant part of slave and plantation culture. The slave bell was rung to regulate the day on slave plantations and in slave societies. They controlled the lives and labor of enslaved people (Marshall 20). Slaves, who were not usually allowed to own pocket watches or clocks to keep time, found that relying on the sun was a difficult way to manage time because of the changing seasons. Most masters or overseers used a bell, horn, or other audible means to communicate with enslaved workers that it was time to start work, time to eat, time to quit work, time to go to bed, and, on rare occasions, time to celebrate (Talbott).

The context of the plantation bell's history is apparent and consistent in *At Fault*. The bell wields power and control as an animated thing in the story. Chopin describes the bell as "great" and associated with harkening the noon hour of "sweet and restful enjoyment." However, to Hosmer, it is a "derisive demon" who is "mocking" his "spirit" (40). Because he can't find peace on Thérèse's plantation, he must leave and return to his lumber mill world. Plantation bells have a long and painful history in slave culture, and a bell's presence in *At Fault* also has a negative association. The plantation's parent-like bell seems to alert Hosmer and Thérèse to the chasm between their two worlds, of industrial life and plantation life, as well as to the problems associated with Hosmer's divorce and Thérèse's religious background.

Similarly, the rose tree around Thérèse forges a reminder about strict codes of honor and religion. Like the plantation bell, the rose tree has thing power and enacts change in the story. The "great rose tree climbs and spreads generously over one side, and big red roses" grow by the hundreds around Marie Louise's house (88). Cole has discussed how the rose tree symbolizes older Catholic ways of life and how it blooms because of a blessing from the parish priest. She also has suggested that Marie Louise's cabin deep in the forest is a refuge for Old World customs and offers a link to Catholicism, which reminds Thérèse of why she encouraged Hosmer to stay with his wife and why she cannot have a romantic connection with him (70). However, the rose tree is more than an object; the scent of the rose seems to be pervasive in Thérèse's life. There is a "faint odor of rose" coming from a "curious Japanese jar on the ample hearth" in the main area of Thérèse's home (35). The rose's omnipresence reminds Thérèse to live within religious traditions, and in this way, it exudes "thingness."

Understanding the context of divorce and Catholicism in the late nineteenth century further illuminates the power of these plantation objects. Even though divorce rates were rising significantly across America by the late nineteenth century, divorce was still considered scandalous in life and in literature. W. E. Gladstone's 1889 *The Question of Divorce* asserts that the "health of the social body depends on the soundness" of family, and that the "hinge of family is to be found in the great and profound institution of marriage" (650). At the time, men and women believed equally in the sanctity of marriage as a mark of civilized living. The idea of a woman loving a divorced man was also scorned. As the country grew, Americans divorced more but disapproved of it no less.

Before 1900, neither fictional works nor magazines (other than the radical *Arena* magazine) defended divorce. For example, in T. S. Arner's 1864[1] novel *Out in the World,* when a divorced man proposes to a woman, she tells him that his offer is an insult. In the late nineteenth century, divorce novels featured lawyers who were given names like Mr. Sly, and repercussions of divorce included alcoholism, business failure, ill health, and even death. Later, in Edith Wharton's *The Custom of the Country* (1913), the heroine is cavalier about divorce and is ironically outwitted by it. Wharton's *The Age of Innocence* (1920) depicts a woman imprisoned by society's prejudice against divorce (Feldman). Given that Victorian society frowned on the idea of divorce, one's being Catholic added further to the condemnation of being divorced or remarried after divorce. The Catholic religion asserts that marriage is a contract for life and that the church has no authority to cancel this contract, based on the interpretations of scriptural writings of Mark, Luke, and Paul (Maiorano). Some Victorian Catholics believed that not even death could break the marriage bond (Gladstone 651). Divorce and remarriage in the late nineteenth century ranged from being perceived as low class to horrific, depending upon one's social circle and/or religion. In *At Fault,* Thérèse's Roman Catholic background exacerbates her perception of divorce and causes her to spurn Hosmer's romantic advances. The rose tree shifts from being an object in the story to being an actant that can deliver a staunch Catholic reminder to the story's protagonist.

Thérèse says that divorce does "not concern her" and that it is an idea "remote" from her "clean existence." Because the "prejudices of her Catholic education" are "coloring her sentiments," she believes that this concept should therefore be "dismissed" and "as far as possible effaced from her remembrance" (34). When Hosmer expresses dismay, Thérèse reiterates her conviction that she won't give him "a false impression that religion doesn't influence" her reason to believe that neither a man nor a woman should be able to undertake a second marriage. Moreover, when Hosmer suggests hopefully that such a "prejudice" could be "set aside by an effort of the will," Thérèse reminds him that "there are some prejudices which a woman can't afford to part with, even at the price of happiness," and that he should "say no more about it and think no more of it" (36). Thérèse's strong beliefs and the sacramental authority of Catholicism contribute to the power of the surrounding objects, such as the rose tree, which eventually help unify Thérèse and Hosmer. The rose tree, like the bell, woods, and plantation, functions like a character in *At Fault*. Because all of these objects seem to impact others' actions and feelings, they function outside their normal capacity and shift from being objects to personified matter.

Not all objects in nature function similarly in their "thing" capacity. For instance, while the plantation and woods in *At Fault* are protective, the river embodies and catalyzes change. Because Louisiana lies completely in the coastal plain, the rivers dominate life in this region (Koloski, introduction viii). The Cane River in *At Fault* borders Place-du-Bois and continually erodes its banks. Many critics have established that the river in *At Fault* is a symbol of motion and change (Anderson 6). Others see it as a motif in the novel that causes Thérèse's life to crumble (Koloski, "Structure" 90). Yet, the river is not a mere symbol in *At Fault;* it is a primary character, a force, and an object that becomes a thing as it no longer functions in its traditional role. Although the river does not make its appearance until part 2, chapter 4, the river is a game changer in *At Fault* when it destroys lives as well as changes others. Not just a pretty, innocuous or dangerous entity, the river is a powerful thing because of its impact upon the lives of those who live near it. The river is a constant "standing worry to Thérèse, for when the water [is] high and rapid, the banks cave constantly, carrying away sections from Place-du-Bois"

(87). The river's presence demands that the inhabitants who live near it move their fences as it changes the landscape of the plantation. Its force demands reverence as much as it acts as a catalyst. In this way it is not just threatening or majestic, but it has a power on par with that of any character in the story. For instance, the river becomes a barrier between Thérèse and Marie Louise. Marie Louise is a mother figure, a voice of conservatism and religion who, like the plantation, tries to keep Thérèse on a traditional path. Because of the river, Thérèse seldom goes to see her former nurse. There are only two occasions that could be "considered of sufficient importance to induce her to such effort" to visit her—when Marie Louise was ill or when she would be a "chef de cuisine" of an important dinner (89). Thérèse understands the river's force, and she even encourages Marie Louise to move her whole house to another location to avoid being so "perilously near the edge." Once far removed from Marie Louise's cabin, the river has "now eaten its way close up to it—leaving no space for the road way" (88). Thérèse warns Marie Louise that someday she will "find herself out in the middle of the river" (90). Unlike Thérèse, however, Marie Louise does not fear the river's power and insists that she is too old to move and will die there.

Ultimately, Marie Louise and Fanny both die because of the river's force and their immovable convictions. We see the river as an object that has become a "thing" through the eyes of Hosmer, who experiences an "undefined terror laying hold of him" when he realizes that Fanny has disappeared and notices that the river is rising to "an unaccustomed height and an added tremendous swiftness" (154). It is suddenly "eddying and bulging and hurrying . . . striking with an immensity of power . . . with a force all its own" in a "seething turmoil . . . demon dance . . . against the projection of land on which stood Marie Louise's cabin" (156). Marie Louise's cabin is a symbol of conservative Catholic ideals. Blessed by the priest, it is a haven. Marie Louise insists that "nothing going to harm Marie Louise" while she lives there. Similarly, Fanny feels "free" and "good" in the cabin; she is "free and moved to exercise a looseness of tongue" with Marie Louise that "was not common with her." In the cabin, Fanny informs Hosmer that, like Marie Louise, she "can take care" of herself and is no longer as lonely as she has been with him. Infused with the cabin's atmosphere of independence, Fanny sits in Marie Louise's big rocker, "balancing comfortably" (157). The cabin inspires Fanny and Marie Louise to live life as they choose, unfettered by the changing, threatening outside world. However, the river "eats" away at the safety of the cabin, now "perilously near the edge" of the river (88). Critics have maintained that the river is a symbol of motion and change that, like a baptism, cleanses Place-du-Bois of its Old South symbols such as Marie Louise and her cabin (Anderson 7). However, the river is not only a symbol in *At Fault;* it is a murderer. Marie Louise and Fanny die, and along with them die Victorian Catholic ideals such as the prohibition of marriage after divorce or death, which opens the door for Fanny and Hosmer's marriage.

The river destroys life, but it also yields new life for Hosmer and Thérèse, as it has forced a wedge between Thérèse and her old way of life. Thérèse embraces the changes that the river brings and, contrary to her initial beliefs, eventually finds happiness with Hosmer. Some critics have suggested that Thérèse becomes free to start a new life and remarry because of an accident. They suggest that Thérèse does not change her beliefs about the Catholic objection to divorce or modify her traditions and customs related to religion's importance in life (Koloski, "Structure" 90). Although Thérèse does not overtly change her belief systems, the river—not an accident or chance—transforms her by making her a new wife and a plantation manager, identities she could not have assumed prior to the river's impactful agency.

Things Are Changing

Similar to the river but in opposition to the stabilizing woods and plantation, the railroad and sawmill propel the characters to change. Many scholars have acknowledged that the train is a symbol of progress in *At Fault* (Anderson 4). Others have noted that a newly empowered Thérèse rebuilds Place-du-Bois to buttress tradition and not to accommodate change, such as the railroad, after her husband's death (Russell 9). Viewing the railroad from the perspective of its "thing power" suggests that it acts as a character in *At Fault,* one that invokes mistrust, one that illuminates Thérèse's reluctant acceptance of change, and finally, one that unifies lives.

An understanding of the nationwide growth of the railroad in the Cane River area of Louisiana highlights the power of the railroad in *At Fault,* which is about the changing social world of the post-Reconstruction South and its effects on the people who inhabit it. The evolution of the railroad industry during this time period had a profound effect on the nation, often determining how an individual lived. This change is seen in the events of *At Fault* as the characters adjust to the appearance of the railroad in both positive and negative ways.

The first carrier of passengers and freight was the Baltimore and Ohio Railroad, completed in 1827. The modern railroad industry was born when the South Carolina Canal and Railroad Company completed the first mechanical passenger train. By 1835, dozens of local railroad networks existed and grew exponentially. By 1850, more than 9,000 miles of track had been laid. With the onset of the Civil War, although production of new railroads fell, usage of this mode of transportation increased significantly. For example, the Battle of Bull Run was won by a group of reinforcements shuttled in on a railroad car. By the war's conclusion, the need for railway extension was apparent when the first transcontinental railroad was constructed, and small railroad companies died out ("History of American Railroads"). Beginning in the early 1870s, railroad construction in the United States increased dramatically. Before 1871, approximately 45,000 miles of track had been laid, and between 1871 and 1900, another 170,000 miles were added ("Railroads"). The railroad appears in the late nineteenth century in the region where *At Fault* takes place.

The influence of the industrial North on the agricultural South highly impacted Louisiana after the war. Until the twentieth century, there were few innovations in Louisiana road construction. Plank road construction did not start in Louisiana until after the 1850s, and prior to the Civil War, Louisiana had very few railroads (only 335 miles of track in 1860). Board roads rotted, and a "shed road" with a roof on posts was built. By the mid-1880s, railroad commerce replaced the shed-road transport (*Transportation* 35). The boom years for railroad construction in Louisiana were between 1880 and 1910, increasing from 652 miles of track in 1880 to 5,554 laid by 1910 (Fricker 8). With the growth of railways during the late nineteenth century, many Louisiana roads were abandoned. Trade centers were established near the railroads, and settlements were moved from roadside to railside, leaving behind ghost towns. The Texas and Pacific Railroad came to the Cane River district of northwestern Louisiana not far from the Texas border in Natchitoches Parish in 1881 (Koloski, introduction viii). As a result, industry grew, people were connected and disconnected in new ways, and lives were changed forever. Set in the Cane River region, *At Fault* reflects the railroad's impact on people's destinies.

Thérèse views the railroad to be of "questionable benefit," but its power drives her "to seek another domicile" because the "old homestead that nestled to the hillside and close to the water's edge had been abandoned to the inroads of progressive civilization." Her former home has become a "mutilated dwelling." Suspicious of the northern influx of industry such as the railroad, she avoids the "temptations offered by modern architectural innovations." Instead, she clings to "simplicity" and things that reflect the endurance of "easy-going and comfort-loving generations." Although Thérèse loves to look at the landscape of Place-du-Bois from her veranda, a "brown and ugly intruder"—the railroad station—ruins her view (6). The railroad has invaded her life despite her "pouting resistance" and "opposing it step by step." She imagines "a visionary troop of evils coming in the wake of the railroad, which in her eyes no conceivable benefits could mitigate." She maintains that this "intruder" and its progeny of other "intruders" are forcing their way "upon her privacy" and destroying the peace of Place-du-Bois (7).

Conversely, the railroad brings empowerment and connections, which ultimately induce Thérèse's development. The railroad appears after she has become mistress of the plantation as a widow and landowner and heralds her acceptance of life changes. The railroad also connects to the inception of a profitable lumber mill in Place-du-Bois, and it is this mill that brings Hosmer to Thérèse and a chance at new love. But, consequently, she must deal with her feelings about Hosmer and navigate the challenges of business and workers. After Fanny's death forces their separation, the railroad reunites Thérèse and Hosmer a year later. Thérèse feels peaceful on the train as she leans "back in her seat with a sigh of contentment" (162). Although Thérèse has previously thought of Hosmer during the year but has not seen him, the train also enables her to feel Hosmer's "presence somewhere near." There in the safety of the train, she encounters Hosmer happily, admits that she was "at fault" for viewing their possible unification as impossible, and muses that "old supports appear to be giving way" beneath her (163, 165). The train is not the "intruder" Thérèse had originally imagined, but instead it inspires the two of them to rebuild their lives together.

Like the railroad, the growth of the timber industry helped revolution-ize the late nineteenth-century Louisiana economy. Following the Civil War, vast quantities of lumber were needed to repair the wartime ravages throughout the South and to supply the demands of northern industry. Louisiana contained thousands of timber acres, and the lumber compa-nies cut numerous logging roads into the interior forests. As railroads became more important, they became the preferred method of trans-porting timber products. The transport of lumbered planks required roads from the rural forests to the plant and to larger urban areas. Lumber companies expanded roads through the woods and located their plants close to waterways or railroads (*Transportation* 35–36). In 1880, Louisi-ana ranked thirtieth in the United States for the dollar value of its timber product. By 1900, it ranked tenth in the nation. The lumber boom's im-pact on Louisiana was immense. Fueled by out-of-state capital, the lum-ber boom changed the look of the state. With a policy of "cut out and get out," priceless natural resources were lost by the millions of acres. Large sections of the state in a short period of time became vast stump-filled, barren land as rapacious mill owners moved on to another stand of vir-gin timber elsewhere in the country. By the mid-1920s, the Louisiana lumber boom ended when the big mills ran out of timber (Fricker 1).

The Louisiana lumber boom is integral to Chopin's *At Fault* and re-flects the changing nature of the region and the lives of its inhabitants during the late nineteenth century. At the end of chapter 1, the timber industry makes an appearance and consequently erodes the woods, a barrier that has shielded Place-du-Bois from the outside world. Chopin's depiction of the rapidly changing economy is realistic, as demonstrated by Thérèse's mixed emotions regarding the arrival of the lumber mill. Though pleased by the financial windfall from the sale of timber on her property, she is wary of the changes to the land and to her community that the mill will bring. She feels "resistance" but acquiesces to this change after bidding a "tearful farewell to the silence" of her "beloved woods" (8–9). The lumber mill also brings a love affair with David Hosmer, the lumber mill's builder, to Thérèse. In conjunction with these changes, Thérèse begins to watch the logs dripping with water at the lumber mill with "fascinated delight." She stands at her "favorite spot," located dangerously "on the edge of an open platform that overhung the dam," and feels "giddy" while watching "the unending work" (13). As with Melicent's forest-fueled transformation, the mill's agency changes Thérèse, but even more permanently. Before the lumber mill's arrival, Thérèse was wedded to her husband and to the traditions of her secluded plantation; however, the lumber mill's power transfigures her into a primary household breadwinner—a working woman who is willing to take physical, financial, and emotional risks.

Although the mill brings love and profit to Thérèse and Hosmer, the mill also brings chaos, sadness, and death to other characters in *At Fault*. The mill brings Hosmer and Fanny to Place-du-Bois, as well as Joçint to work at the mill, leading to Fanny's, Joçint's, and Gregoire's tragic demise. Joçint is frustrated by the new demands his job at the mill place on his time. At the mill, he rides "all day long" on a car, "back and forth, back and forth with his heart in the pine hills" thinking "that his little Creole pony was roaming the woods in vicious idleness" (13). Although critics agree that as a lover of fishing and hunting, Joçint resents the timber mill's infringement on his formerly carefree life, they do not discuss that the mill is a thing, a character in the novel, that causes Joçint's "surly open revolt" (Green and Caudle xxiii). His resentment leads him first to sabotage Hosmer's mill and then to commit arson. Grégoire Santien is as out of place as Joçint in the new industrial South (Ringe 180) and is also changed by the mill. The mill causes Melicent, Hosmer's sister, to remain at Place-du-Bois, and her presence contributes to Grégoire's early death. Although he is at ease traversing the swamp and navigating the lake when he is with Melicent, he cannot deal with her inability to love him freely. Grégoire also cannot accept the mill's impact on Joçint, and after murdering Joçint, Grégoire leaves Place-du-Bois when he realizes that it cannot shield him from the anguish from his crime and unrequited love. The mill is a powerful thing that has transformed Grégoire from being the son of a wealthy slaveholder who does as he pleases into a lovesick murderer who must escape to Texas, only to find his own death.

The mill's power over Joçint and Grégoire is a reflection of industrialization's disruption of late nineteenth-century Louisiana and suggests an alternative interpretation of *At Fault*. Critics have noted that Joçint's wish to adhere to a primitive way of life destroys him, as he can oppose the chaos of industrial society with only violence (Arner 152). Joçint's and Grégoire's inner natures will not allow them to adjust to the new industrial South. Joçint cannot remain himself and work at the mill, and Grégoire cannot change himself to make Melicent love him. However, viewing the mill as a powerful thing in *At Fault* reveals that the mill brings the dawn of a new South, and fuels Joçint's and Grégoire's rebellion and demise. The presence of the lumber mill pushes Joçint and Grégoire over the edge in an already unstable post–Civil War community.

Natural forces and industrial objects in *At Fault* yield a domino effect of changes, perhaps more multidimensional and powerful than previously explored. Some critics of *At Fault* have argued that the industrial changes to a traditional southern pastoral way of life are negative, while others have suggested that these changes are beneficial (Anderson 3). Scholars have also maintained that the plantation and the mill are symbolic opposites (Arner 152). The union of Thérèse and Hosmer has been seen as a representation of the shotgun wedding of agriculture and industry that was occurring all over the post-Reconstruction South (Green and Caudle xxiii). In this vein, other readers assert that *At Fault* preaches the power of the northern male to construct new social realities and reflects the submission of the plantation mistress (and metaphorically, the South) to that power (Menke 44). However, the idea that powerful "things" in *At Fault* find a way to connect and conflict with humans as well as other things, suggests a new interpretation of *At Fault*. This juxtaposition of opposing "things" in *At Fault* highlights the forced union between North and South. The plantation and the woods of the Old South have thing power that conflicts with the power of the northern-influenced railroad and mill. The river, a vector for change, seems to bridge the connection between these two worlds. The plantation and nature protect the inhabitants of Place-du-Bois, whereas the river, railroad, and mill bring disturbance and change to a previously static environment. Viewing *At Fault's* objects as "things" that wield power over humans suggests that objects in the novel do not serve their typical function and therefore have to be categorized differently as empowered "things." Without these objects' presence, these relationships and events would not be possible.

"Things," and not objects, in *At Fault* enact changes that improve and destroy life and cause people to reimagine their identities. Consideration of the power of the things in Chopin's novel helps us to cultivate a "bit of anthropomorphism—the idea that human agency has some echoes in nonhuman nature" and to balance our ideas of humans' control over the world (Bennett xvi).

NOTES

1. The publication date of T. S. Arner's *Out in the World* is recorded variously; it has been dated as 1850, 1864, and 1865.

WORKS CITED

Anderson, Maureen. "Unraveling the Southern Pastoral Tradition: A New Look at Kate Chopin's *At Fault*." *Southern Literary Journal* 34, no. 1 (2001): 1–13. doi:10.1353/slj.2001.0016.

Appadurai, Arjun. *The Social Life of Things: Commodities in Cultural Perspective.* Cambridge: Cambridge University Press, 1986.

Arner, Robert D. "Landscape Symbolism in Kate Chopin's *At Fault*." *Louisiana Studies* 9 (1970): 142–53.

Bennett, Jane. *Vibrant Matter: A Political Ecology of Things.* Durham, NC: Duke University Press, 2010.

Briggs, Asa. *Victorian Things.* 3rd ed. Gloucestershire, UK: Sutton, 2003.

Brown, Bill. "Regional Artifacts (the Life of Things in the Work of Sarah Orne Jewett)." *American Literary History* 14, no. 2 (2002): 195–226.

———. "The Secret Life of Things (Virginia Woolf and the Matter of Modernism)." *Modernism/modernity* 6, no. 2 (1999): 1–28.

———. *A Sense of Things: The Object Matter of American Literature.* Chicago: University of Chicago Press, 2003.

———. "Thing Theory." *Critical Inquiry* 28, no. 1 (2001): 1–22.

Chopin, Kate. *At Fault.* 1890. Edited with an introduction and notes by Bernard Koloski. London: Penguin, 2002.

Cohen, Jeffrey. "In the Middle." *Flash Review: Jane Bennett, Vibrant Matter.* January 1, 1970. www.inthemedievalmiddle.com/2010/05/flash-review-jane-bennett -vibrant.html.

Cole, Karen. "A Message from the Pine Woods of Central Louisiana: The Garden in Northup, Chopin, and Dormon." *Louisiana Literature* 14, no. 1 (Spring 1997): 64–74.

Feldman, Ellen. "Till Divorce Do Us Part." *American Heritage* 51, no. 7 (November 2000). americanheritage.com/till-divorce-do-us-part#4.

Freedgood, Elaine. *The Ideas in Things: Fugitive Meaning in the Victorian Novel.* Chicago: University of Chicago Press, 2006.

Fricker, Donna. *The Louisiana Lumber Boom, c. 1880–1925.* Fricker Historic Preservation Services LLC.

Gladstone, W. E., et al. "The Question of Divorce." *North American Review* 149, no. 397 (December 1889): 641–52. University of Northern Iowa. jstor.org /stable/25101903.

Glenn Menke, Pamela. "Fissure as Art in Kate Chopin's *At Fault.*" *Louisiana Literature* 11, no. 1 (Spring 1994): 44–58.

Green, Suzanne Disheroon, and David J. Caudle. "A New Generation Reads *At Fault:* Introduction to *"At Fault": A Scholarly Edition with Background Readings,* edited by Green and Caudle, xix–xxxii. Knoxville: University of Tennessee Press, 2001.

Hill, Ethan Meyer. *Articulating Matter: New Materialisms in Contemporary American Fiction.* Honors thesis, Wesleyan University, Middletown, CT, 2016. wesscholar.wesleyan.edu/etd_hon_theses/1588.

"History of American Railroads." *Rise of Monopolies.* Stanford University, 1996. *Case Studies,* cs.stanford.edu/people/eroberts/cs181/projects/corporate -monopolies/development_rr.html.

Koloski, Bernard J. Introduction to *At Fault,* by Kate Chopin, vii–xxii. London: Penguin, 2002.

———. "The Structure of Kate Chopin's *At Fault.*" *Studies in American Fiction* 3, no. 9 (1975): 89–95.

Latour, Bruno. *Reassembling the Social: An Introduction to Actor-Network-Theory.* Oxford: Oxford University Press, 2008.

Lindner, Christoph. *Fictions of Commodity Culture: From the Victorian to the Post-modern.* Farnham, UK: Ashgate, 2003.

MacKethan, Lucinda Hardwick. *The Dream of Arcady: Place and Time in Southern Literature.* Baton Rouge: Louisiana State University Press, 1999.

Maiorano, Hannah. "Women of Divorce in High Society." Molly Brown House Museum. mollybrown.org/women-divorce-high-society/.

Markovits, Stefanie. "Form Things: Looking at Genre through Victorian Diamonds." *Victorian Studies* 52, no. 4 (2010): 591–619.

Marshall, Lydia Wilson. "The Comparative Archaeology of Slavery." Introduction to *The Archaeology of Slavery: A Comparative Approach to Captivity and Coercion,* edited by Marshall, 93–115. Carbondale: Southern Illinois University Press, 2014.

Millar, Andrew H. *Novels behind Glass: Commodity Culture and Victorian Narrative.* Cambridge: Cambridge University Press, 1995.

Mills, Victoria. "Introduction: Victorian Fiction and the Material Imagination." *Interdisciplinary Studies in the Long Nineteenth Century* 19, no. 6 (2008).

Plotz, John. *Portable Property: Victorian Culture on the Move.* Princeton, NJ: Princeton University Press, 2008.

Price, Alexander. "Beckett's Bedrooms: On Dirty Things and Thing Theory." *Journal of Beckett Studies* 23, no. 2 (2014): 155–77.

Pykett, Lynn. "The Material Turn in Victorian Studies." *Literature Compass* 1 (2003): 1–5.

"Railroads in the Late 19th Century." American Memory Timeline: Rise of Industrial America, 1876–1900. Library of Congress. loc.gov/teachers/classroommaterials/presentationsandactivities/presentations/timeline/riseind/railroad/.

Ringe, Donald A. "Cane River World: Kate Chopin's *At Fault* and Related Stories." *Studies in American Fiction* 3, no. 2 (1975): 157–66. doi:10.1353/saf.1975.0030.

Russell, David. "A Vision of Reunion: Kate Chopin's *At Fault.*" *Southern Quarterly* 46, no. 1 (Fall 2008): 8–25.

Sattaur, J. "Thinking Objectively: An Overview of 'Thing Theory' in Victorian Studies." *Victorian Literature and Culture* 40, no. 1 (2012): 347–57.

Talbott, Tim. *The Bell—Plantation Time Pieces,* January 1, 1970. randomthoughtsonhistory.blogspot.com/2013/04/the-bell-plantation-time-pieces.html.

Transportation in Louisiana. New Orleans: Goodwin and Associates, 2012.

Waters, Catherine. *Commodity Culture in Dickens's Household Words: The Social Life of Goods.* Burlington, VT: Ashgate, 2008.

"Thérèse Was Love's Prophet"

The Emotional Discourse and the Depiction of Feelings in At Fault

EULALIA PIÑERO GIL

> Most emotions and feelings are essential to power the intellectual and creative process.
>
> —ANTONIO DAMASIO, *The Strange Order of Things*

In 1884 Kate Chopin and her six children returned to her hometown, St. Louis, two years after her well-to-do Creole husband, Oscar Chopin, died of swamp fever in Cloutierville, Louisiana, on December 10, 1882. Chopin began to write sketches inspired by the time she spent in Louisiana, as a healing emotional experience after the devastating loss of her lifetime companion. Almost certainly, Oscar Chopin understood her emotional needs, and he probably became a source of inspiration for her most significant fictional male characters, or "Chopin's enlightened men," as Koloski has observed ("Chopin's Enlightened Men" 15). In St. Louis, Chopin began a new life as a young widow with her five sons and daughter in Eliza O'Flaherty's home, whose help and support were crucial during that period of her life: "Kate was proud of her mother's speech, and in her mother's home again, she felt secure and loved in the world of women she knew best" (Toth 102). Nevertheless, death struck hard again as her devoutly Catholic mother died of cancer in June 1885. Once more, Chopin was "literally prostrate with grief" (Toth 102), and she had a faith crisis that made her leave the church as she found life meaningless and arbitrary. Eventually, Chopin abandoned Catholicism and began reading agnostic writers such as Charles Darwin, Herbert Spencer, and Thomas Huxley (Batinovich 74).

Chopin's life was truly difficult in that period as both her husband and mother had passed away within three years; she felt emotionally devastated, deeply lonesome, and distressed. As the omniscient narrator of her first novel, *At Fault,* intriguingly inquires, "Who of us has not known the presence of Misery?" (148). Fortunately, Dr. Kolbenheyer, Chopin's obstetrician and close friend, believed in her talent and encouraged her to write and publish in order to recover from her profound sense of loss. Chopin turned to writing as a way "to master her emotions" (Ayers 355) and channeled them into artistic creativity. Her literary calling found a powerful voice that developed into a new professional life centered on imagination, self-exploration, and autonomy.

In 1889, Chopin began writing her first novel, *At Fault,* which, in many ways, explores her complex personal experiences as a widow and the strong urge to adapt to the challenges of her new life in a very conventional society. After several attempts to publish her novel with different companies, she finally published one thousand copies of *At Fault* at her own expense in 1890. Although it seems that her investment was not profitable, it at least launched her literary career (Toth 120).

Scholars do not regard *At Fault* as one of Chopin's best works. In fact, Nancy Walker has argued that it is not a major artistic achievement, but she suggests, at the same time, that Chopin showed "the depth of her interest in and affection for the culture and landscape of the region inhabited by Creoles and Acadians" (62). Walker highlights two fundamental aspects of this early novel: the writer's "affection" for the cultural scenery of Louisiana and her insightful knowledge of the peoples of that area. Indeed, those aspects are precisely related to Chopin's greatest achievement in this novel: her reliable depiction of the characters as they are not mere abstractions, but flesh-and-blood human beings with emotions and feelings that shape their personalities.

At Fault is a multifaceted romance novel that clearly depicts "a potpourri of the things" (Toth 114) on the writer's mind during a difficult period of her life, but above all it portrays a powerful and violent love triangle between Thérèse Lafirme, David Hosmer, and Fanny Larimore. Thus, physical and emotional violence are inherent aspects of the narrative that reflect the social tensions and the great changes during the historical period of the novel. The novel is set on an isolated cotton plantation in the Cane River district of northern Louisiana during post-

Reconstruction and reconciliation in the American South. One of the major changes of the rural South was the incursion of modern industry into the agricultural world of postplantation culture and economy. Consequently, it was a time of adaptation and transformation of the old social structures to a society that was changing rapidly and moving into a new social and economic order.

As a realist writer, Kate Chopin treats controversial social issues such as alcoholism, sex, marriage, divorce, family, religion, and racism in *At Fault*. Her characters experience the emotional tensions of a period of crisis and awakenings, when people struggled against the old values of the South represented by the plantation culture and the need to move forward to a new technological society. These transformations are embodied in the novel by freethinkers, liberals, and those characters who challenge conventional values through the use of rational thinking such as David Hosmer, Homeyer, and Mr. Lorenzo Worthington.

This essay is concerned with the ways this early novel presents a complex microcosm of characters who experience deep emotional tensions and express their feelings according to their need to adapt their lives to a changing social and cultural environment. These characters show that some aspects of their affective lives have been shaped by culture and history, so they themselves also embody historical and sociological conflict. As a result, emotions and feelings are crucial affective experiences in *At Fault,* as all characters of the plantation who live in Cane River society and culture are affected by and affect other bodies. Thus, Chopin's novel is a compelling reflection of how human beings emotionally faced the ordeals of an unstable time. The novel offers insight into many features of human behavior of a specific past and the ways it "sticks" to their embodied experiences. In this regard, Sara Ahmed has convincingly argued in *The Cultural Politics of Emotion* that "through emotions, the past persists on the surface of bodies. Emotions show us how histories stay alive, even when they are not consciously remembered; how histories of colonialism, slavery, and violence shape lives and worlds in the present. The time of emotion is not always about the past, and how it sticks. Emotions also open up futures, in the ways they involve different orientations to others" (202).

This essay explores Kate Chopin's representation of affect in *At Fault*. For this purpose, I analyze the significance of the emotional discourse and the representation of feelings as a fundamental epistemic source. The affective life of the main characters is a crucial aspect of the novel, and Chopin creates a very powerful emotional portrait of her protagonists, as emotions and feelings can be considered an essential and unifying characteristic of human experience and move people to take action. The characters' emotions have a bodily expression that connects the individual to other social bodies. In order to explore these aspects, it is also important to take into consideration how female and male "emotional communities" (Rosenwein 55–56) expressed themselves in the post-Reconstruction period in Cane River society.

Before moving into the analysis of the novel, it will be helpful to define the theoretical grounds of my inquiry and the terminology I use for this purpose, and in so doing draw a connection between the theories of cultural philosopher and feminist Sara Ahmed (2014) and the scientific breakthroughs and discoveries of neuroscientist Antonio Damasio (2003, 2018). On the one hand, Ahmed focuses on the relationship between emotions, language, and bodies and their sociocultural representations from a feminist perspective. She investigates them as collective corporeal expressions, which materialize and circulate between the individual and social bodies. Therefore, Ahmed develops a new methodology for reading the emotionality of texts where it is fundamental to study the real impact emotions have in society. On the other hand, Damasio concludes that the body is the origin of emotions and that the mental experiences they create are feelings that are always "hidden, like all mental images necessarily are" (*Looking for Spinoza* 28). Thus, for the neuroscientist, emotions and feelings play a crucial role in social cognition and decision-making processes. In addition, cognitive processes always have a corporeal basis, and he suggests that "Emotions play out in the theater of the body" and "Feelings play out in the theater of the mind" (*Looking for Spinoza* 28). In this essay, I refer to primary or basic emotions as described by Damasio, who considers "emotions [to be] actions or movements, many of them public, visible to others as they occur in the face, in the voice, in specific behaviors";

the primary or basic emotions include fear, anger, disgust, surprise, sadness, and happiness (*Looking for Spinoza* 28, 44). Social emotions, according to Damasio, include sympathy, embarrassment, shame, guilt, pride, jealousy, envy, gratitude, admiration, indignation, and contempt (*Looking for Spinoza* 45). In the same way, the neurologist argues that a feeling is "the perception of a certain state of the body along with the perception of a certain mode of thinking and of thoughts with certain themes" and concludes that "feelings translate the ongoing life state in the language of the mind" (*Looking for Spinoza* 86, 85).

With this theoretical framework in mind, I explore how the main characters in *At Fault* manage to control their emotions and struggle to find a balance between them and their own hidden feelings. Most importantly, Chopin unveils the characters' affects in the context of their "emotional community" (Rosenwein 55–56) in a specific time and place. Furthermore, I study the affective world and the corporeal expressions as generative forces in a specific sociocultural context and how these characters respond emotionally to these circumstances. In my view, emotions and feelings can determine character development and narrative form, as Chopin brilliantly achieved in her first novel.

Thérèse Lafirme's Emotional Discourse: A Mistress of Her Own Emotions

At Fault begins with the chapter titled "The Mistress of Place-du-Bois," introducing Thérèse Lafirme, the only owner of a cotton plantation in Cane River. She is a powerful woman in an old rural society that is vanishing after the unexpected irruption of technology. The narrator describes Thérèse's emotional distress and "deep lethargy of grief" (5) as she has recently lost her husband, Jérôme Lafirme. The young Creole widow "had wanted to die with Jérôme, feeling that life without him held nothing that could reconcile her to its further endurance" (5). It seems that Thérèse truly loved her husband, and her marriage was satisfactory in every possible sense. But this vital loss triggered an emotional crisis of unforeseen consequences. Her husband's demise also affects the laborers of the cotton plantation community, who feel "demoralized" (5).

Cane River's emotional community mourns the death of a significant member of their social group. Chopin's language of grief "aligns
this body with other bodies; the surface of the community comes to
be inhabited differently in the event of being touched by such loss"
(Ahmed 39). In fact, the primary emotion of sadness, according to
Damasio, gives rise to more feelings (*Looking for Spinoza* 70). This is
exactly what happens with Thérèse Lafirme's early emotional state:
she is literally "trapped in her grief" (Koloski, introduction xv), but
her embodied affects have significant outcomes for other bodies in the
community as when her servant Uncle Hiram wants to rouse Thérèse
from "her lethargy of grief" (5), so that she could take charge of her
husband's business. Thérèse Lafirme is a proactive woman, "a clever
enough business woman" (9), who decides quickly to take on the responsibility to own and manage the plantation. Her encounter with St.
Louis businessman David Hosmer dissipates the tearful silence of her
widowhood, and her emotional paralysis eventually disappears as she
confronts her reality and awakens to a new emotional and productive
life. In fact, Thérèse falls in love with David Hosmer and assumes the
role of the plantation owner as a New Woman who is also determined
to adapt to the new changes industrialization and technological modernity have brought to her property and community. In this light, Leo
Marx's famous trope of "the machine in the garden" becomes relevant
to understanding the implications of the changes experienced by Cane
River's community and its pastoral scenery as a consequence of the
technological advances and the rapid industrialization of the American
South. The notion of pastoralism as a cultural symbol is "an image that
conveys a special meaning—thought and feeling—to a larger number
of those who share the culture" (Marx 5). The old order of plantation
life was transforming rapidly, and Thérèse, a woman of commercial vision, has to adapt to inevitable changes such as the railway tracks or the
new industrial machines David Hosmer brings to build a new sawmill
for the timber industry. The predictable disruption of noisy machines
in the quiet pastoral landscape has emotional effects in the collective
and literary imagination, as Marx has noted: "The ominous sounds of
machines, like the sound of the steamboat bearing down on the raft or

of the train breaking in upon the idyll at Walden, reverberate endlessly in our literature. . . . Indeed it is difficult to think of a major American writer upon whom the image of the machine's sudden appearance in the landscape has not exercised its fascination" (Marx 15–16). The idyllic pastoral America vanished with the Civil War and the period of the Reconstruction. Nevertheless, there was a belligerent resistance to those values, and many plantation owners praised the old simple life in contrast to the complexities of urban life. As a result, a new period of uncertainties and anxiety required an emotional adaptation and reinvention. In this context, Chopin's *At Fault* captures the emotional unrest experienced by her protagonists, facing these technological changes and their emotional adjustment to the demands of modernity. In this sense, Thérèse is a character who shows a significant emotional balance and her determined pursuit for happiness informs her resolutions. Her self-reflection and decisions save Place-du-Bois from economic ruin and ensure an important source of income and financial prosperity for her cultivated area, her workers, and the entire community. The narrator emphasizes the fact that she is a "warm-hearted woman, and a woman of clear mental vision; a combination not found so often together as to make it ordinary" (30). Like Chopin's other literary heroines—Edna Pontellier, Paula von Stolz, Charlie Laborde, Adrienne Farival, or Athénaïse Miché—Thérèse Lafirme has the clarity of mind, the emotional balance, and the determination to face the challenges of life in a decisive way. All of these qualities enable her to evolve emotionally from "her lethargy of pain": "Being a woman of warm heart, she had loved her husband with the devotion which good husbands deserve, but being a clear-headed woman, she was not disposed to rebel against the changes which Time brings, when so disposed, to the human sensibilities" (30–31).

Certainly, Thérèse represents the independence and strength of a New Woman, and she is not ashamed to share social emotions such as tenderness and sympathy. However, the narrator surprisingly categorizes these emotional features as "un-American" (82). Her spontaneous behavior and her warm affectivity are emotional aspects that make Thérèse an exceptional "un-American" character who unmistakably contrasts with other characters of the novel. Possibly, the fact that she is a Creole woman is related to her un-Americanness, though it is also true that she struggles to find a difficult balance between her emotions, her own hidden and private feelings, and the social emotions of her community. As for Chopin's representation of Thérèse's feelings, she develops them as her perceptions adapt to the circumstances. That is, her sexual and emotional needs become more central in her life as she awakens to the physical embodiment of love. As Damasio argues, the body and feelings "translate the ongoing life state in the language of the mind. Feelings are perceptions, and they occur in the *brain's body maps.* These maps refer to parts of the body and states of the body. Some variation of pleasure or pain is a consistent content of the perception we call feeling" (*Looking for Spinoza* 85). As previously noted, Thérèse is a woman who speaks from her emotions and feelings: she is open, generous, and shows solid social virtues. Like Edna Pontellier, she is a very sensorial woman (Piñero Gil, "The Pleasures" 83–100), and emotionally generous as she shows an uncommon hospitality and care about her neighbors and friends: "Thérèse with her pretty Creole tact was not long in bringing these seemingly incongruent elements into some degree of harmony" (131).

Needless to say, Thérèse's most important emotional challenge is to manage her passionate love for David Hosmer and the emotional pain over the fact that he is a divorced man. The attractive young widow's personal moral code and her religious prejudices make her demand that he remarries Fanny, and he obediently complies. However, she cannot avoid being Hosmer's "Love's prophet" (50), and she still loves him. Her demands make her experience the pain of knowing that she has sent Hosmer back to his ex-wife (Campbell 29). Consequently, in part 2 of *At Fault,* Thérèse's "world begins to crumble from order into chaos as her plans to organize other's lives go awry" (Koloski, "The Structure" 90). The protagonist's feelings reflect this emotional turmoil through the episodes of pain and pleasure that emerge along her psychological evolution. Specifically, that emotional pain shapes her body, her language, and as has been mentioned, her decisions: "She said no more and he was glad of it, for her last words held almost the force of action for him; as though she had let him feel for an instant her heart beat against his own with an echoing pain" (100).

In spite of these moments of emotional pain, Thérèse strives to control her emotions and maintain a sense of dignity: "Her native pride rebelled against the reticence of this man who had shared her confidence while keeping her in ignorance of so important a feature of his own life" (33). The thoughts and feelings that accompany Thérèse's "native pride," which according to Damasio is a social emotion (*Looking for Spinoza* 45), are based on her previous social and personal experiences. In short, Thérèse is always a "mistress of herself" (27), of her own emotions and social performance, but she is also a member of what Rosenwein describes as "an emotional community," and she feels she has to respond to the social consequences of marrying a divorced man.

"Who Determines What Is Right or Wrong?": How Emotions Move Communities

Thérèse Lafirme rejects David Hosmer's proposal of marriage because, as a Roman Catholic, she considers divorce against the law of God. As Koloski notes, "she is Catholic more in tradition than in conviction" ("Chopin's Enlightened Men" 21). In my view, Chopin represents Thérèse's dilemma in the significant context of an "emotional community" (Rosenwein 2011) with its own particular norms of affective expression. The heroine's private emotional reactions coexist with the conventional norms of the Cane River community's emotional valuation and expression: a Creole culture with social traditions, security, and order. At the same time, Thérèse belongs to a Catholic emotional community with its religious doctrine and moral values that she apparently accepts. Critical approaches to the novel have not noticed that Thérèse is a relevant member of both communities and has a social responsibility that is expressed by emotional codes of behavior. Thus, she shows "unwavering Catholic convictions" (Ostman 11) that reaffirm her emotional compromise with her religious community. Nevertheless, her deep love for Hosmer and her emotional bond with him will eventually overcome the pressure of the community's religious dogmatism.

Chopin expresses a similar dichotomy between the individual and the community in *The Awakening*. In the latter case, the narrator describes Edna Pontellier's dual existence: "At a very early period she had apprehended instinctively the dual life—that outward existence which conforms, the inward life which questions" (57). The protagonist of this exceptional novel learns to negotiate the tensions deriving from society's restrictions on her as a wife and mother and her quest for independence and autonomy. In Thérèse's case, she also learns to live in a dual existence: the individual who conforms to her emotional or religious communities, and the individual who, at the same time, questions the emotional rules and the religious dogma of her social group. Even though she might be a New Woman who "possessed an independence of thought exceptional enough when considered in relation to her life and its surrounding conditions" (34), and might claim an individual right to pursue her own happiness, she also has a social responsibility and code of behavior. Thus, Thérèse is trapped between "the prejudices of her Catholic education coloring her sentiment" (34), which are an essential part of her community, and her New Woman attitudes, which challenge the traditional stereotypes of women as delicate, domestic, passive, and obedient. In this sense, Ahmed sheds light on how communities interpret affect and how we inherit those interpretations as members of a community: "Emotions are what move us, and how we are moved involves interpretations of sensations and feelings not only in the sense that we interpret what we feel, but also in that what we feel might be dependent on past interpretations that are not necessarily made by us, but that come before us" (171).

Even though Thérèse is negotiating emotionally with her community, it is also clear that Chopin shows in her fiction "little patience with those who so value the stability of the group that they are willing to sacrifice the lives or the happiness of individuals to achieve it" (Koloski, introduction xxi). In fact, Chopin advocated for her heroines' autonomy and independence, as well as their right to decide freely and to pursue their own happiness. However, *At Fault* shows how the central female character also acts according to the particular norms of emotional valuation and expression of a given community. In particular, the writer shows how American women have been traditionally constrained by Catholic culture, which reinforced social emotions such as shame, guilt, and the moral conflicts derived from them. As Ostman argues: "Catholicism functions as an aesthetic as well as the subject of critique in *At Fault*" (125), and emphasizes the relevance of moral rules this religion placed on men and women as well (129).

Eventually, Thérèse acknowledges her error and admits to David that she was at fault in demanding that he remarry Fanny because she realizes that her primary emotional need is to pursue her own happiness. Her individual emotional fulfillment is more important than the community's religious constraints because, in spite of being an independent woman, she is affected by and affects other bodies. As Koloski points out: "Within her world, within the context of her nineteenth-century, Southern, rural conservative, tight-knit, Roman Catholic community, Thérèse makes the best choice she can. To leave her community, to marry Hosmer, to become his lover, to banish him from her life, or to do nothing, to leave the matter as it stands—all are unacceptable for her. So she chooses the best opportunity available" (introduction xvi). In this respect, Chopin's categorical view about Thérèse Lafirme's wrong decision is very revealing; she "is the one who was at fault—remotely, and immediately. Remotely—in her blind acceptance of an undistinguishing, therefore unintelligent code of righteousness by which to deal out judgments" (quoted in Toth 119).

David Hosmer: The Affectionate Man and His Emotional Turmoil

David Hosmer is one of the most fascinating male characters in Chopin's fiction. He is "a sallow, earnest, humorless Yankee" (Toth 113), a man of action, an honest and brave gentleman who tries to manage his emotions during turbulent personal and social circumstances in which the only certainty he has, according to the narrator, is that "Love was his god now, and Thérèse was Love's prophet" (50). From my perspective, his only vital assurance is his passionate emotional awakening to the experience of love, "What ever I do, must be because you want it; because I love you" (40). Nevertheless, David's emotional turmoil is a direct consequence of his frustration as his remarriage makes all three main characters unhappy. In spite of these unhelpful emotional circumstances, Hosmer looks for personal coherence throughout the novel and is very critical about his actions and decisions regarding his wife, Fanny Larimore. He has no religious constraints, a crucial fact in the novel because, as he states, his only God is love. Even though Ewell notes that "Hosmer acknowledges with complacency his inability to comprehend human emotions and relationships. Neither the inner life nor society holds much interest for him" (38–39). In my view, Hosmer is a convinced agnostic, a man whose ethical grounds are based on a profound skepticism about the human condition: "The truth in its entirety isn't given to man to know—such knowledge, no doubt, would be beyond human endurance. But we make a step towards it, when we learn that there is rottenness and evil in the world, masquerading as right and morality—when we learn to know the living spirit from the dead letter" (165). In addition, he is a down-to-earth businessman who shows pragmatic reasoning based on evidence and his own affective experience. In chapter 5, Hosmer makes a very open and significant confession to Thérèse about his real feelings and emotional needs: "It doesn't make it any the more bearable to feel that the cause of this unlooked-for change lies within myself—my altered feelings. But it seems to me that I have the right to ask you not to take yourself out of my life; your moral support; your bodily atmosphere. I hope not to give way to the weakness of speaking of these things again: but before you leave me, tell me, do you understand a little better why I need you?" (100). Hosmer is, at that moment of the novel, convinced that he has made a terrible mistake in remarrying Fanny Larimore and sacrificing his real feelings for the wrong woman.

As for Hosmer's wife, Chopin depicts a female character who lacks empathy with her family and friends as she is uneducated, unsophisticated, and manipulative. In fact, Fanny, who is one of the first female alcoholic characters in American literature (Toth 113), is a dishonest woman who exerts emotional pressure upon Hosmer and the rest of the community. The truth is that the elation she had felt with Hosmer ten years before "had soon died away, together with her weak love for him" (51). Further, she constantly whines and uses her drinking problem to control her husband and friends. Her addiction makes her an aloof and selfish woman who is unable to appreciate her husband's sacrifice and compassion toward her. She even lies to Hosmer and makes no effort to overcome her addiction, "after shedding a few maudlin tears over the conviction that he intended to leave her again, and clinging to his neck with beseeching enquiry whether he loved her" (101–2). As a matter of fact, they have a very toxic relationship, which is a source of permanent emotional conflict between them. Consequently, Hosmer loses his temper most of the time and cannot get rid of the "haunting dread of having wounded her nature cruelly" (153). In chapter 15, the narrator defines Fanny as a "small, weak, irresponsible creature" (153) as her life of leisure and uselessness gives her no significant social role. Indeed, her unproductive and self-destructive life contributes to the fact that she is also deformed psychologically and her figure is indeterminate in the novel (Campbell 41). Moreover, the narrator describes her existence as haunting and careless: "Fanny alone was the ghost of the feast" (134). And, in another instance: "Oh bother," was Fanny's careless reply. "This suits me well enough; I don't care how long it lasts" (157). In short, her only physical craving stems from her alcoholism, and her affective life finds a close connection with the tearful scenes of sentimental novels, "of one of those prolific female writers who turn out their unwholesome intellectual sweets so tirelessly, to be devoured by the girls and women of the age" (78). Fanny's fascination for this kind of "morbid literature" (51) clearly portrays her emotional unbalance as well as her need to be provided for as compensation for the emotions that life has denied her, as she has always felt "of little consequence, and in a manner, overlooked" (78). Sadly enough, Fanny feels fulfilled with alcohol and the emotionally extravagant sentimental novels. Obviously, Chopin is making a point about the dangers of these "unwholesome intellectual sweets" (78), discussed further in the essay in this volume by John A. Staunton. By focusing upon the perils of sentimental literature, Chopin draws attention to the excesses of a fiction that, in most cases, reinforced traditional gender roles and the exploitation of superficial emotions and feelings. Fanny's addiction is as toxic as her fascination with the sentimental novels, especially as they offered an idealized depiction of patriarchal domesticity and marriage as the only institution that provided women with a social identity.

Thérèse points out that Hosmer's attitude toward Fanny had contributed to a certain extent to her condition: "You married a woman of weak character. You furnished her with every means to increase that weakness" (39). But Fanny's physical craving and her demands are part of her survival strategy as she has the feeling that sooner or later she will lose Hosmer. When she realizes that Hosmer loves Thérèse, the social emotion of jealousy drives her crazy. Her unhappiness and anger lead to a lack of emotional control that will eventually cause her tragic death by drowning. On these grounds, Chopin was very clear with the psychological depiction of Fanny and her frailty. She responded to a reviewer of the novel that "Fanny is not the heroine. It is charitable to regard her whole existence as a misfortune" (quoted in Toth 119).

The Emotional Body: Love and "Violent Passions"

In her fiction, Kate Chopin conveyed the ways emotions mediated human experience of the exterior world and the importance of the connection between mind, body, and emotion (Piñero Gil, "The Pleasures" 84–92). She also strived to depict characters who have sensorial bodies and represent everyday embodied experiences from a realist perspective: they breathe, touch, see, smell, hear, taste, and feel pain, anger, sadness, happiness, and look for body-to-body contact. In other words, their "emotions play out in the theater of the body" (Damasio, *Looking for Spinoza* 28), and they are expressed with a powerful body language. In this regard, Campbell has pointed out the relevance of bodies in relation to the realist construction of Chopin's characters: "Chopin writes about bodies not merely as vehicles for expressing the oppression and pain . . . but as sites of knowledge that contribute to the novel's realism. Bodies constitute a means of measuring the character's grounding in reality: the more substantial the character's body, the better she understands real life" (35). Chopin developed an original emotional portrait of her characters based on a poetics of verisimilitude

EULALIA PIÑERO GIL

that literalized their affective life. At the same time, she depicted them as they evolve psychologically and are affected by a historical and social context. She explored how emotions work to shape her characters and "the surfaces of individual and collective bodies" (Ahmed 2). Ahmed's analysis can be applied to the embodiment of emotions in *At Fault* and can help us see "what emotions do and how emotions circulate between bodies, examining how they stick as well as move" (Ahmed 4). A case in point is David Hosmer, a deeply emotional character affected by the painful experience of being married to Fanny Larimore, as has been previously argued. His "hasty and violent passions" (153) show how Chopin depicts her characters' contrary emotions and how they act in a reliable and realistic way. Thus, Hosmer rejects Fanny but at the same time remains genuinely sorry about being cruel with her: "Hosmer passed the day with a great pain at his heart. His hasty and violent passion of the morning had added another weight for his spirit to drag about, and which he could not cast off" (153). The experience of pain is personal, private, and lonely, but Hosmer's pain is the result of his deep frustration and he needs to disclose it, to share it with the members of his family and community. His physical suffering is also portrayed by Chopin as a bodily sensation, "Physical suffering, thwarted love, and at the same time a feeling of self-condemnation, made him wish that life were ended for him" (124).

Chopin wrote extensively about how people felt love and sexual attraction in and out of marriage. She also projected emotion and physical desire onto the bodies of others, as in "The Storm," "La Belle Zoraïde," and *The Awakening*. When the leading characters of her fiction describe the unexpected feeling of falling in love or sexual attraction, they express it as a sensation that affects their body through touching, smelling, seeing, tasting, and hearing. In *At Fault*, Hosmer, an extremely sensitive man, needs Thérèse's "bodily atmosphere" (100), that is, her physical contact. The narrator emphasizes throughout the novel this physical desire with the symbolism of her sensual body: "But he felt that when he saw her there, waiting for him, he would cast himself at her feet and kiss them. He would crush her white hands against his bosom. He would bury his face in her silken hair" (124). In the former description, Hosmer's desire is channeled through a sensual fantasy where he literally opens to the dream of being loved and of loving physically, and in this daydream experience he finds the only compensation for a frustrated existence. Therefore, his sensual emotions shape the surfaces of his dreamed body and circulate between bodies: "She should know how strong his love was, and he would hold her in his arms till she yield back tenderness to his own. But—Thérèse met him on the steps" (124). The projection of those emotions onto the characters' bodies is an essential device in the fictional construction of Hosmer's and Thérèse's love with the allusion to body parts, as the passage echoes their first encounter "for it was in utter blindness to everything but love for each other, that their lips met" (40).

As Koloski has concluded, *At Fault* is Kate Chopin's "novel of hope" and "celebrates the redemptive power of love" (introduction vii, xxii): as the protagonist couple marries and finally achieves the fulfillment of their passionate love. In spite of their struggles for happiness, they learned through painful experience that their own feelings were more important than the community's beliefs or religious dogma: "But of the opinions, favorable and other, that were being exchanged regarding them and their marriage, Hosmer and Thérèse heard little and would have cared less, so absorbed were they in the overmastering happiness that was holding them in thralldom" (166). The couple's emotions can tell us about the time and space of their social context in the Cane River world. Those emotions become, in Ahmed's words, the "very flesh of time" (202), and through them the historical past persists on the surface of the characters' bodies and in their stories of the love, passion, and violence that shaped their lives.

What I hope to have achieved in this essay is grounds for reading the affects depicted in Kate Chopin's *At Fault.* The writer's first novel is a powerful realist work, as emotions and feelings determine character development and narrative form. The embodied characters show that, though they might claim independence, they are affected by and affect other bodies at the Cane River plantation. Those characters are thinking-feeling bodies that unveil much about a crucial historical moment of crisis and awakenings during the post-Reconstruction period in the American South. In the same way, the novel shows how people lived in emotional communities with their own affective discourse and codes of behavior. Chopin depicts how emotions register on the characters' bodies and how their emotional lives create a complex image of a society in transition and reinvention. In the end, the American writer represents how affects are a fundamental aspect of human existence and how social, cultural, and economic contingencies can influence the way in which her main characters experience and express them.

WORKS CITED

Ahmed, Sara. *The Cultural Politics of Emotion.* Edinburgh, Scotland: Edinburgh University Press, 2014.

Ayers, Edward L. *The Promise of the New South: Life after Reconstruction.* Oxford: Oxford University Press, 2007.

Batinovich, Garnet Ayers. "Storming the Cathedral: The Antireligious Subtext in Kate Chopin's Works." In *Kate Chopin in the Twenty-First Century: New Critical Essays,* edited by Heather Ostman. Newcastle upon Tyne, UK: Cambridge Scholars Publishing, 2008.

Campbell, Donna. *"At Fault:* A Reappraisal of Kate Chopin's Other Novel." In *The Cambridge Companion to Kate Chopin,* edited by Janet Beer. Cambridge: Cambridge University Press, 2008.

Chopin, Kate. *At Fault.* 1890. Edited with an introduction and notes by Bernard Koloski, London: Penguin, 2002.

———. *"The Awakening" and Selected Stories.* Edited by Sandra M. Gilbert. London: Penguin Classics, 1984.

Damasio, Antonio. *Looking for Spinoza: Joy, Sorrow, and the Feeling Brain.* Eugene, OR: Harvest, 2003.

———. *The Strange Order of Things: Life, Feeling, and the Making of Cultures.* New York: Pantheon, 2018.

Ewell, Barbara C. *Kate Chopin.* New York: Frederick Ungar, 1986.

Koloski, Bernard. "Chopin's Enlightened Men." In *Kate Chopin in Context: New Approaches,* edited by Heather Ostman and Kate O'Donoghue, 15–27. London: Palgrave Macmillan, 2015.

———. Introduction to *At Fault,* by Kate Chopin, vii–xxvi. London: Penguin, 2002.

———. "The Structure of Kate Chopin's *At Fault." Studies in American Fiction* 3 (1975): 89–95.

Marx, Leo. *The Machine in the Garden: Technology and the Pastoral Ideal in America*. Oxford: Oxford University Press, 1964.

Ostman, Heather. *Kate Chopin and Catholicism*. London: Palgrave Macmillan, 2020.

Piñero Gil, Eulalia. Introducción to *El Despertar de Kate Chopin*. Madrid: Cátedra, 2012.

———. "The Pleasures of Music: Kate Chopin's Artistic and Sensorial Synesthesia." In *Kate Chopin in Context: New Approaches,* edited by Heather Ostman and Kate O'Donoghue, 83–100. London: Palgrave Macmillan, 2015.

Ringe, Donald A. "Cane River World: Kate Chopin's *At Fault* and Related Stories." *Studies in American Fiction* 3, no. 2 (Autumn 1975): 157–66.

Rosenwein, Barbara H. "Emotional Communities and the Body." *Médiévales* 61, no. 2 (2011): 55–75.

Toth, Emily. *Unveiling Kate Chopin*. Jackson: University Press of Mississippi, 1999.

Walker, Nancy A. *Kate Chopin: A Literary Life*. London: Palgrave Macmillan, 2001.

CONTRIBUTORS

Natalie Aikens is currently a postdoctoral teaching fellow in American literature and culture at Utah State University. She is currently writing a book that explores the effects of plantation colonialism in multi-ethnic literatures of the circum-Caribbean.

Michael P. Bibler is the Robert Penn Warren Associate Professor of English at LSU. He is author of *Cotton's Queer Relations: Same-Sex Intimacy and the Literature of the Southern Plantation, 1936–1968* (2009) and coeditor of *Just below South: Intercultural Performance in the Caribbean and the U.S. South* (2007) and the first reissue of Arna Bontemps's 1939 novel *Drums at Dusk* (2009). He is currently finishing a book manuscript about literalism and queerness that discusses John Waters, the B-52's, Truman Capote, RuPaul, plays and films about small-town Texas, and the artist Nick Cave.

Nadine M. Knight is the director of the Center for Interdisciplinary Studies, an associate professor of English, and affiliate faculty in the Africana Studies concentration at College of the Holy Cross in Worcester, Massachusetts. Select previous publications examine the Civil War diaries of Union soldiers; contemporary texts setting *The Odyssey* during the Civil War; and the complications of freedom in contemporary neo–slave narratives.

Bernard Koloski is the editor of the Penguin Classics edition of Chopin's *At Fault* as well as *The Historian's Awakening: Reading Kate Chopin's Classic Novel as Social and Cultural History.* He edits the Kate Chopin entry in the *Oxford Bibliography of American Literature* and coedits the website of the Kate Chopin International Society.

Susan Moldow founded an educational consulting business in 2001 and has shared her research at literature conferences nationwide. Susan is pursuing doctoral studies in American literature.

Heather Ostman is a professor of English and the director of the Humanities Institute at SUNY Westchester Community College. She is the author of *American Women Activists and Autobiography* (2021), *Kate Chopin and Catholicism* (2020), *The Fiction of Junot Díaz* (2017), and *Writing Program Administration and the Community College* (2013), and the editor/coeditor of *Kate Chopin in Context: New Approaches* (2015), *Kate Chopin in the Twenty-First Century: New Essays* (2008), and *Teaching Writing through Immigrant Stories* (2021). She also serves as president of the Kate Chopin International Society.

Eulalia Piñero Gil is a professor of American literature and gender studies of the Universidad Autónoma of Madrid, Spain. She is the author of the translation and critical edition of Kate Chopin's *The Awakening/El despertar* (2012). She has coedited *Visions of Canada Approaching the Millennium* (1999); *Voices and Images of Women in 20th Century Theater: Anglo-American Women Playwrights* (2002); *Women and Art: Visions of Change and Social Development* (2010); *Breaking a Sea of Silence: Interdisciplinary Reflections on Gender Violence* (2013); and *Live Deep and Suck all the Marrow of Life: H. D. Thoreau's Literary Heritage* (2020). She has authored several peer-reviewed articles on Kate Chopin and other American women writers. In 2020, she edited *Kate Chopin's Complete Short Stories/Cuentos Completos* in Spanish with an introduction. She is the president of the Spanish Association for American Studies (SAAS).

John A. Staunton is associate dean of the Honors College, a professor of English education and American literature, and affiliate faculty in women's and gender studies at Eastern Michigan University. He is author of *Deranging English/Education: Teacher Inquiry, Literary Studies, and Hybrid Visions of 'English' for 21st-Century Schools* (2008), and coeditor of *Teaching the Literature Survey Course: New Strategies for College Faculty* (2018).

Emily Toth has written the definitive biography of Kate Chopin, *Unveiling Kate Chopin;* coedited *Kate Chopin's Private Papers;* and published the first edition of Chopin's last story collection, *A Vocation and a Voice.* The first of her eleven published books, *The Curse: A Cultural History of Menstruation,* has been in print for forty-five years, and her *Inside Peyton Place: The Life of Grace Metalious,* has been sold to Sandra Bullock for a feature film. Emily Toth writes academic advice columns and books as "Ms. Mentor" and is the Robert Penn Warren Professor of English at Louisiana State University.

Deborah Lindsay Williams is a clinical professor in the Liberal Studies Program at NYU and in the Literature and Creative Writing Program at NYU Abu Dhabi. She is the author of *Not in Sisterhood: Edith Wharton, Willa Cather, Zona Gale, and the Politics of Female Authorship* (2001); she is coeditor, with Cyrus R. K. Patell, of *The Oxford History of the Novel in English,* volume 8: *US Literature from 1940,* for which she also wrote the chapter on US children's literature. She is currently writing a book for Oxford's Literary Agenda series about the ways that young adult fiction helps shape contemporary political and cultural discourse. From 2014 to 2019, she was a columnist at the *National,* the English-language newspaper of the UAE; her nonacademic writing has appeared in such places as the *New York Times,* the *Paris Review Daily, Inside Higher Ed,* and the *Rumpus.*

INDEX

Acadians, 100, 109, 197

affect, 199, 201, 205, 211

agency, 11, 33, 39, 47, 58, 101, 111–12, 148, 151, 179, 187, 191, 193

Ahmed, Sara, 211–12

alcoholism, 3, 23, 35, 42, 71, 74–75, 100, 117, 122–23, 139, 153, 184, 198, 208

American South (US South), 4, 8, 16, 27, 157, 198, 201, 212

Anderson, Maureen, 42, 53, 65, 75, 163–65, 167

antebellum, 51, 59n2, 64–65, 67, 70–72, 75–81

Arner, Robert D., 7, 103, 192–93

Arobin, Alcée (*The Awakening*), 91, 108–9

aspirations, 10, 99, 108, 112

"Athénaïse," 104

"At the 'Cadian Ball," 109

Aunt Belindy (*At Fault*), 21–22, 70, 101

"Aunt Lympy's Interference," 158, 172

autonomy, 1, 10, 24, 26, 30n9, 70, 97, 99–102, 105–7, 109, 112, 143, 164, 167–68, 173, 197, 205

Awakening, The, 1–2, 6–8, 10, 14, 27, 29, 30n9, 86, 88–89, 91, 94, 97, 99, 101, 104–5, 108, 111, 116, 118, 137, 150, 156, 205, 210

Ayers, Edward L., 37, 43, 197

balance, 29n2, 68, 108, 110, 131, 193, 200, 202–3

Batinovich, Garnet Ayers, 196

Baym, Nina, 100, 110

Beauregard, P. G. T., 71–72, 74, 81n4

Belford's Monthly, 2

Bender, Bert, 127, 171–73

bilingualism, 21, 104, 179

Black anger, 74

Black laborers, 4, 9, 52, 56, 64–67, 69–71, 73, 76, 80

Bonner, Thomas, Jr., 65

Brontë, Charlotte, 6

Brown, Bill, 176, 178

cabin, 25–26, 54, 66, 74–75, 77, 97, 123, 126, 183, 186–87

Calixta ("The Storm"), 91, 109, 112

Campbell, Donna, 14–16, 22, 24, 51, 61, 69–70, 100, 125–26, 128, 203, 208–9

Cane River, 3, 5, 7, 13, 25, 28, 29n2, 39, 66

Cather, Willa, 6

Catholic Church, 5, 94

Catholicism, 22, 30n6, 90, 106, 161, 183–85, 196, 206

Caudle, David J., 2, 6–7, 103, 142, 149, 191–92

Chopin, Oscar (husband), 2, 60n18, 88, 91, 137, 196

Civil War, 1–2, 41, 65–66, 68–69, 73, 77–78, 90, 110, 142, 157, 163, 165, 188, 190, 202

Cixous, Hélène, 111

classical liberalism, 34, 51, 58, 59n9

Cloutierville, LA, 88, 91, 133n4, 196

Compromise of 1877, 32, 34, 38, 40

219